DATE DUE

UPI 201-9509   PRINTED IN USA

Procedures for Library Media Technical Assistants

Procedures for Library Media Technical Assistants

Barbara E. Chernik

Chicago 1983

American Library Association

Designed by Randi Brill
Composed by Modern Typographers, Inc.
    in Linotron Times Roman and Helvetica
Printed on 50-pound Warren's 1854,
        a pH-neutral stock, by the University of Chicago
        Printing Department and bound in B-grade Holliston
        linen cloth by Zonne Bookbinders, Inc.

Library of Congress Cataloging in Publication Data

Chernik, Barbara E., 1938–
    Procedures for library media technical assistants.

    Bibliography: p.
    Includes index.
    1. Library science.   2. Library technicians.
3. Library science—Handbooks, manuals, etc.
4. Library technicians—Handbooks, manuals, etc.
I. Title.
Z665.C539   1983   023′.3   83-7070
ISBN 0-8389-0384-3

*This book is dedicated with love
and affection to
my family, Glenn and Lee,
and to my parents*

Contents

Acknowledgments

In writing this book, I am indebted to my colleagues for sharing their time, their ideas, and their talents with my students and myself. I am also indebted to all of my students who have helped shape the content and context of this book. Their learning has made this effort worthwhile.

Introduction

Ever since Melvil Dewey opened the first school of library science in 1887, there has been training for librarians who will administer and direct the operations of libraries. However, there has seldom been any specific training for the library worker below this professional level who will perform library routines and procedures. Instead, the library worker has been taught on the job by someone who has performed a routine for many years and who can show the beginner the "way it is done in our library." This latter training system may have been effective in the early days of the 1900s, but libraries have moved into a cost-conscious world of technology, information processing, and rising salaries. Library administrators have therefore begun taking closer looks at this method of training their nonprofessional staff members.

In this process, library administrators recognized that jobs could be separated into categories performed by different levels of personnel. These personnel levels required varying degrees of knowledge and skills and different types of education and training. Instead of two personnel categories—professional and nonprofessional—library administrators devised four—clerical, technical, subprofessional, and finally professional librarians. As they did this, they found that personnel in these categories not only performed different kinds of jobs but also needed different types of training to make them proficient.

To help standardize such jobs and training at all levels, the American Library Association adopted and published a policy statement entitled *Library Education and Personnel Utilization* in 1970. This statement established two types of library personnel—professional and supportive—and defined three distinct categories of support personnel—library clerk, library media technical assistant, and library associate. It identified the type of education or training and the major responsibilities for each of the supportive categories.

According to the policy statement, a library clerk needed general clerical and secretarial skills; it recommended on-the-job training. This employee was usually closely supervised and performed repetitive library routines requiring few library skills.

A library media technical assistant (LMTA) was not just an advanced clerk but was an employee who had specific library-related or technical skills based on post–high school training. This employee could exercise judgment within guidelines set by the librarian and could be responsible for a work unit within the library such as the circulation area or the order department. The LMTA could also perform the duties of the library clerk but usually supervised such clerks and sometimes also supervised other LMTAs.

The library associate had a bachelor's degree and might have some library education below the master's degree level. The associate often performed high-level supportive tasks in areas such as reference assistance or bibliographic searching which required good judgment and a broad general background.

The ALA personnel statement included suggestions about library education for these categories. Librarians and specialists were to have master's degrees, while library associates might have a bachelor's degree with a minor in library science or library work experience, or be working on a master's degree. Library clerks needed only on-the-job training in specific library skills.

Library media technical assistants, on the other hand, required specific training of a type not found in the library world before. This employee level could require two years of post–high school training in graphics or data processing or perhaps two years of college-level training with an emphasis in library and media technologies. In order to provide this training, many community colleges in the United States and Canada began to develop library media technical assistant programs. This development was guided by several divisions of the ALA when they established *Criteria for Programs to Prepare Library Technical Assistants* (1979).

These criteria defined the LMTA's role in the library and the type of education this employee should receive. The criteria suggested educational programs at the community college level in which curricula covered three broad areas—general education, library technology courses, and other related courses. The library technology courses were to include an introduction to libraries and library operations as well as provide laboratory experience and practical, supervised fieldwork.

This book is designed as both a textbook for a library technology course on library operations and as a handbook for laboratory exercises, fieldwork, and in-service training programs. It describes basic operations such as circulation, filing, serials, and processing, which are commonly performed in most libraries. It is written for people who have never worked in libraries and explains both procedures and terminology.

Through the chapters and study units, readers can learn to perform and supervise those procedures that are common to most library operations. They will also be introduced to the philosophy and principles behind those rules and procedures. Emphasis is placed on the purposes of such procedures, what to consider in performing them, and efficient methods in completing them. The attitudes and philosophy a staff member should develop are specifically discussed. Commonality of procedures is stressed, but individual libraries differ; so LMTAs must adapt efficiently to these local variations.

To help the reader accomplish this learning task, the relationships between various library operations are presented. For example, the importance of accurate circulation records and files is reinforced in the shelving and inventory units. Also, the chapter on filing should help students realize the complexity of the catalog, so they will learn to help patrons use the card catalog rather than tell them to look up the information.

Since a library media technical assistant also serves as a supervisor and instructor, the techniques needed to teach and motivate others are also discussed. These techniques are based on the principle that a good supervisor should be thoroughly knowledgeable about a job in order to instruct others. In addition, the supervisor must develop the ability to communicate well with a new employee and be able to explain procedures understandably. Frequently, a supervisor has been taught on the job and can perform an operation exceptionally well but cannot teach anyone else to perform the same job. The techniques and procedures presented in this text should enable a supervisor to instruct employees and help them understand the purposes behind the procedures.

By learning the relationships between these procedures and their underlying principles, the clerical and technical staffs will contribute to effective library service. Study of the subject matter of this text will enable the reader to learn these relationships and to (1) carry out instructions of the librarian and demonstrate correct work habits and methods, (2) perform and supervise procedures presented in the text, (3) define library terms and use them correctly, and (4) review library procedures and suggest the best ones in relationship to objectives and policies.

1 The Library: Its Policies, Procedures, Personnel, and Service

Unit Objectives:

Identify the major purposes and objectives of various types of libraries.

Discuss the effects of these purposes on the development of library policies and procedures.

Emphasize the importance and effects of procedures in a library on good public library service.

Describe personal qualities that are needed and why they are required by library personnel in all jobs.

Identify rules of library etiquette and ethics which are important ingredients of good library service.

The Library

Before we can identify the policies and procedures that a library will follow, we should first define what a library is.

A library can be defined as an institution for the acquisition, preservation, and dissemination of information in all of its forms. This information may be contained in books, magazines, pictures, film, records, tapes, and even computer data bases. And yet, although all libraries will acquire and preserve these materials and make them available, they will usually differ from one another in the policies and procedures they adopt to fulfill these basic functions.

Each library has been established to satisfy the specific needs of the society it serves. These needs have been translated into purposes or objectives that libraries try to achieve. Historically, a review of the purposes of libraries from their beginnings shows that, among other purposes, they have preserved the archives, records, and ideas of their times; encouraged the exchange of information during great periods of learning; and supported education on both an informal and a formal basis.

Today's libraries acquire their collections and encourage their use for many different purposes. Besides preserving archives and supporting education, they also provide recreational reading, encourage aesthetic appreciation, satisfy informational needs, and support research. However, not all libraries try to fulfill all these objectives. Instead, libraries tend to satisfy a few specific needs of special groups of patrons. Those libraries that attempt to fulfill similar objectives are often considered to belong to similar categories or types of libraries.

Basically, there are four major types of libraries: public, school, academic, and special.

Public libraries are supported by local public taxes and provide free library services to every resident of the taxing community. They usually have six major objectives which can be identified as recreation, education, information, research, culture (or aesthetic appreciation), and social responsibility.

The purpose of school libraries is to support the educational curriculum of elementary or secondary schools (kindergarten through the twelfth grade). Since today's American schools are interested in educating the total child, their school libraries provide information on many subjects in a great variety of formats. This variety of materials and an increase in library activities have influenced their reorganization into first instructional materials centers and then into school media centers. At the same time, library staff such as audiovisual specialists, librarians, audiovisual and library clerks, and aides have been transformed into media specialists, media technicians, and aides.

Academic libraries serve post–high school institutions such as junior colleges, colleges, and universities. Their major purposes are to support the educational, informational, and research needs of their faculty and students.

Special libraries are defined by the Special Libraries Association as those sponsored by an organization or group. They serve members by providing special services and often have a special subject collection. They include business, industry, church, hospital, and prison libraries. They also include special-subject libraries such as medical or music libraries. Their major purposes are to provide information to and support the research of their organization's members.

The major purposes of the various types of libraries are not mutually exclusive, and many libraries have purposes other than those stated here. However, understanding the types of libraries and the major differences in their purposes will clarify the direction that their policies and procedures will take.

Once libraries have determined their major purposes and acquired their materials, they should concern themselves with disseminating this information in accordance with these goals. This dissemination is the library's most important function because policy should be based on the idea of service to patrons. A library is *not* a collection of materials to be stored and seldom used—it is designed to be a dynamic source of information. A library's existence should depend upon giving the best possible service to its patrons.

Policies and Procedures

A library can ensure that it will provide "good library service" if it follows several basic principles. First, it should adopt *stated* purposes and objectives. Then, it should develop policies and procedures based on these objectives and designed to satisfy the needs of the patrons. Finally, these policies and procedures (and the purposes behind them) must be understood and supported by every staff member. Only if these steps are followed can a library effectively fulfill its objectives.

Who formulates these library purposes and objectives? It will come as a surprise to many people to find that "the librarian" is not the person who controls library policy. The head librarian or library director is usually responsible to some governing authority that represents the citizen or controlling institution.

In a public library, the governing agency may be a board of trustees or library board. The library may also be a department of the local government with the librarian responsible to the mayor or city manager. If there is a board of trustees, it is responsible to the public for the operation of the library. The board hires the librarian and library staff, states the library objectives and policies, and is generally responsible for any actions taken by the library and its staff.

The librarian is responsible to the board for implementing the objectives and policies set by the board. To do this, the librarian customarily recommends the hiring and organizing of the library staff and is responsible for efficient operation, public relations, and development of good service.

In libraries of other types there is similar responsibility for library policies and operations. The librarian is the professional who guides and assists the board of trustees, school board, or administration in stating the objectives of the particular library. The librarian then directs the library staff in developing policies and procedures to carry out these objectives.

The policies and procedures that a library will develop to carry out its objectives will usually be determined by its type. Because each type of library serves the needs of different patrons, these policies and procedures can differ a great deal.

The size of the library, regardless of type, will also affect policies and procedures. Large libraries of every type will tend to have more stringent policies than smaller libraries and to follow them more strictly. However, regardless of their size, libraries of each type will generally have similar policies.

For example, public libraries try to satisfy the educational, recreational, cultural, and informational needs of all the people in the community by designing policies to make materials and services available to the largest number of people. Policies such as those for reserving items for a patron, charging overdue fines, and borrowing items from other libraries will be designed to provide equal service for every taxpayer.

However, the policies of a public library could also be influenced by the size of the population it serves. A large public library might require a proof of residence before issuing a borrower's card, while a library in a smaller, more stable community might not need to do so. Although any fines or fees charged by a public library are applied equally to all patrons, a large public library might collect them immediately, while a small public library might be more flexible. In each case, the policies will be based upon individual objectives and purposes.

A school library media center's needs and purposes will produce slightly different policies. Materials in great demand may be placed on reserve shelves so that all students will have access to them. Overdue policies may be more informal, since school policies make it easier to locate students and hold them responsible for their materials. School media center hours may be much more restricted than public-library hours because of policies concerning the hours students can be in the building and because the school media center is not necessarily designed to provide recreational summer reading.

The basic purposes for school media centers are undergoing serious discussion in the library and educational worlds, and these changing goals will inevitably influence the media center's purposes and policies in the future. For example, some educators and librarians are striving to make the facilities available to students and others beyond the normal hours of the school day. Other educators and librarians are establishing satellite resource centers away from the main media center. These satellite centers provide materials and staff to support subject departments such as the science or English department. Thus, libraries are always reevaluating their purposes and objectives and do not remain static.

Academic libraries also design their policies to serve their educational objectives. These libraries usually choose policies and procedures providing the greatest use of and access to their library materials. For example, many academic libraries remain open very late in the evening, and some are even open on a twenty-four-hour basis. Also, most academic library circulation systems show the location of every item checked out, so that any item can be recalled immediately if it is needed. These libraries also provide reserve materials collections to ensure that many students can have access to a limited supply of materials.

Special libraries are usually designed to provide information and assist in research for their clientele. Therefore, many searches that the patron would have to undertake in other libraries are provided by the staff in special libraries. The special-library patron is most concerned with the speed in which the information is obtained and not in how or where it is found. Since business and industrial libraries are supported by profit-making organizations, they are designed and operated according to policies intended to enhance the organization's ability to make a profit.

In the future, distinctions among the various types of libraries may become less pronounced. More and more, libraries are forming cooperative systems composed of more than one type. As this continues, their objectives may become more similar so that all libraries will serve the needs of a wider variety of patrons. As objectives are combined, policies and procedures will change as well. Catalog and resource sharing may lead to cooperative borrower registration and circulation systems. For example, in one cooperative system, a small academic library issued public library cards to its students and faculty. All of the community's public-library cards could then be used at the large university library nearby. Such policies may become common in the future.

Whether policies serve one library or many, they must be designed well if they are to be effective in achieving a particular purpose or objective. In addition, *the procedures to carry out these policies must be as carefully designed to achieve an objective as the policies*. Good policies can be negated by procedures that carry out the objective inefficiently. For example, a library's objective to encourage and facilitate the patron's use of the library might have to be combined with a need to issue all branch-patron cards from the main library. The procedures to carry out this policy could follow several different routes. One procedure could have all cards filled out by a staff member on a particular day of the week, regardless of when the application was taken, and held for the patron to pick up (requiring the branch patron to travel to the main library). Another procedure could have a staff member fill out cards every day for the preceding day's applications and mail out the cards to the patrons. The first procedure might at first glance seem to be more efficient and cheaper for the library, but the second procedure would enable a patron to return more quickly and check out books.

The preamble of the American Library Association's *Code of Ethics for Librarians* (1938) states that "the library as an institution exists for the benefit of a given constituency." If all library procedures were evaluated with this in mind, many procedures now in use by libraries might be redesigned. The major purpose of any procedure should not be to make its operation easier for the staff but to satisfy the objectives of good library service. Many times these two purposes go hand in hand, but at other times librarians and supervisors must introduce procedures that are more complicated or more difficult for the staff. If all library personnel understood the purpose behind each procedure and why it was chosen over others, they might accept it more readily and perform it better.

It is this human element that is most important in carrying out library procedures. Only if the staff members understand *why* they must perform a procedure and how it fits into the total picture of the library's objectives will they perform it willingly and well so that they can contribute to effective library service.

Personnel

A library staff is divided into two major categories of personnel, professional and supportive, to carry out all its functions. The titles and responsibilities of these personnel levels were designated by the American Library Association in 1970 (*American Libraries* 4 (1970): 341–44). These titles are librarian, specialist, library associate, library media technical assistant, and library clerk (see appendix A).

The professional responsibilities fall to the librarians, specialists, senior librarians, and senior specialists. Primarily, their duties involve managing the library services and operations and administering library policies. Personnel in these positions possess at least master's degrees in library, media, or other specialized areas and will supervise the rest of the staff in the performance of their duties.

Personnel who hold bachelor's degrees are called library associates. Their responsibilities are sometimes termed subprofessional because they fall just below those of the professional librarian or specialist. Often, the library associate may have a special subject expertise that enables that person to perform a particular function in the library.

Personnel with bachelor's degrees may also sometimes be considered professionals if they fulfill assignments with professional librarian responsibilities. For example, persons serving as librarians in special libraries, or persons with majors or minors in library science or media technology who function as school media specialists are often considered to be professionals or librarians.

Library media technical assistants should have at least two years of college-level study (or post-secondary training.) This personnel level, also referred to as paraprofessional, supports the associate and professional staffs. LMTAs follow established rules and procedures, and many supervise other LMTAs or clerks in performance of library tasks and duties. (For an LMTA job description, see appendix B.)

Library clerks are often referred to as nonprofessionals because they need no training beyond high school to enter the library field. They will receive any library training they may need through on-the-job programs.

All members of a library staff must work together when performing their duties if the library is to achieve its objectives. Unless the various staff members accept their responsibilities for effective library service, they may work at cross purposes and destroy the very thing they are trying to build.

Personal qualities

Library personnel are the key to whether a library satisfies its patrons and achieves its objectives and purposes. No amount of formal public relations by a library can offset a staff that is efficient but considered unfriendly and unapproachable by the public. The personal qualities of every staff member reflect on the image of the library, and library etiquette and ethics practiced by the personnel can make the library a vibrant, well-used facility or turn it into a mausoleum.

The two most important personal qualities needed by every staff member are a liking for people and an interest in helping them. Personnel in every department in the library need these qualities because people are important in every aspect of library work. Good personal relations between staff members are as important as good public relations with the patrons.

The first qualities a librarian will look for in an employment interview with a prospective staff member are those outward qualities that indicate that a person is interested in others. Some of these qualities are enthusiasm, a wide-ranging interest in many subjects (not just a liking for books), interest in others, ability to communicate well, willingness to admit lack of knowledge, and a friendly and pleasant personality. Prospective employers are also interested in the human-relations qualities of politeness, patience, tact, helpfulness, and consideration for others.

Qualities such as judgment, perception, and imagination which indicate an ability to think are equally important and are usually thought to be those a person either has or does not have. However, these latter qualities can be broken down into abilities that a person can work to develop. Perception and a good memory often come from paying close attention to detail and the observation of routines. Imagination can be strengthened by investigating situations with an open mind and dreaming of "things that could be" rather than dwelling on "things that are." Good judgment can be developed by practicing the decision-making process. This process includes looking at all the factors involved in a situation, thoroughly evaluating every point, and selecting and implementing the most effective way to handle the situation. Persistence and dependability in pursuing a job to its end, along with punctuality in performing assignments, are characteristics that will help the employee perform well on the job.

Good personal appearance and grooming have been left until last because they are often the most difficult area for employers to deal with. Daily personal hygiene and grooming are essential for persons who will have contact with other people. This area is one of the hardest for employers to correct tactfully, and many persons have not been hired or have been given false reasons for their dismissal from jobs rather than told of their hygiene problems. Each person must be his or her own guardian in such personal matters.

Personal appearance is as important in library work as it is in banking, sales, or any other patron-oriented service position. In dressing for jobs that deal with the public, staff members should remember that the patron may be judging their character partly by their appearance. If a library staff member wears clothes that are five to ten years out of style, the patron may assume that the person's ideas and thoughts are also outdated. Library personnel should dress appropriately for a library work situation and follow the guidelines set by library policy.

Library etiquette

Equally as important as the personal qualities of staff members working with the public is the etiquette they practice. Library etiquette is based on the premise that the patron is a person important to the library and its staff. If library personnel would treat patrons as they do other people in social situations, there might be no need for such a term as *library etiquette*. However, all too often the personnel are involved in their various assignments and forget that the library exists to serve the patrons.

There are several basic rules that should be followed when working with patrons. The patron should be treated with the same respect and courtesy as a social acquaintance would be. Staff members should look at patrons when talking with them, listen to them when they speak, and show an interest in helping them. It should not be taken for granted that the patron knows anything about the library. Personnel working in an establishment often assume that everyone knows the rules or arrangement of a particular library. Instead, library terms should be explained, library staff members' names and positions pronounced distinctly, and clear directions given so that the patron knows what to do or how to get where he or she wants to go. It should always be remembered that the patron is a human being and that the library is staffed by human beings; they are known to make mistakes at times, but the mistakes usually are not disastrous and can be corrected. If a problem arises with a patron, the staff should be pleasant and helpful, for the problem may just as easily have been caused by the library as by the patron. There is a phrase that sums up these rules of library etiquette: *Good patron relations are the best public relations*.

Library ethics

Library personnel should follow a code of ethics such as the *Statement on Professional Ethics* adopted by the American Library Association (ALA 1981). This statement emphasizes that personal views and activities of employees may be interpreted as being representative of the library. Therefore, care should be taken to distinguish between private actions and authorized responses or actions. All library personnel have a responsibility to maintain the principles of the Library Bill of Rights and to protect the confidentiality of the library user. Library ethics require staff members to be loyal to the spirit of the Library Bill of Rights as well as to the libraries in which they work. If these two come into conflict, the staff members should work within the library structure to bring them together.

If a staff member disagrees with library policies, personnel, or services, he or she should only offer criticism of them to the proper authority for the sole purpose of improving the library. Criticism should never be expressed to patrons, and information concerning patrons should be considered confidential and not discussed with others. Library personnel, whether public or private employees, must conduct themselves in an ethical manner.

By their behavior, library personnel can develop a friendly and inviting library environment, or they can present a forbidding point of view that discourages patrons from using the facilities and calling on the staff for help. It is up to each staff member to do his or her best to develop a library environment that will foster good library service.

Library Service

Every aspect of a library should be aimed at providing service to its patrons. A library's objectives, policies, procedures, personnel, and programs or services must all have this goal in mind, or it will not be reached, and the library will become an archaic institution. Each aspect is like a part in a jigsaw puzzle—if one part is missing or distorted, the picture will not be complete.

One major part of this jigsaw puzzle is expressed in the Library Bill of Rights and the Freedom to Read statement which have been adopted by the American Library Association. These documents provide a foundation for library service which is based on the principle of intellectual freedom. This principle recognizes the library's responsibility for providing materials that represent all points of view. It also acknowledges that materials should not be excluded or removed from a collection because someone disagrees with or disapproves of them. This freedom of access to information has been recognized as one of the basic tenets of a democratic society.

Another major puzzle part is governed by a library's ability to identify its patrons' needs and to provide materials and services to satisfy these needs. Many libraries have accepted this challenge by attempting to provide "the right material to the right patron at the right time." How well they do this is determined by how well they design their policies and procedures to facilitate rather than hinder the satisfaction of their patrons' needs. It is in satisfying these needs that a library fulfills its *raison d'être* (reason for being).

Conclusion

Libraries have developed throughout the centuries to satisfy specified needs or objectives. However, their major purpose has always been to acquire, preserve, and make available information in all of its many forms. In achieving this purpose, four major types of libraries have developed; they are public, school, academic, and special libraries. Although libraries within each of these types may differ, they generally fulfill similar objectives and develop policies and procedures to fulfill these objectives. However, these objectives and policies can only be as effective as are the staff members who carry them out. Libraries must develop such staffs by encouraging personal qualities and behavior that will contribute to effective library service and satisfy their patrons' needs.

Student Work Unit

Based on chapter 1, the student will be able to:

1. Identify all the major purposes of each of the four types of libraries.
2. In a short paragraph, discuss the importance of designing library procedures that are based upon library objectives.
3. List five personal qualities needed by all library personnel and describe the importance of each in a short paragraph.

4. Identify five guidelines of library etiquette and illustrate two of them by describing example library situations.

Teaching Unit

Students list personal qualities needed by library personnel in class and discuss the importance of each. Students can also discuss guidelines for library etiquette and illustrate with example library situations. Students can role play interviews between patrons and library staff members.

2 The Circulation Department

Unit Outline:

Circulation System Objectives
Circulation Systems
Circulation Personnel and Their Duties
Conclusion
Student Work Unit
Teaching Unit

Unit Objectives:

Identify the purposes of the circulation department and the objectives of the major types of libraries in this activity.

Describe the principles of the basic circulation systems and their variations.

Emphasize the importance of the circulation department in public relations.

Describe example circulation responsibilities and duties of various types of library personnel.

Describe three guidelines to follow when the librarian's assistance should be requested.

The circulation department is one of the most important areas in a library because it provides the patron's first contact with the library. It is the one department with which most patrons come into contact on every visit. Therefore, all the library rules, procedures, and personnel should be directed toward making this contact a satisfying one. This public-relations value of the circulation department cannot be overstressed and must be taken into consideration by every staff member.

The major purposes of the circulation department are to provide a record of the items charged out of the library and to get materials to and from the reader as quickly and efficiently as possible. When these purposes are translated into policies and procedures, they can involve a large number of the library staff and many staff hours to perform jobs which are often repetitive and time consuming. Library staff members should constantly be looking for ways to simplify and improve these procedures in the light of the major purposes of the library and its circulation objectives. These procedures must be kept relevant and continue to contribute to satisfying library contacts for the patrons. In this light, every library should make its regulations as flexible as possible except when the convenience of one patron might cause great inconvenience to others.

Circulation System Objectives

Each of the major types of libraries has its own circulation needs based on its purposes. Public libraries need to make their materials available on an equitable basis to all patrons. School and academic libraries need to provide a few materials to many students at one time. Special libraries need to provide materials to a patron as quickly as possible and for as long as needed. Therefore, the circulation system that a particular library will choose will depend on its type and the individual requirements of its local situation.

Fry (1961, p. 15) indicates that the accepted minimum objectives for a circulation system for public libraries are to: (1) identify the materials charged out, (2) identify the borrower, (3) provide a means for recalling overdue material, and (4) keep statistics of the total number of materials charged out. Other objectives are also sometimes considered, and these might be: (5) provide an efficient reserve system, (6) identify delinquent borrowers, and (7) report detailed borrower and circulation statistics, which can enable a library to evaluate the use of its collection. However, the cost of keeping these statistics in some circulation systems may outweigh the value gained from gathering the statistics. Detailed circulation statistics are being kept less often by libraries because they found that the value gained from the statistics was not enough to warrant the cost of collecting them.

School and academic libraries have the same minimum objectives as public libraries plus the additional objective of an efficient reserve and recall system. The academic library must be able to locate its materials at all times so that they may be recalled as promptly as possible. This one objective may largely determine the type of circulation system an academic library will choose.

Special libraries are concerned most often with the needs to (1) identify the material charged out, (2) identify the borrower, and (3) have an efficient reserve and recall system. Compared to public libraries, special libraries are usually less concerned with overdues, because special libraries have less need to provide all patrons equal access to their materials. Sometimes special libraries also have the objective of maintaining records of all items checked out by each borrower. This may be necessary in order to recover the materials if a borrower leaves the organization.

Considering these minimum objectives and its own local needs, a library can establish its own objectives and choose a circulation system that will satisfy its individual purposes.

Circulation Systems

A wide variety of circulation systems is used in libraries today, and there will be more in the future. In determining which system to choose, libraries should keep in mind the minimum criteria a system should meet. First of all, it should be simple for the public and staff to use and understand; second, it should be economical in relation to the total library budget; third, it should be adaptable to a library branch system and compatible with other library operations, such as acquisitions or cataloging. Needless to say, it must also satisfy the library's circulation objectives.

Other criteria that will influence the choice of a circulation system are economy in terms of staff and patron time and the provision of safeguards from error. It should be usable with all types of material and provide for various loan periods. A good circulation system should facilitate the execution of other library operations and require as few steps and as little equipment as possible. In choosing a new circulation system, another important consideration is that it should not require excessive change-over costs and problems. All these criteria may be met by several types of circulation systems that will be described here.

There have been many types of circulation systems, and the earliest ones were very simple. The *daybook* system simply recorded each borrower and book title, one right after the other, in a record book. The *ledger* system divided the record book by borrower and recorded each borrower's books on a separate page. When a book was charged out in the *dummy book* system, blocks of wood with the borrower's name attached were placed in the book's place on the shelf. This system allowed a staff member or patron to easily tell who had the wanted book.

The Newark system

After these simple systems, libraries next used temporary charge slips. The borrower's name and the book title were written on a slip when the book was checked out, and the slip was destroyed when the book was returned. Later, permanent slips were put in books, and these became the forerunner of the book card. Next, borrowers were given cards showing that they were patrons of the library. The Newark (New Jersey) Public Library in 1900 became the first to use a two-card system utilizing both book and borrower cards, which became known as the *Newark charging system*.

The Newark system, including its many variations, has become one of the most common circulation systems in libraries today (see fig. 1). Its popularity stems from its simplicity and its usefulness in small and medium-sized libraries of all types. Borrowers' cards either use the patron's name or assign numbers to borrowers in sequential order. Records of these cards are then kept in alphabetical or numerical registration files or, in some cases, both. When a book is charged out in the Newark system, the book card is withdrawn from the book, the borrower's number and the due date are written or imprinted on the book card, and this card is filed by due date at the circulation desk (see figs. 1 and 2). The due date is also stamped in the book so that the patron knows when to return the book. When the book is returned, the book card is pulled from the appropriate due date file and replaced in the book. This system has many variations. For example, the due date may be stamped on the borrower's card rather than in the book; predated due-date cards may be placed in the book pocket; or patrons may write their own borrower's number rather than having a staff member do it.

The system had many advantages that speeded its adoption. It provided a permanent record of all book charges and a permanent record of the circulation for each individual book. The loan record identified the material, the borrower, and the date the material was due, thus helping the librarian deal with overdues. It provided a book charge that could be located in the files and marked for reserve requests, and it provided data for many types of statistical studies. The system's disadvantages were that routines were slow and time-consuming, and inaccuracies could develop because of illegible borrowers' numbers or names and misfiled book cards. Some of these disadvantages were offset by the introduction of mechanical charging systems by companies such as Gaylord, Demco, and Brodart. Among other functions, these machines eliminated written borrower names or numbers by using imprinted metal or plastic numbers.

The transaction card system

Public libraries used the Newark system for many years because of its advantages. As the economy changed, however, the Newark system became less and less economical in relation to the total library budget. Public libraries with a circulation of more than 50,000 began to adopt a new type of circulation system called a *transaction card system* (see fig. 3). This system is based on a series of sequentially prenumbered cards, called transaction cards, which are used to keep track of all book charges. When a book is charged out, the transaction card number, the borrower information, the book information, and the due date are usually recorded on microfilm by such machines as the Recordak or Regiscope (see fig. 4). The due date is recorded on the transaction card, and the card is placed in the book. Borrower information can be obtained from any form of

(a)

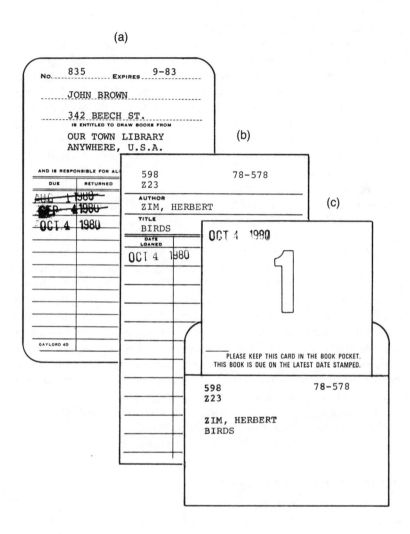

Fig. 1. Newark charging system records.

(a) Borrower's library card; (b) Book card; (c) Due-date card is placed in book pocket.

sharing. Although many vendors have entered and left this market, libraries have been generally satisfied with the automated systems they have adopted.

Several types of automated circulation system have emerged in recent years. Although they may be replaced tomorrow by new technology, most of them are designed along similar lines. They require book or item identification, borrower identification, a due date, and different codes to indicate whether an item is being charged, discharged, reserved, or handled in some other way (see fig. 5). Many on-line systems use identification bar codes, or "zebra labels," which are placed on every item and on the borrowers' cards. To charge out an item, the "charge" code is selected, and a light pen or wand (similar to a small pocket flashlight) or laser beam is passed over the bar codes of the item and borrower's card to optically "read" the numbers and enter them in the computer's data bank (see fig. 6). To check in an item, the "discharge" code is chosen, and the light pen or laser is again passed over the item's bar code. Thus, all circulation information is recorded immediately in all library files.

Most automated circulation systems also provide features not available in other circulation systems. On-line systems can often indicate to the staff member that a borrower is ineligible to check out a book because of overdues or other problems. They can also indicate that a particular item has been reserved or needs attention for some reason. Libraries that belong to library systems can communicate with other branches or library agencies by means of computer, and reserves may often be made instantly on any copy of an item anywhere in the library system. Some automated systems even enable patrons to perform self-service charging or to query the computer about the status of items in the collection. However, these automated circulation system features may be very costly.

Generally, libraries have considered the expense of a computer system to be justified when they have an annual circulation of over 250,000 and can recover the cost of the system in five to seven years. In spite of heavy costs, libraries have been satisfied with their automated systems and list the following principal benefits: user satisfaction, improved patron service, and faster charging and discharging. Contrary to most expectations, when automation is introduced into a system, the staff is generally not reduced. Instead, staff members have been released from circulation duties to spend more time in direct contact with library patrons. Thus, many libraries have finally found circulation systems that enable them to serve their patrons more fully and to provide good library service.

Although larger libraries seem most likely to use automated circulation systems, other libraries can also take advantage of their many benefits. Turnkey library systems using minicomputers or microcomput-

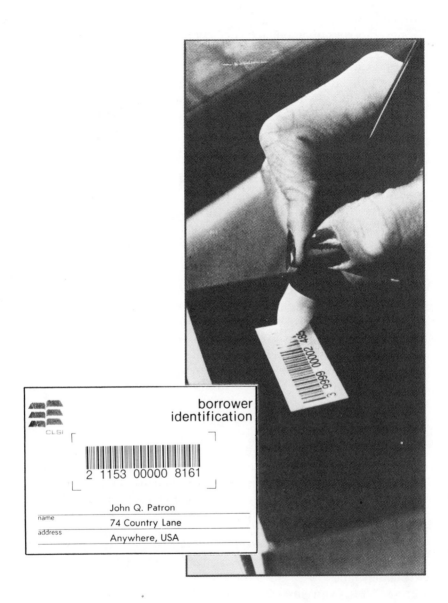

Fig. 5. Computer circulation system.

(a) Borrower's card; (b) Book being charged out with light pen. (Courtesy of CL Systems, Inc.)

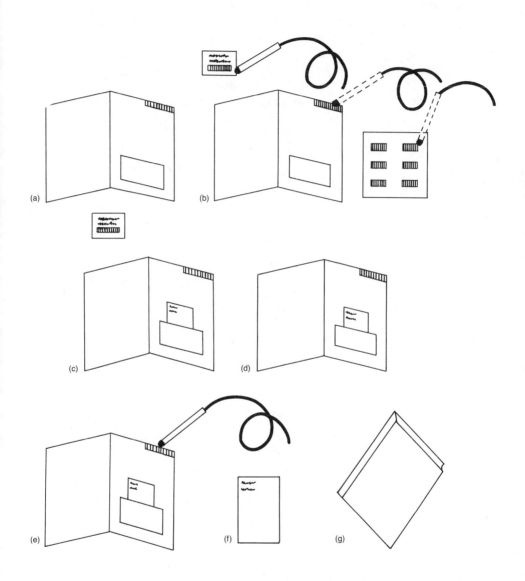

Fig. 6.   Computer circulation system.

(a) Book to be charged out and borrower card; (b) Light pen "reads" borrower code on zebra label, due date, and book code on book zebra label; (c) Due-date card placed in book; (d) Book returned; (e) Light pen "reads" book code label; (f) Due-date card pulled from book; (g) Book is ready to be shelved.

ers are being offered by vendors at prices reasonable enough to attract medium-sized and small libraries. Their capabilities are ideal for academic libraries that must be able to recall items instantly or to exclude a student from borrowing until library obligations are paid. Public libraries also appreciate having information about their circulating materials that exceeds that provided by the Newark system, while also enjoying the simplicity of use offered by the transaction systems.

Generally, however, small public libraries still use the Newark system or a variation of it. School and special libraries most often use a simple charging system requiring only the borrower's signature and room or company identification number on the book card. These libraries use the school or organization's records for locating borrowers rather than keeping duplicate borrower-registration files.

Double-record charging system

The need for academic libraries to locate their material at all times determines their choice of circulation systems. Some may use a double-record charge system that requires two identical charge slips for each book charge. One slip is filed under its due date for overdue purposes. The other slip is filed in call-number or shelflist order, the order used to file the books on the shelves (see fig. 7). This file provides one location file for all the books not on the shelves. When the book is returned, both slips must be pulled from their files.

McBee-keysort system

Another system often used, the McBee-keysort system, utilizes charge cards on which the borrower, book, and due date information are written. The margins of the card have holes that can be notched out to represent the due date or type of borrower information (fig. 8). The charge cards may then be filed in call-number order. When due date or borrower information is needed, a long needle can be inserted into the appropriate hole in a group of cards. When the needle is lifted, the cards notched for the desired information will fall out of the pile. This system satisfies most of the objectives for a circulation system, but the initial notching procedure is time-consuming.

These are some of the charging systems currently used in libraries because they meet today's circulation objectives. In the future, objectives may change, especially as libraries and library patrons become more concerned with maintaining the privacy of circulation records. Although today's major circulation systems may satisfy a library's objectives in various ways, there probably never will be a "perfect" system. Instead, a system will be chosen because, at the time, its advantages outweigh its

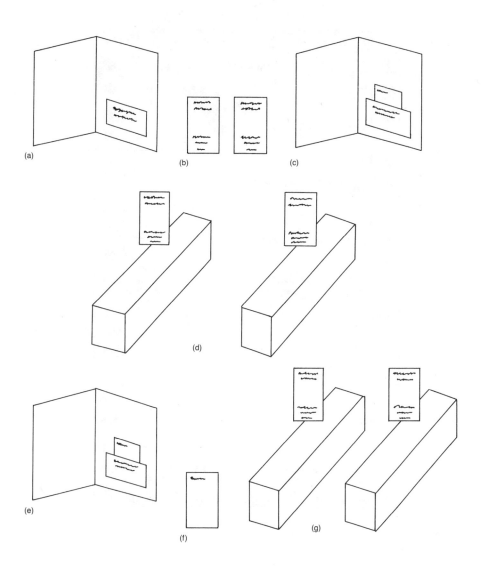

Fig. 7.   Double-record charging system.

(a) Book is ready to be charged out; (b) Two charges are made for the book; (c) Due-date card is placed in the book; (d) Book charges are filed, one by call number and one by due date or borrower's name; (e) Book is returned; (f) Due-date card is pulled from book; (g) Both charges are pulled from the files.

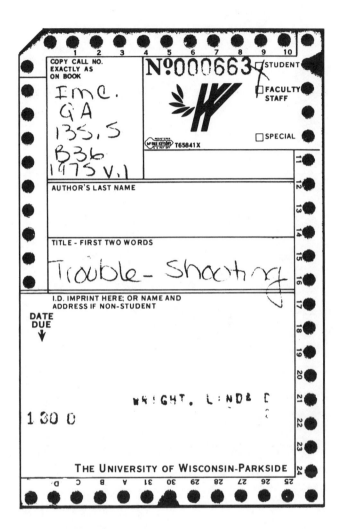

Fig. 8.   McBee-keysort circulation charge.

Book is due on January 30, 1980 (1 30 0).

disadvantages. In this case, library staff members must be observant and continually analyze the operations of the library system to simplify methods and procedures and minimize waste and unnecessary motion. Only in this way can a library effectively carry out the purposes of the circulation department.

Circulation Personnel and Their Duties

The circulation department and its personnel have many routines, procedures, and duties to perform to operate a circulation system. Since the next chapter will discuss these procedures in detail, they will be mentioned only briefly here.

The circulation department's major purpose, to provide a record of the items charged out of the library, involves many procedures and routines. Staff members charge materials out, check in or discharge returned items, maintain records of these loans, recall overdue materials, and assess fines. They also maintain registration files of borrowers and keep statistics. The circulation department is also a service area and assists patrons in using the library, reserves material that a patron may request, and even borrows material from other libraries for a patron's use. Staff members also shelve materials, maintain the collection so that all items are kept in place, and assist patrons in finding materials of their choice. Periodically, inventories are taken so that lost books and materials can be replaced, torn or damaged items repaired, and out-of-date materials withdrawn and replaced by current materials. Circulation staff members do much more than charge books in and out or read books when there are no patrons at the desk!

A new staff member may wonder who performs all of these circulation routines—that is, whether everyone performs all of the jobs or if the jobs are divided up in some way. Larger libraries with separate staffs in the circulation and reference areas may have distinct divisions among the professional, technical, and clerical responsibilities in the circulation department. The staff in small libraries may appear to share circulation duties; however, even here there are distinctions when decisions must be made.

Usually, three areas of responsibility exist in a circulation department: (1) establishing and supervising policies, (2) establishing and supervising procedures to carry out the policies, and (3) carrying out the procedures. Each area is usually the responsibility of a different level of personnel (see appendix C).

The professional librarian's primary function in the circulation department is to establish circulation policies and supervise the staff members in this department. The librarian also acts as a liaison between the circulation department and other departments and handles unusual patron complaints or compliments. Until several years ago, many libraries assigned professional librarians as circulation librarians to supervise the daily operations of this department. However, their other duties often kept them away from the circulation area attending meetings or consulting with others.

A recent trend to improve utilization of library staff members has encouraged librarians to delegate supervision of the circulation procedures and daily operations to subprofessional or paraprofessional staff members. Library administrators have found that such personnel can effectively supervise clerical employees and handle routine operations. They can also be trusted to request professional assistance when it is needed to resolve complicated issues.

Staff members at the technical or paraprofessional level have been assigned important duties in the circulation department. In many libraries, LMTAs supervise and train clerical, student, and volunteer personnel. They also schedule such personnel. They may, in some cases, establish circulation procedures and routines in consultation with the librarian. LMTAs may supervise the charging, discharging, overdue, reserve, and shelving procedures. Although the LMTA in charge of the circulation area will know how to perform these circulation routines, his or her primary responsibility may be to supervise others in carrying out these duties.

The responsibility for performing these normal circulation routines is usually given to the clerical staff or the newest staff members. Library clerks and aides will charge and discharge library materials, count circulation, type overdue notices, shelve materials, and file cards. If questions or problems arise concerning an item or a patron, clerical personnel are expected to turn for assistance to the LMTA in charge. Thus, a library can build a strong circulation team by developing a chain of command or chain of responsibility from student and clerical to technical to professional personnel.

This team approach is important to the library because many patrons believe that the person who checks the books in and out is "the librarian" in charge of everything. Since the person at the circulation desk is more often than not the newest person hired, it is important for even the most junior staff member to understand the part that he or she plays in the image the patron has of the library.

The circulation department is much more than a circulation system, circulation procedures, or a department that provides a record of the items charged out of the library. This department usually represents the pulse of the library. It is the place where patrons can sense whether the library staff is interested in them and their use of its services or more concerned with preserving the collection.

How can patrons tell this about a library? They need only observe whether the staff members notice them when they enter. Does the staff talk to them? Does the staff offer to assist the patrons when they rummage through the card catalog? Do they suggest a book to borrow on interlibrary loan that the library does not have? Do they suggest a new book on the same subject when a patron returns a book?

These are simple and obvious gestures of interest in a patron, but many staff members are so caught up in their daily tasks that they treat the patron as an intruder. Worse yet, they may even groan when a patron returns a large stack of materials or asks for an item that will require them to make a trip to the basement or attic. The staff member may only be doing this in jest, but the bad effects that these remarks or negative body language has on public relations may remain a long time. Likewise, carelessness in such areas as discharging materials, filing circulation cards, and preparing overdue notices can create unnecessary problems and ill will on the part of the patron.

Courtesy is particularly important when patrons ask questions of staff members. The kinds of questions normally answered at the circulation desk and the manner in which they are handled will vary from library to library. Some librarians would recommend that questions answered by nonprofessional and paraprofessional employees be limited to directional questions such as "Where is the card catalog?" or "Where is the Art Department?" This practice may be followed in academic libraries or large libraries that have separate reference staffs trained to answer all other queries. However, in small libraries of all types, a lone staff member may have to assist the patron to the best of his or her ability before calling for assistance from professional staff members either within the building or at a central or regional library center.

Library clerks and assistants often find it hard to ask for assistance or to know when they should ask for such aid. A few guidelines are presented here that may be useful in solving this problem. Circulation clerks or assistants should be able to answer directional questions. If they do not know the answer to such questions, they should find out; they can then answer the question at hand as well as future inquiries. If staff members do not know or cannot easily find the answer to a question, they should refer it to someone who can answer it.

Library clerks and assistants do not have the authority to say no to a patron. If they cannot help, they should turn the patron over to another staff member who may be able to help. Librarians follow this rule themselves, even if they have worked in libraries for many years. A question that may baffle one staff member may have just been answered by another. A book one person cannot find may have just been charged out by another. This happens so often in libraries that it seems to go beyond the realm of coincidence and becomes an accepted fact. Clerks or assistants should feel no stigma if they cannot help a patron further. They should simply say to the patron, "I don't know, but I will help you find out."

The following examples may help illustrate this referral principle. If the questions can be better answered by another department, the question should be referred to that department. If the patron requests a particular person or department, he or she should be directed to that department; staff members should not feel offended that they were not asked for help.

If staff members do not know the answer to a reference question, and after looking in one or two reference sources cannot find the answer, they should ask their colleagues or supervisor for help. One guideline limits the search of a professional or paraprofessional to a maximum of two to three sources or an eight- to ten-minute search. It is believed that if the answer cannot be found by an assistant in that time, his or her knowledge may be too limited to answer the question.

Staff members should follow their own library's policies when asking for help from others. This might mean the patron would be referred to the reference department for such assistance or to other departments for other help. It might also mean that a problem or complaint in the circulation area should be referred to the supervisor immediately.

In any case, staff members should remember that a patron is waiting, patiently or not so patiently, for an answer to a question or problem. Patrons will remember the courtesy and prompt assistance they received long after they have forgotten the question that prompted it. When staff members refer the patron to another staff member for help, they should introduce the patron politely so that the patron feels helped and not just passed on. Sometimes, despite all of a staff member's efforts, some patrons become offended or offensive or just object to library rules. When this happens, the supervisor should be politely called and the patron referred to a higher authority. Often, just talking to the "head" librarian will calm the patron.

Circulation staff members should know their place and responsibility and should understand others' as well. The librarian will not be expected to charge books in and out because he or she is involved in policy decisions and other professional tasks for the entire department. Likewise, LMTAs who supervise a procedure may help perform it but will not perform it as often as a clerk or new assistant. This ladder of duties and responsibilities is designed to produce an efficient and effective personnel team.

Conclusion

The circulation department and its personnel have a very important influence on the public's view of the library. Since every patron who enters the library usually has some contact with this department, it is important for all circulation personnel to see that the library's objectives are fulfilled by its circulation policies and procedures.

The choice of a circulation system by a library will also reflect this emphasis. That is why public libraries tend to use Newark, transaction, or automated systems; school and special libraries use Newark systems; and academic libraries use Newark, double-record, semiautomated, or automated systems. Many libraries have adopted automated circulation systems as the costs of such systems have become more economical in relation to their objectives.

Finally, effective library service is the result of shared efforts by the whole circulation staff. Each level of employee from professional to student has specific duties and responsibilities in this department. If each person accepts these responsibilities, performs his or her duties carefully and willingly, and searches out and receives assistance when needed, a circulation team will be developed that will have a positive effect on the library's public relations.

Student Work Unit

Based on chapter 2 and appendix C, the student will be able to:

1. Identify the major purposes of the circulation department.
2. Identify the minimum objectives of the circulation system of each of the major types of libraries.
3. In a short paragraph for each, describe how books are charged out with the Newark, transaction, and automated circulation systems. Then list two major features of each system that would be important to consider in choosing a circulation system.
4. Write a one-page essay commenting on the following statement: "The public-relations value of the circulation department cannot be overstressed and must be taken into consideration by every staff member in the performance of duties."
5. Describe the reasons for differences in the responsibilities of the librarian, LMTA, and library clerk in charging and discharging books.
6. Describe what should be done by a staff member who cannot answer a patron's inquiry.

Teaching Unit

Representatives of various companies may be willing to present their charging systems to the class, or students could make reports to the class on the various charging systems. Students can role play in staff-patron situations.

3 Circulation Procedures

Unit Outline:

Learning a New Procedure
Instituting a Procedure
Registration
Circulation Loan Periods
Charging Materials
Circulation Statistics
Circulation Charge Files
Discharging Materials
Overdue Policies and Procedures
Overdue Notices
Reserve Materials
Interlibrary Loans
Circulation Desk Routines and Priorities
Conclusion
Student Work Unit
Teaching Unit

Unit Objectives:

Identify guidelines for analyzing and evaluating library procedures.

Describe purposes of and best methods for performing typical circulation procedures.

Identify differences of procedures in various types of libraries and circulation systems.

Present procedures for each section of the chapter.

Choose best methods for performing circulation procedures.

Circulation procedures will be determined largely by the type of circulation system that a library chooses. If a Newark system is used, very detailed manual procedures are needed to search through all of the permanent charge cards. Transaction systems, on the other hand, require fewer procedures, and computer systems replace these manual procedures with automated ones. Because most U.S. libraries still use Newark systems, the procedures for such systems will be described in detail in this chapter. However, all circulation procedures follow common guidelines and principles. Once a person learns to perform routines in one system, this knowledge should be easily transferable to a new system.

Learning a New Procedure

A staff member must always follow library policies in any procedure. When learning a new circulation procedure or when setting one up, a person should follow several steps. First, the objective of the procedure should be determined; this may mean asking questions. Second, the staff member should find out how the procedure is usually carried out.

Instituting a Procedure

When reviewing or setting up a new procedure, all the ways the procedure can be performed should be listed. It should be determined whether each of these methods will achieve the desired objectives. The advantages or disadvantages of each method should be listed. It is then necessary to identify that procedure which requires the minimum physical and mental effort. There are many excellent books on time and motion study available to assist in this area. A procedure that meets all the other requirements but is so disliked by the staff that they will not perform it well can become detrimental to library service in the end. Finally, based on this analysis, the procedure that will best satisfy the library's needs and provide the best library service should be chosen.

In performing a library procedure, each staff member should consider several factors. The first (and most obvious) is to set up a routine that is the easiest physically and mentally for that particular individual to follow. This will produce the most efficient use of time and energy. Second, the same individual should consider how the performance of a routine will affect other staff members. Consideration of others is sometimes forgotten by individuals in work situations. Many times, in fact, library staff members have become so engrossed in their own methods of doing things that they have kept others from performing effectively. The qualities of awareness and interest in others should come into focus; they will help make a staff member one with whom others will enjoy working.

A primary principle to follow when working with circulation procedures is to talk with fellow staff members. There are many circulation activity problems that can be eliminated or solved if good communications take place. If a staff member cannot read a borrower's name and address, he or she should check with another staff member instead of guessing. If a person preparing overdue notices finds that a patron has moved, the staff member in charge of borrowers' registration should be notified so that these records can be made current. Even casual conversations with patrons may turn up information such as a forwarding address for the family that left town and could not be reached by the library regarding seven overdue books. Again, the human factor becomes an important element in providing effective library service.

The most important rule to follow in every library situation is that a staff member should be sure to date and initial every item handled and every note written. This enables the registration assistant to know whom to ask when a borrower's name or address is illegible. Anonymous notes or forms can hinder or complicate the performance of a procedure because the information provided may be incomplete or unclear. The best way to avoid such problems is always to initial everything. This also will contribute to better service for the patron. If patrons have a question about an overdue notice or a reserve book, they can ask for the person who initialed the notice and will feel they are getting personal attention.

These guidelines should help a staff member perform a procedure well. The following sections will discuss the various circulation procedures to which these guidelines will be applied. Detailed instructions for various procedures will be presented that have proven effective and most practical in many library circulation operations.

Registration

Registration creates the official record of a borrower. It provides a file of the patron's or borrower's name, card number, address, phone number, and references. This file is used to locate information for overdue procedures as well as to provide statistical information about the library's patrons. In addition, some libraries use the application card which is signed by the patron as a contractual agreement between the library and the patron (see fig. 9). By signing, the patron agrees to abide by the library's regulations and fulfill any financial obligations that are incurred.

Libraries of different types have different registration procedures. School, academic, and special libraries usually use school or organization records for their registration files rather than create their own borrower records. These libraries can use school or company directories of students or employees to locate information needed for acting on overdue materials. They may either charge out materials by borrower name or by any school or company identification number. The administrative policies of the school or organization usually require the patron to comply with any library obligations. A student may not graduate or an employee may not receive a final paycheck until obligations are met.

Public libraries serve a wider and more diverse public and usually need registration files that provide a verified record of a patron's name and address. Many public libraries require that a patron be listed in the

(a)

No. ___836___

DOE, MARY JANE

Expires ___9-83___

DO NOT WRITE ABOVE THIS LINE

I apply for the right to use the Library and promise to comply with all its rules, to pay promptly fines or damages charged to me, and to give immediate notice of change in my address.

Sign Full Name _Mary Jane Doe_

Address _401 Walnut St.,_   Phone _654-1082_

Occupation _Homemaker_   Business Address _____

Reference _Mrs. Walter Smith_

Address _403 Walnut St.,_

Age _____   Parent's
IF UNDER 14 YEARS   Signature _____
GAYLORD 175   _9-10-80_   _fec_   PRINTED IN U.S.A.

(b)

No. ___836___   EXPIRES ___9-83___

___MARY JANE DOE___

___401 Walnut St.___
IS ENTITLED TO DRAW BOOKS FROM

OUR TOWN LIBRARY
ANYWHERE, U.S.A.

AND IS RESPONSIBLE FOR ALL BOOKS TAKEN ON THIS CARD

(c)

No. ___836___   Expires ___9-83___

Name ___Doe, Mary Jane___

Address ___401 Walnut St.___

Phone No. ___654-1082___

Fig. 9.   Borrower's registration forms used in Newark charging systems.

(a) Application or registration card; (b) Borrower's card; (c) Numerical registration card.

telephone book or city directory. New residents may be required to show proof of residence such as utility or tax receipts or any mail that they have received at their new address. Libraries in small communities might accept the patron's own word as proof of residence since the staff tends to know most members of the community. Public libraries often require a patron to list another person as a reference, but this reference is used only to seek a forwarding address if the patron moves.

How does a library staff decide who may use the facilities? The policies of school and special libraries usually limit their borrowers to members of the school, institution, company, or organization. In academic libraries, borrowing privileges may extend beyond students and staff to alumni or to taxpayers if the institution is publicly supported. Public libraries usually provide free access to residents or taxpayers of the community that financially supports them.

The policies of many libraries also provide for service to the community at large and make provision for special borrowers so that persons otherwise ineligible may use the facility. Public libraries usually issue special-borrower's cards to all students and teachers and to those who work within their legal community. Sometimes a fee may be charged for these special cards, and if so, it may be based on per capita support from local taxpayers. The special-borrower's card may be issued for a shorter or more specific time period than a regular card but usually entitles the patron to the same privileges as a regular card.

Many libraries of all types are now involved in reciprocal arrangements with other libraries. Multiple-library organizations are developing that enable patrons from one library to borrow items from another or to use its facilities. Joint library cards may be issued by several libraries, or each library may use another library's cards as its own. Some states have already developed statewide public library cards. In the future, multistate or national library service may be available to borrowers when they register at a local library.

In light of these developments, libraries have begun reevaluating their registration policies and procedures and reexamining the cost of these procedures in relation to their usefulness. Although the registration forms have traditionally contained invaluable information about their patrons, few libraries have tabulated such information to take advantage of it. (Only computerized circulation systems enable libraries to use such information easily.) Thus, many libraries found that they used their registration files primarily to locate information regarding overdue books and delinquent borrowers. As early as 1961, the Fry study had indicated that a more efficient method for gathering this information would be to keep records only for such problems and eliminate the unnecessary record keeping for the majority of patrons. Instead, the staff member would check a borrower's card or name against a list of delinquent borrowers as many stores check a customer's name against credit card records. The Fry study also recommended that libraries use other types of patron identification. For these reasons, libraries began to look for cheaper and easier ways to keep track of their patrons.

Library circulation systems were developed that eliminated the costly registration routines of the Newark numeric system. Companies such as Gaylord, Brodart, and Demco sold machines that could imprint the borrower's name and address—not just a borrower number. If the borrower signed the card, this could also serve as the contractual agreement. Besides using library cards, some of these machines could also print the information found on credit cards. Transaction charging systems could also use any kind of borrower identification that indicated the borrower's name and address. Libraries with these systems could still assign borrower's cards to show that a patron was eligible to use a library. However, because these cards could also include the information needed for overdues, the registration files could be eliminated.

When libraries reviewed their needs for registration files, they had to be sure that they weren't throwing away information that would be needed in the future. Libraries that adopted computer circulation systems found that they had to maintain registration files and assign numeric borrower numbers because it was too expensive to charge out items by borrower name. These libraries would continue to register patrons and assign borrower numbers, but the information would be entered into the computer data base. This information could be manipulated by the computer so that statistical data could be easily tabulated about borrowers, borrowing patterns by types of patrons, overdue notices, and many other reports.

However, no matter what kind of circulation system is used by a library, the process of issuing a borrower's card or explaining the library's rules is an integral part of a patron's first contact with the library. For this reason, every staff member should understand the function of the registration activity and be able to explain it to new library patrons. The following policies and procedures may serve as useful guidelines for staff members to follow.

Registering a borrower

When registering a new patron, a staff member should make every effort to make the patron feel at ease. A friendly voice and smile will be especially welcome to a new resident, employee, or student. The staff member can then inquire to see if the applicant is eligible to use the library. If the library uses registration cards, the applicant should be invited to fill out an application form. Any confusing items, such as "reference," should be explained to the patron. The staff member should then check to see that the application form is filled out completely and legibly.

Some libraries verify the information using school, company, or local telephone directories. Public libraries may check a city directory to ensure that the patron's address is within the tax district of the library. Although the applicant who lives in a borderline area may not know it, one side of the street may be within the city's legal boundaries and vice versa. Children's applications must usually be signed by parent or guardian because children cannot be held legally responsible for borrowed materials and other obligations. The library may also check the borrower's registration files to see if the borrower already has a library card. The patron may have forgotten about a card or an overdue fine or lost book records which must be cleared up before a new card is issued. If the application is complete and accurate, the staff member usually initials the application. Then the staff member either issues the patron a card or explains when the card will be delivered and what borrowing privileges the patron will have until then.

The staff member should take a few extra minutes and explain the library rules to the new borrower and, if possible, show the person around the library. This will help the borrower to feel welcome and to become acquainted with the library's collections and services.

Issuing a borrower's card

Libraries without application forms may or may not issue library cards. An academic or special library may require a patron to sign a card accepting library obligations before his or her ID card is coded for library usage. Some school and special libraries may not use library cards at all but still keep borrower records at the circulation desk indicating which items a borrower has checked out. This system is useful for any library that needs immediate access to such information when a patron leaves the institution.

Libraries serving children may differ in their policies for issuing library cards. Policies in public libraries have varied from issuing cards to children when they could write their own names to doing so when they entered first grade to allowing them to have cards at any age. When children reach the age of fourteen or enter ninth grade, public libraries usually issue adult cards to them. School libraries, particularly elementary schools, do not issue library cards, but some secondary school libraries use the student's school identification cards. Some school libraries have also restricted use of the library by children in the lower grades.

Libraries have often limited children's privileges to the children's section of a library, but this practice should be eliminated whenever possible. A child's mental and emotional maturity is not dependent upon his or her physical age, and the child's mental growth should not be hindered by limited library policies. The library should encourage the greatest possible use of its facilities by children.

Most libraries issue their cards for a specified length of time because this enables them to keep their borrower's records fairly current. School, academic, and special libraries usually limit their cards or library privileges to persons while they are students, employees, or members in good standing. Many public library cards are good for three-year periods. However, the Fry study recommended that libraries with fairly stable populations issue five-year cards to cut down unnecessary record keeping. Libraries that can use other forms of identification may avoid this problem altogether since people tend to keep their drivers' licenses and credit cards more up-to-date than their library cards.

Maintaining registration records

Libraries that assign numerical borrower numbers must have numerical access to their borrowers. Libraries may either keep this information in manual files or computer files. All files include the borrower's number, name, address, phone number, and card expiration date. Numerical files are used for overdues and for weeding expired borrower's cards on a predetermined periodic basis.

Application cards are usually filed alphabetically by borrower's name. Alphabetical files are used to check for numbers, lost cards, delinquent borrowers, and duplicate borrowers, but the Fry study recommends their elimination because their use is limited. Instead, it recommends a library keep an alphabetical delinquent borrower's file if school or public libraries feel this is important.

These registration records are used for many statistical purposes by libraries. By subtracting the first borrower's card number issued at the beginning of the month or year from the last one, a library can count its new borrowers. By reviewing borrower's applications, it can obtain other statistics about borrowers, such as the number from a particular area, their occupation, or their school district. Juvenile and adult statistics are usually kept separate by issuing color-coded cards with separate number sequences. Sometimes branch statistics may be kept by adding designated branch letters to the number on the borrower's cards.

Other procedures in the registration area include recording the change of address on the library records and ordering lost cards (usually for a small fee to cover the cost of reordering cards or plates used in mechanical circulation systems). Sometimes records of overdues are attached to the borrower's application card. If the fine owed exceeds an amount set by library policy, the application may not be weeded at the expiration date but be kept for a certain number of years or until the fine is paid.

Registration prepares borrower's records for the whole library system. It is most important that these records be kept accurately. Mistakes in this area can cause inaccuracies in other activities that can harm relations with borrowers.

Circulation Loan Periods

Loan periods are designed to facilitate the public's use of a collection by providing equal access to the materials for all patrons. Each library should decide upon circulation loan periods appropriate for its own particular needs. If its collection is small but demand is great, a library may have a more limited loan period than one with a much larger collection. As a library grows, it should review its loan policies.

Public libraries have usually had two circulation loan periods, each for specific types of materials. The more frequently used combinations have been two weeks and one week and four weeks and two weeks. (Some libraries, however, have a two-week loan period for all materials.) The shorter loan periods are used for materials in limited supply but in great demand, such as new books or magazines. Such loans usually cannot be renewed. Sometimes a shorter loan period may also be used for children's books, because some libraries believe that children might forget their books if they had a long loan period.

There seems to be a trend toward lengthening loan periods and eliminating renewals. For one reason, a single loan period cuts down on the circulation workload. Also, library collections have generally grown large enough to handle longer loan periods. Another reason for lengthening the loan period for new books is that their average size has increased so much (from about three hundred to eight hundred pages) that patrons need more time to read them. Finally, many libraries now recognize that children can be trusted to return their books on time and that parents appreciate having the same loan period for adult and children's books. This is particularly true for families that must make special trips to obtain library materials.

In recent years, many libraries have adopted the loan periods recommended by the Fry study. This study recommended that public libraries adopt three-week loan periods with no telephone renewals (which are impossible with a transaction system anyway.) It also recommended that libraries have only one due date per week. This latter practice would mean that all books would be due on the same day of the week and that borrowers would have a loan period of two to three weeks depending on which day of the week their books were charged out. The study also recommended that academic libraries have single loan periods of a month, quarter, or semester. Special libraries were recommended to have indefinite loan periods with an option to recall an item if needed. (Since the Fry study did not discuss school libraries, no recommendations were made for these.)

Libraries have found that single or indefinite loan periods save staff time, reduce overdues, and eliminate renewal procedures. They have also maximized service by enabling their patrons, especially students working on term papers in academic libraries, to keep materials until they have finished with them. A single loan period can also eliminate the need for unusual loan periods such as long teacher or vacation loans which require extra records and files.

School libraries may be the exception to this practice of providing longer loan periods. Because collections in school libraries are generally smaller than those of other types of libraries, they commonly maintain shorter loan periods so that their limited resources can be shared among more patrons.

In the past, libraries sometimes restricted or limited the number of loans that could be made by a person at one time. The philosophy behind this policy was that the library was a custodian of books. Libraries now conceive of themselves as providers of books. Thus, few libraries today restrict the number of books charged out at one time. An exception to this "no limit" policy may apply to books in great demand such as new books or holiday books. New or delinquent borrowers may also be limited in book loans until they receive their cards or clear up their obligations. Some libraries do not loan adult books on children's cards. These limiting policies should be reviewed periodically by the librarian and perhaps revised. Clerical and student staff members must follow their library's policies in dealing with any of these matters. If there are any questions, they should check with their supervisors. The supervisors, if they are LMTAs, may be allowed to use their own judgment, but they also should know their limitations and clarify points of confusion with the librarian.

Charging Materials

Charging procedures differ according to the charging system used in a library. However, the following information is needed in almost every system: (1) accurate and legible borrower information, (2) the due date of the material, and (3) the title and author or a number that identifies the item such as its call number (see fig. 1). In most circulation systems, the call number is used not only in locating the material on the shelf but is also used as the filing symbol for retrieving the circulation charge record.

Without such basic information, the circulation charging record will be incomplete and problems will develop.

When a patron comes to the circulation desk to charge out material, the staff member should smile and pay complete attention to the patron. The patron should be made to feel that his or her business is welcomed, for the patron is giving business to the library just as a customer does when buying an item in a store. Patrons should be directed in a tactful manner in the circulation procedures if they don't know them; library slang and terminology should not be used. If patrons are supposed to assist the staff by opening their books, they can be politely asked to do this. Some libraries find that this help reduces the staff time involved by 10 to 25 percent. If a patron should participate more in the charging system, the staff member should be sure that any instructions are explicit and clearly understood by the patron.

In many libraries, particularly smaller-school, academic, and special libraries, the borrower must write his or her name and room or identification number on the material charge card. In other libraries, a staff member may use a machine to stamp this information on the charge card. Systems using temporary charge slips may require the borrower to write not only name, address, and identification number, but also the call number and perhaps the author, title, and copyright date. In automated computer systems, staff members enter all of this information by passing either an electronic or laser-light pen over bar codes identifying material and patron. Public libraries using transaction systems may take a microfilm picture of the borrower's library card or identification, the transaction number with its due date, and the book information (fig. 10). This book information may be taken from a book card, book pocket, or even a catalog card pasted into the book.

The staff member who checks out a patron's library materials (except in transaction or computer systems) should also ensure the legibility of each charge and that it matches the material being charged out. It is surprising how many of these charges can be illegible and how a quick perusal can save hours of staff time in overdue procedures and poor public relations. The staff member should also verify that the borrower has a valid library card or identification. In automated systems, the computer will indicate this, sometimes by triggering a warning buzzer and light signal. The staff member should quickly glance at the expiration date to see if the card is valid. In some libraries, the borrower's name or number may also be checked against a list of delinquent borrowers. If this validation check turns up a problem concerning the borrower, it should be cleared up before the staff member proceeds to charge out any materials.

The date the material is due is usually put somewhere in the book or

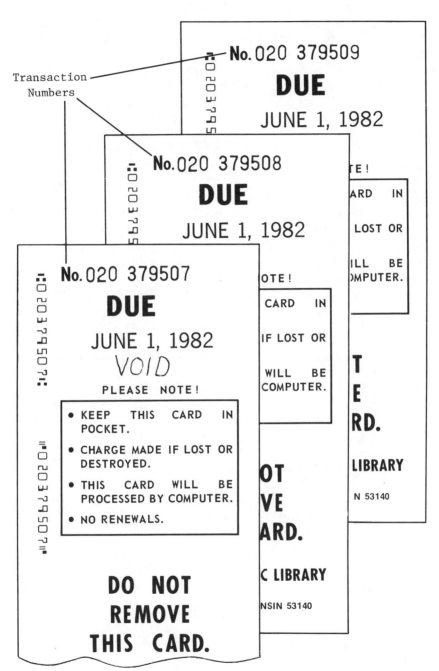

Fig. 10.   Transaction charges.

material. A slip can be used on which the due date is stamped, or a predated due-date or transaction card may be placed in a book pocket. This due date must be correct and legible, or else the library cannot hold the borrower responsible for overdue material. It would be helpful (particularly with new borrowers) if the staff member would state when the material is due, show the due date in the material to the patron, and explain that the last date shows when the item is due. Staff members in libraries with theft detection systems would then follow procedures described in the section on theft-detection systems below.

To complete a materials charge in the Newark system, the attendant may separate and file the cards or charges in an interim file so that they may be counted for statistics and filed at the end of the day. If school or special libraries also keep a separate record for each borrower indicating the items charged out, one more step is needed before the charge is complete. The borrower's record may have the due date and total number of items or the call numbers written on it. When the materials are returned, this information will either be crossed off or the return date will be stamped next to each item on the record (fig. 1a).

Charging procedures for magazines, pamphlets, and other special-print materials may be slightly different from those followed for books. (Because the procedures for audiovisual items may vary so much in different libraries, they will be discussed in chapter 5.) Sometimes, charge cards may be made out for each pamphlet or issue of a magazine. Transaction systems may need the name and date of the magazine or the pamphlet title typed on a label that can easily be filmed. Oftentimes, a temporary charge slip must be written for a magazine or pamphlet. The information recorded must be accurate and complete and may include the title, date, volume, and issue number for magazines. For pamphlets, the information may include the subject, title, and total number of items charged out (fig. 11). These items are then charged out like books except that they usually have a shorter loan period and cannot be renewed. In automated systems, a bar-code label may be placed on each pamphlet or magazine, or such a label may be placed on a charge card for each magazine title. When a magazine issue is charged out, the issue information is written on this card.

Renewals

Library policies on renewing items may differ because of such factors as the length of loan period allowed for certain types of materials and the size of the collection. Often, new books, periodicals, pamphlets, and audiovisual materials may not be renewed. Thus, libraries that do renew items usually renew only books. They are renewed for the same length of time as the original charge. If a patron brings in a book to renew, it should

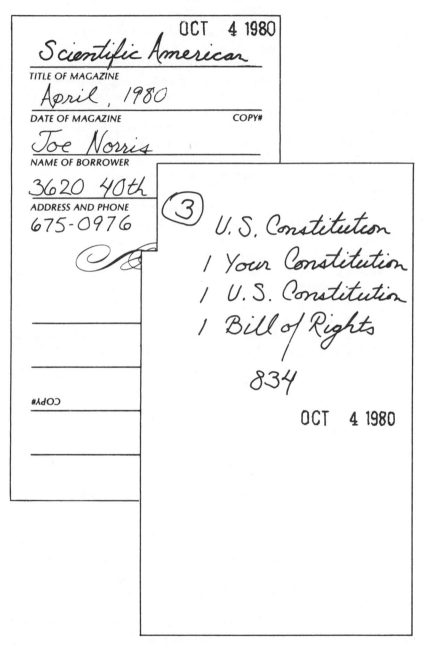

Fig. 11. Temporary circulation charges.

(a) Periodicals; (b) Pamphlets.

be discharged and charged out again as if it were a new book charge. (This is the only way that materials may be renewed in a transaction system.)

If the library accepts renewals over the telephone, the following procedures should be followed. Locate the original book cards or charges for every book to be renewed. Then, stamp the new due date on the charge with the word *renewal* in place of the borrower information, and file the book charge in front of the renewal file to be counted and interfiled later (fig. 12). The patron should be told when the books will be due and asked to write this new date or the word *renewed* on the due-date cards, a step that could save much searching when the books are returned. If the book charges cannot be found in the due-date file, the chances are that they may already have been renewed. If that is the case, follow the library's policy concerning second renewals.

Many libraries allow a second renewal if there has been no request to hold the item. Others may allow a second renewal only if the patron brings in the item to renew, thus certifying to the library that it has not been lost.

Some libraries allow unlimited renewals, while others allow only one or none at all. In some instances, patrons are customarily told they may check out the material on someone else's card. If this is allowed, the owner of the second card should be told that he or she will be responsible for the loan. However, this is not an acceptable library practice, and libraries that follow it should review their loan and renewal policies in light of their objectives and their aim of providing good service to their patrons.

Theft-detection systems

In recent years, many libraries have installed theft-detection systems. This deterrent factor has proven to be very effective; the average reduction in material losses for libraries using such systems has been reported as 75 to 85 percent.

The detection systems use sensitized targets that are placed in library materials. These targets can be either sensitized strips hidden in the books or sensitized labels placed under the book pockets or camouflaged as library identification labels. They can be placed in all types of library materials, including audiovisuals. When a person attempts to remove marked materials from the library without properly charging them out, an alarm system detects the targets and may lock an exit gate and trigger a buzzer or light.

Libraries use two basic types of detection systems: bypass systems and full-circulating systems. In a bypass system, the item is always magnetically charged to activate an alarm system. A patron leaving the library must hand all materials to a library staff member. The staff

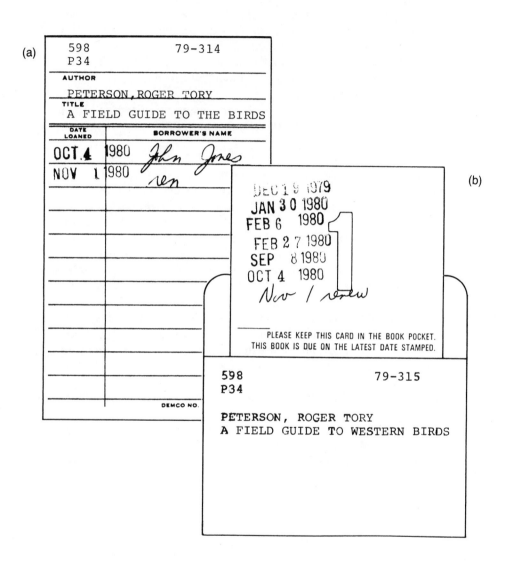

Fig. 12. *Renewal circulation charge made from a patron's telephone call.*

(a) Book card renewed from the circulation file; (b) Book patron wished to renew. Notice that the staff member renewed the wrong book.

member will check each item to ensure that it has been properly charged out and that the charge record matches the item. The staff member will then pass the items around a protective shield to the patron who has passed through a detection point. This system is less expensive than a full-circulating system because a library need not purchase deactivating equipment or protective-shield cards. However, it does require that a staff member check every item that is removed from the library. This may be done at the time the item is charged out at the circulation desk or by an exit guard at the library door.

A full-circulating system uses electromagnetic targets that remain sensitized until deactivated by the circulation assistant. To do this, the assistant can pass the material through a desensitizing unit; the assistant may also place a protective-shield card (usually a special due-date card) in the library pocket or place a protective tab on the target label. The material can then be taken through the system's detection unit (usually located at the library entrance or exit) as many times as the patron wishes. This latter characteristic is the major advantage of the full-circulating system over the bypass system and often offsets the fact that it is more expensive to install. When a charged-out item is returned to the circulation desk, the circulation or shelving assistant either passes the material through the sensitizing unit to resensitize it or removes the protective card or tab.

Most libraries have been very satisfied with theft-detection systems. The system's effectiveness in ensuring that library materials are available when a patron needs them has more than offset the additional complexity of library procedures and the cost of the system. Also, the cost has not been considered exorbitant; libraries have been able to amortize the cost of such systems in from 2½ to 3 years, depending on their original loss rate.

Psychological deterrence seems to be the major contribution of the theft-detection systems. Since few of the systems were designed to be completely theftproof and the detection units in all of the systems have limited detection ranges, determined patrons can find ways to get around any system. However, the success of such systems seems to hinge on the fact that their existence indicates to patrons that libraries *do* care if their materials are stolen.

The manner in which staff members handle situations when the alarm system is activated has a great effect on the patron's response to such systems and can affect the relations of the library with the public. When the alarm is activated by a patron, he or she should be asked in a pleasant manner to return to the circulation desk. At the desk, the staff member should ask the patron courteously if all library materials have been charged out. This interchange with the patron should be handled with great tact. For instance, the patron may be the victim of a prankster colleague or may truly be attempting to "beat the theft-detection system." Since the patron may be embarrassed, insulted, or angry about the situation, the staff member should speak in a quiet voice so that others in the library do not get concerned or involved. Also, the system may have been activated by something other than a library item. One university found that the bookstore sold briefcases that set the library alarm system off.

The staff member should also ask to recheck each library item that a patron has or ask to look inside a briefcase or tote bag. If an item is found that is not charged out, the staff member should make no accusations but just charge out the item to the patron. The patron should be thanked for returning to the desk and allowed to continue on his or her way. The circulation assistant should always be pleasant and objective with patrons in these situations. If the patron objects or if problems arise, the library supervisor or librarian should be called. The library should have a backup policy if the cause for setting off the alarm cannot be determined, and the library staff members should always follow this policy.

Priorities at the charging desk

Service to the patron at the charging desk comes before any other duties the assistant is performing. The patron should not have to wait for a staff member to finish other tasks such as looking up reserves, calling about overdues or reserve notices, or checking in or shelving materials. To prevent this, some libraries schedule their staff so that the charging desk is never left unattended. Other staff members should be aware of busy periods at the charging desk and offer assistance if needed. Also, each staff member should cooperate with fellow staff members if the desk is crowded. Physical routines should be devised so that several attendants may charge out books at one time. If all the staff members work as a team, the charging routines can be performed smoothly and busy circulation periods will not become disasters.

Circulation Statistics

Libraries should keep only circulation statistics that they will use in planning and evaluating their programs and satisfying their objectives. Too many libraries have kept circulation statistics determined by the type of circulation system rather than by their needs.

In the past, libraries often kept very detailed circulation statistics of the type of borrower, type of material, and call number. Some school and academic libraries even kept count of the number of patrons who used the library. However, as library needs began to change, some libraries began to reevaluate their needs for such detailed and isolated circulation statistics. In doing so, they discovered some gaps in the information provided by the traditional statistics that had been kept. For example, academic libraries found that many of their items were used within the library and never brought to the charging desk. School libraries found that study halls in the library provided false figures concerning true media center usage. Public libraries found that circulation of library materials may have declined but that attendance at film programs, story hours, and library clubs had increased tremendously as well as generated a lot of in-library usage.

When libraries discovered these statistical gaps, they began to design new methods of recording circulation statistics and correlating this information with other factors. Academic libraries began to count all the items reshelved from in-library usage, and one library found that this count equalled 50 percent of the circulation of materials charged out of the library. School and public libraries began to compare their circulation statistics with the number of borrowers in the library at any one time.

Libraries also began to evaluate the cost of gathering their statistics in relation to the benefits derived from them. What they found was that, due to rising labor costs, the detailed circulation statistics were very expensive to gather and record. These new methods enabled libraries to better evaluate the usage of their facilities rather than relying on circulation figures alone. Also, libraries with large circulations could not afford to continue using the manual Newark circulation system that enabled them to gather such statistics. Instead, these libraries found that the cost of gathering such data was out of proportion to their total value to the library. In fact, some libraries found that the data that they had been so carefully gathering were not really needed or used at all.

Using these evaluations of circulation needs as guidelines, some libraries began adopting circulation systems that did not provide such statistics. Transaction systems were adopted that provided only the total daily circulation count. This count was obtained by subtracting the first transaction number used at the beginning of the day from the last number used that same day. Other mechanical systems could be adopted that would not provide extensive statistical information. Libraries could even adopt temporary charge systems if they did not need to keep permanent records of their borrowers' charges.

Automated circulation systems were available for those libraries that could afford them or that needed to keep detailed circulation records. These automated systems used the computer's capabilities to record and total such library statistics as circulation by type of borrower, by class of material, and even by each individual item. They could also keep a running tally of the charges made by individual borrowers as well as indicate the number of requests made for a particularly popular item.

These statistics could also be calculated daily, stored in the computer, and printed out on a regular basis or whenever needed.

However, many libraries felt that they still needed some indication of their circulation. For libraries with Newark systems, it was a relatively easy matter to separate daily charges into specific categories and count the charges before they were put in the circulation files (fig. 13). Other libraries began to develop newer methods for providing such usage figures. Measuring techniques were borrowed from the social sciences and introduced to libraries. The principle behind such sampling was that a small sample of library usage could be used to project that of a longer time period.

DAILY RECORD		
Date *September 18, 1980*		
BOOK CIRCULATION	ADULT	JUVENILE
General Works 000		
Philosophy 100		
Religion 200		
Social Sciences 300	2	
Language 400		
Pure Science 500	5	
Technology 600		
The Arts 700	3	
Literature 800	2	
History 900-909 930-999	1	
Geography, Travels 910-919		
Biography B-920		
Periodicals *MAGAZINES*	2	
Pamphlets		
Total Non-Fiction	15	
Fiction	5	
Rental Collection		
Foreign Books		
Total Book Circulation	20	
(Over) Signature *bec*		

Fig. 13.   Sample circulation statistics form.

One method for such sampling would be to select a specified time period and manually tabulate or count the number and kind of material charges, patrons, or other events that occur during this period. Another sampling method would be to count the number of returned items during a specific time period. A third method useful in Newark systems would be to record the circulation information from a specified number of books at specified locations in the library collection. For example, to sample the use of science books, the circulation could be counted for ten books at the end of every shelf in the science section. These random methods have the double advantage of providing a fairly objective and accurate sample of a library's usage as well as being an economical method for gathering such data. However, the most-used books would usually be charged out and seldom counted.

Circulation Charge Files

Although libraries use different types of charging systems, almost all of them maintain some type of circulation files. Newark and double-record charging systems require manual charge files that must be updated daily. Transaction and computer systems have enabled libraries to eliminate these involved manual files, but they may still need some circulation files. Circulation files usually contain entries for every item known to be someplace other than the library shelves. Circulation files may include records of current charges, overdues, telephone renewals, faculty charges, reserve collection materials, lost materials, bindery materials, and sometimes charges for materials that the library keeps in storage. All staff members use circulation files to locate specific library materials. For these reasons, they should be organized for maximum efficiency and convenience.

Newark system

The circulation charge files for Newark and double-record charging systems are very complicated to maintain. Each day, the material charges must be arranged in some predetermined order and added to the circulation-charge files. In addition, most libraries keep a statistical count of the number of items charged out within specific call numbers or categories. Daily procedures of sorting, counting, and filing require accuracy and are time-consuming. Any mistakes in filing the charges can cause problems later in the discharging process.

In typical Newark and double-record charging systems, the charge slips for items currently due are kept at the front of the files for easiest access. The due dates are then filed in calendar order. Behind each due date, the material charges are usually filed according to a library's designated pattern. Some libraries keep adult- and juvenile-book charges separate, while others interfile them. Fiction may be filed alphabetically by author and title, while nonfiction is filed by call number and author. Circulation charges for magazines, pamphlets, and audiovisual (AV) material may be filed separately. However, a library should organize its files for easy access, and having too many categories may hamper their use. For libraries that charge out materials for two loan periods on one day, the charges for the two periods should be separated and interfiled with other charges for the two due dates. If two or more circulation files are due on one day because of a holiday, they should be interfiled.

Libraries may also have separate sections in their files for special categories of charges. As the dates of the circulation charges become overdue, some libraries move them and place them behind an overdue marker to remind the staff members that fines are due on these books. Telephone renewals may be kept in a separate file for easier use in discharging books, especially in case the patron fails to record the new due date. The permanent book charges for materials in reserve collections may be charged to a special teacher's reserve section and kept in a separate file in call-number order. This will enable the staff to determine quickly if a particular item is on reserve and, if so, for which teacher.

Double-record

Double-record charge systems require two charge cards and two charge files. Some libraries keep one charge file by due date and the other by call number. Other libraries keep one charge file by due date or call number and the other by borrower's name. Such two-pronged approaches enable libraries to find information quickly but are very cumbersome to maintain. They are doubly time-consuming in both charging and discharging, and the chances for errors to occur are greater than in other systems.

Automated systems

Libraries that have automated circulation systems may still have to maintain some manual circulation files. Manual files may sometimes be kept for special material charges such as magazine issues, pamphlets, and AV equipment if these items do not have individual bar-code labels.

McBee-keysort

The McBee-keysort system enables libraries to file all charges in one category, usually call number. When adding charges to these call-number files, libraries must interfile each day's circulation charges with those already in the file. Special care should be taken to ensure that all charges are correctly interfiled. The McBee system also requires the staff member to notch each material charge for the due date and perhaps for the status of the patron, for example, student or faculty member.

These systems give easy access to library charges, but their charging and discharging procedures are somewhat involved for the same reasons that Newark systems are. However, having all charges interfiled in one order carries several advantages, namely, the charge for a material can be found even if the due date slip has been removed, and it is easy to learn whether an item is in circulation. Moreover, if the file is in shelflist order, it is easy to learn which areas of the library's holdings are being heavily circulated; for instance, it is easy to tell whether many books on oceanography are charged out at any one time.

Discharging Materials

Materials returned to the discharge desk are either brought by a patron, dropped in a book-return box, sent by another agency, or sent by mail. The staff member should check the due date of the returned material. If it is not overdue, it may be put aside in the returned-book area until it can be discharged. If it is overdue, the book charge should be located and the fine calculated and collected.

When a patron returns materials, he or she should be thanked and asked to place them in the correct area. (This is often a hard-to-see box or a return slot in the charge desk.) If a patron continues to wait, the staff member should ask the patron if the books are on time or overdue and then direct the patron accordingly. The staff member should not make the patron wait for assistance only to find that the books were on time. If the materials are overdue, ask the patron to "please wait a moment; a staff member will be right here." Courtesies are valuable to the patron, and they help the staff avoid writing fine slips that must be mailed.

Accuracy and speed are important in discharge routines. If the staff member devises an efficient technique when learning the discharge procedures, speed in performing them will quickly develop. The following routines have been proven efficient in discharge procedures.

When discharging materials, it is useful to arrange them in easy-to-handle piles according to type of item. All materials should be placed facing the same way and perhaps opened to the card pockets.

Newark system

In systems with circulation charge files, such as Newark systems, the staff member should check the due date in the item and then search the files under the current due date or other filing order. When the card seems to be located, do not pull the charge from the file; first check the call number, author, title, and other identifying information on the card against the item. Pull the correct card carefully from the circulation file and place it in the pocket of the item. If temporary charges are used, they should be checked against the item returned and then discarded or kept for statistical purposes. If predated due-date cards are used, they should be removed when the charge card is inserted. It is most efficient if the staff member can use one hand to handle the materials and leave one hand in the file, thus keeping a place in the file in case several returned books are due on the same date or are by the same author. This is also a good time for examining materials for damage and assessing any fees for damage. The item is now discharged and ready to be returned to the shelves. It may be placed on a waiting cart or in a separate area to be reshelved.

When charge cards cannot be located in the file, several factors may be considered. The item may have been renewed, so the renewal file should be checked. The due date can be checked again to ensure that the correct date is showing—predated due-date cards are often placed in the pocket wrong side up. Also, check the date that is one loan period earlier or later because the wrong date may have been put in the item. If the material is adult, the juvenile files can be checked and vice versa. If there is a charge card almost identical to that of the material to be discharged, the shelves can be checked to see if the charges were interchanged. If the charge card still cannot be found, the item may be considered a "snag." A notation such as "searched" should be put in the material next to the date, and the material then placed in the snag area. The library will search periodically for the cards belonging to snag materials and, after a predetermined length of time, make duplicate cards. After the designated time, perhaps six months, duplicate charge cards are made and the item returned to the shelves. There may also be a snag file of charge cards for materials that cannot be found.

Transaction systems

Materials charged out in other systems are much easier to discharge. In transaction systems, the transaction card need only be removed from the item and the item checked against the reserve request list. The transaction card is put aside to be filed in numerical order or checked off against a numbered sheet that includes all transaction numbers. The transaction cards are usually sorted several weeks or one loan period after their due date. Sometimes, libraries have contracted with local banks or schools to have computers sort these transaction cards and deliver a list of missing cards to the library.

Automated systems

Automated computer systems need only be set in the discharge mode and a light pen or laser drawn over the item's bar code to discharge an item. If the item is reserved or if there is a problem with it, the computer will trigger a buzzer or signal light.

Materials that are ready to be reshelved may be sorted by type of material or by the areas to which they will go; it will then be easier to shelve a large number of materials. This is another example of a good time to check returned materials to see if they need to be mended. In some systems that use visible-record reserve lists, each returned item should be checked against the current reserve list (in other systems, it was checked when discharged). Each staff member should develop the habit of flipping the item open, whenever handling it, to the charge card and pocket to verify that they are correct. The habit shows awareness and permits assistants to find mistakes before they become troublesome.

Discharge errors are embarrassing because they can easily be traced back to a particular activity. The closer attention a staff member pays to detail and accuracy here, the fewer mistakes there will be to correct.

Overdue Policies and Procedures

The philosophy that a library is mainly a storehouse for books dies hard in many staff members' hearts, so that too much time and energy are expended on frustrating overdue procedures. Even though the Fry study in 1961 found that a public library only sent first overdue notices for 1.8 percent of its total circulation, few libraries have redesigned their library policies to take this fact into account. Many staff members still perform overdue routines and operations as if most patrons deliberately kept books out to prevent others from using them or to complicate the staff members' duties. These ideas are far from the truth; most borrowers do honestly forget when their materials were due or believe they returned their books. This is the first truth a staff member should understand when working with overdue books because this belief will foster good public relations.

In overdue policies and procedures, the staff member must follow the library's stated policies. If constructive changes can be made in these policies, these should be suggested to the proper authorities.

Established policies should be practiced by every agency so that no patrons are shown favoritism. For example, if the main library follows policies to the letter and the branch libraries are lax, the patrons using the main library are being discriminated against.

What should be the purposes behind overdue policies and fines? The primary purpose is to obtain return of the materials so that they may be used by other patrons. A secondary purpose is to encourage patrons to return the materials on time and to penalize them for infringing on the rights of others. The emphasis in library policies should be on encouraging patrons to return materials on time by having reasonable loan periods and fine rates. Fines as punishment hurt public relations and may encourage theft.

Since fines are charged by libraries to encourage patrons to return their overdue materials, libraries should often review their policies concerning fines. In the 1970s, several completely opposite policies towards fines and overdue materials began to appear. At one end of the scale, some libraries experimented with eliminating fines; at the other end, some libraries went to court to retrieve long overdue and costly items. These two dissimilar policies were both influenced by the same factor—money. Inflation had increased library salaries and materials so much that overdue notices and routines were costing libraries more than they were collecting in fines. At the same time, the rising cost of materials made it difficult for libraries to absorb the cost of replacing materials not returned. By designing new policies for fines, libraries were searching for ways to solve these money problems.

In reexamining their fine policies, libraries took many factors into consideration. Some libraries looked on fines as a deterrent to overdue items. However, since most fine rates had not kept up with inflation, libraries found that patrons did not object to paying fines five or ten cents per day on overdue materials. Also, libraries that did not place a maximum on their fines found that patrons would keep the items rather than return them and pay an exorbitant fine. Either way, fines did not seem to deter patrons from keeping overdue books.

Some libraries began to experiment with fine-free grace periods that varied from one to two weeks. If the overdue items were not returned during this time period, a fine was usually levied for the entire overdue period including the grace period. Depending on the library, fines for such periods varied from one to five dollars and daily fines ranged from ten cents to one dollar. Libraries with grace periods had less record keeping and approximately the same amount of revenue from fines.

Some libraries became altogether free of fines. These libraries believed that the gain in public-relations value and reduction in overdue procedures more than offset the loss of revenue. Many of these libraries conducted studies and found that the overall return rates of overdue materials with and without fines were about the same. Overdue materials did, however, take longer to be returned under the fine-free system.

Other libraries found that they needed the library fines as revenue. In earlier times, libraries had turned over their fines to the general accounts of their governing authorities. However, as budgets became tighter, libraries fought to retain fines for their own budgets. Many librarians were allowed to keep this money in lieu of budget increases. Thus, these libraries were put in the unenviable position of needing to collect overdue fines to finance other library services. (This practice is considered by some people to be a form of double taxation.)

Some libraries were also put in the position of trying to retrieve overdue library materials without the support of their governing authorities. Schools, colleges, and universities would not withhold grades or degrees unless significant amounts of money were involved. Public libraries found that city police and civil courts would not prosecute library patrons for "just failing to return a few books." To enlist these institutions on their side, libraries produced cost studies that indicated how much it could cost the library to replace an unreturned item.

Even librarians and their staffs were surprised at how much this could be. Libraries set fees of twenty to forty dollars for lost materials or instituted a processing fee added to the list price of the item. Many libraries raised their fines and fees for damaged and unreturned materials to reflect these costs. Maximum fines of fifty dollars or the list price of the book became common. Charges for lost audiovisual items were usually for the list price of the item, which could be very high.

When libraries applied these higher prices to patron overdue materials, they found that some patrons could be charged with fines of up to several hundred dollars. The higher fines made it worthwhile for their parent institutions or the courts to help them retrieve materials and collect fines. Finally, the publicity that usually surrounded such stringent action also tended to discourage other patrons from keeping materials past their due date.

Because of the importance of public relations in dealing with patrons having overdue materials, the staff member should use tact and courtesy in assessing and collecting the fine. When a patron returns an item that seems to be overdue, the charge card should be cleared before the fine is calculated and collected. This will uncover any discrepancy that otherwise might occur. If the charge cannot be cleared immediately, e.g., in a transaction system, the fine should be calculated according to the material's due date and collected, and the word *paid* written next to the due date. Because library overdue policies differ, the assistant should explain them to the patron, especially the charge per day and how the library calculates the fines. If the patron is not satisfied with the assistant's explanation, the circulation supervisor should be called. The patron should always be thanked for returning the material and should not be made to feel like a criminal.

The borrower may not pay the fine when the material is returned. Libraries have various policies for such situations. Often, the fine must be over a minimum amount for any record to be made of it because of the high cost of record keeping. If the fine is above that minimum amount, a record of the borrower and item information may be put in a visible record file or Rolodex, which can be easily updated. It may also be attached to the borrower's registration card. The borrower's card may be kept at the library until the fine is reduced. An automated system may be set to reject the borrower's number. If an item is returned to a library by deposit in a book-return box, these same policies may be followed. However, if it is returned from another agency, the fine may be forgiven because the item might have been returned on time to that agency.

Sometimes, borrowers claim that they never had a particular book out or that they have already returned it. When this occurs, a library clerk or aide should turn the patron over to the supervisor. The supervisor will check the charge to see if there is an error or if the patron's name or number has been misread. Also, the material may already have been returned and the charge cleared from the records. A borrower may insist that he or she has returned an item that is still charged out according to library records. Libraries make mistakes just as patrons do, so the shelves should be checked to see whether the item is indeed in the library. If the item is found, the patron should be thanked and given an apology for this error and inconvenience. If the item is not found, the question then becomes one of the borrower's word versus the library's word. Rather than cause this confrontation, libraries have developed policies for "claims returned" materials. The supervisor should fill out the appropriate form and explain to the patron that the book charge will be marked "claims returned." The patron should also be asked to continue looking at home, at school, or in the car and to return the material if it shows up. The completed form is usually put with the card in the "claims returned" file for a designated period of time and later attached to the borrower's permanent record. Some libraries only allow a patron two "claims returned" items and then take away borrower's privileges.

If a patron reports a lost item, it may be renewed in order to give the patron time to look for it. If the material is renewed, the patron should be instructed to contact the librray at the end of the renewal period to indicate whether the item has been located. When the patron has determined definitely that the item is lost and notifies the library, the fines are stopped. The staff should check the book shelves to see if the item has been returned.

The cost of the material should be determined according to the library's policy. Some libraries charge the original price of the item, others charge the list or replacement price, and some may even add a set amount to the material price to cover reordering and processing costs. When the patron pays for the item, the lost material and refund policies should be explained. The patron pays the material price and any fines which may have accrued and is given a receipt. After the material cost has been paid, the card should be dated and marked "lost and paid." This card is given to the librarian for withdrawal or reordering. If the patron returns the material and receipt within a year of the date of receipt, its price is often refunded, depending upon the physical condition of the item. Fines and processing fees, however, are not refunded.

Sometimes patrons return materials that are damaged and deny that they have caused the damage. If this cannot be easily determined, the library should not pursue the matter further. False accusations can ruin a patron's relationship with the library. If a patron accepts responsibility for the damage, the damage cost will be determined by the librarian or library policy. Usually, the charge is based on the condition of the book. The charge should be collected and a receipt given to the patron. This charge is never refunded. If the book is damaged beyond repair, it may be withdrawn and given to the patron. A notation of the date and extent and type of damage should be placed in the book, on the book card, and on the shelflist card for the book.

Overdue Notices

Most libraries notify their borrowers when their books are overdue to expedite their return. Overdue notices should be as easy and economical as possible for the library to use. The Fry study recommended postcards with a preprinted overdue message as most economical (fig. 14). The name and address of the borrower and the book information are added. Many libraries use multicopy overdue notices (some already sealed in an envelope) that require only one typing to produce records for several notices or departments. Libraries may send from one to four notices for an overdue book, but the Fry study noted that second, third, and fourth notices did not produce results commensurate with the effort spent in sending them. Instead, the Fry study recommends that one notice sent two weeks after the material is due and then an official letter from the city attorney, police, or school or organization administration would be more effective.

The process for overdue notices changes with the type of library. Many school libraries send notices to students through their room number or homeroom teacher. Some school libraries post lists of borrowers with overdue books. Others rescind a student's library privileges until the record is cleared up. This practice should be discontinued because it prevents the library from providing students with materials for their coursework. Academic and special libraries notify their patrons of overdue materials, but the final notice usually comes from the administration.

Our records show you have the following overdue
materials:

                    TITLE   DATE DUE

American marriage   Oct. 27, 1980

Please return at any of the campus libraries
to avoid being charged for lost materials.

Library - LRC Notice ___KENOSHA CAMPUS___

Date __9/19/80__

FORGET SOMETHING?

The following material(s) is overdue:

___Zim___   ___Birds___

Due Date __9/2/80__   *by bec*

Fig. 14. Example postcard overdue notices.

The borrower often cannot receive grades, graduate, or receive a final paycheck until the library records are cleared. Public libraries usually choose overdue notice forms and procedures that represent a compromise between expense and good public relations.

Libraries must consider the public-relations aspect of sending overdue notices as well as the economic aspect. The public may complain a great deal because overdue notices sent out four weeks after the due date cause them to accumulate large fines. A letter from the police or the organization administration may upset many patrons unless the letter is carefully worded. Complaints about these policies will naturally be received by the circulation assistants. They should be able to explain the official library reasoning for these policies and pass on any patron with complaints or suggestions to the supervisor or librarian.

Overdue notices should be sent out on a regular basis. Often this is daily, but some libraries find it just as effective to send out notices on a certain day of the week for the previous week's overdues. Special libraries may not send overdue notices but may send a request to the individual borrower to return a book when it is needed for someone else. Libraries whose charge systems do not specify a due date may send reminder notices asking the borrower either to return the material or to indicate if they are still using it.

No matter what overdue-notice procedures are used in a library, there are several procedures that should be followed to eliminate errors. First, the assistant should calculate the due dates for materials currently falling overdue and then locate the material charges for these dates. It is useful then to take these cards to the shelves to see if the items have been returned. Sometimes materials are inadvertently shelved without being discharged; sometimes new borrowers (especially children) return the items to the shelves themselves. If any items are found, they should be properly discharged. After the shelves have been checked, overdue notices may be prepared. These notices usually include the titles and authors of the items charged out because libraries have found that patrons like to have this information as well as their due dates. In addition, the staff member should either sign or initial the notice so that, if there are any questions about the notice, the patron can call and ask for a specific staff member. This saves the staff time in handling overdues and is good for public relations.

Newark system

The Newark system requires the staff member to pull charge cards from behind their due-date guides, locate the borrower's name and address in borrowers' files, and use this information to complete the overdue notice.

After the notices are written and mailed, the charges are refiled in the overdue section of the charge file.

Transaction systems

Transaction card systems have similar procedures. The transaction numbers that are missing from the file of returned transaction cards or have not been crossed off the number list are considered overdue. The charge system equipment is used to locate the charge represented by the transaction number. If this is kept on microfilm, a printout of the book charge may be made. This printout gives an accurate record of the book charge and may be sent to the borrower as the overdue notice. If no printout is available, the transaction information should be transcribed accurately and completely onto an overdue notice. The transaction number should be included since this is the library's official record of the charge.

Computerized systems

Computerized circulation systems prepare overdue and fine notices automatically. The computer can be programmed to search its records and determine which materials are overdue and which were returned with fines due and not paid. It can then print overdue notices for the borrower and an overdue and fine list for the library records. Shelves can be double-checked before notices are actually mailed.

Some charge systems provide multiple copies of charges (one original and carbons). A copy of the charge may then be sent to the borrower as the overdue notice. This eliminates errors in transcribing information onto the overdue notices and cuts down the time involved in overdue procedures.

Libraries that send additional overdue notices should also send them on a scheduled basis and at a specified time after the first notice. The overdue files should be searched for the appropriate materials charges. The next overdue notice should be written accurately, its information identical to that of the first notice. If multicopy forms were used, another copy may be ready to send. The notice is sent to the patron and the material charges returned to the overdue file with a notation made of the second notice.

If the notice will be sent out from a police department or administration office, the notices are forwarded to these departments. If the notices are sent out by the library in the name of one of these departments, the department should be so informed. When the materials are returned, the library must be certain to notify the police department or other office of this fact.

A library may make telephone calls to notify patrons of overdue materials. Academic or special libraries may make such calls to retrieve materials quickly (especially those needed for reserves). Public libraries may make such calls as a public-relations gesture and because the postal service can often be very slow in delivering notices. In telephone calls for overdue materials, the staff member should speak clearly and politely. Staff members should identify themselves as calling from the library and give the borrower the author, title, and due date of the materials. If possible, a commitment that is definite should be gotten from the borrower. If the borrower is a juvenile, the staff member should follow these procedures with the parent or guardian.

Overdue notices are designed primarily to induce borrowers to return their materials. For this reason, some libraries have designed overdue notices with humorous messages. Other libraries may make telephone calls as their first overdue notices. Libraries with overdue grace periods may even send their first notice before this grace period has expired so that the patron can return the materials before incurring any fines. Many libraries sponsor fine-free library weeks or provide free collection boxes for a specific time period throughout the community or institution. A few ingenious libraries have provided coupons in newspapers or with utility bills. These coupons entitle the bearer to return one overdue item free of charge. All these methods are designed to encourage patrons to return library materials, not to discourage patrons from using the library again. Once patrons have returned overdue materials and cleared all records, they should be considered as being in good standing.

Reserve Materials

Specific items requested by patrons or books in great demand are put on reserve. School and academic libraries often have separate reserve collections for materials that teachers have assigned to students. In this case, many students need to use a few copies within a short time. Reserve collections are discussed below. Reserve procedures are a method by which libraries provide an important service to their patrons by fulfilling their individual needs.

Individual requests for particular books are received in every type of library. The requests may be for new books that have a short loan period, for a specific title, or sometimes for any work by a certain author. The staff member who receives the request should not wait until the patron asks if the library will hold an item, but should make the patron aware of the reserve service. The staff member should also explain the reserve policies to the patron. Sometimes there is a nominal charge to cover the cost of a postcard mailed to the patron or to cover the cost of the reserve search.

Usually the patron fills out a reserve request postcard or form with the call number, author, title, subject, or any other specific information (fig. 15a and b). Patrons must also give their name and address or phone number to be notified when the book comes in. The staff member should check to see all the information is given and collect any reserve fee, noting its receipt on the reserve request. The staff member should also be certain to date the request and initial it.

The reserve request form is used to place the material on reserve. This means either finding the material itself or finding its charge card in the circulation file and noting that a patron has requested it.

The card catalog should first be checked to ensure that the request carries correct information. Then the shelves should be searched to make sure it is not in the library. It is best to do this before the patron leaves the library. Sometimes the material is found on the shelf because the patron does not have the correct call number or the item was shelved in a special section not known to the patron. The reserve-request file should be checked to see if the requested material has already been reserved. New books often have a long waiting list. If there are already reserves for the material in the file, the new reserve should be placed behind the earlier ones so that the earliest request is always sent first. Sometimes, the card catalog shows that the item requested belongs to another branch. In this instance, the material should be requested from the other branch. If the order file shows that the item has been ordered, the order card should be marked to show that it is requested by a patron and should be processed as soon as received.

If the material is not found on the shelf or located through any special files, steps to recover the item from circulation are taken. In Newark charge systems, the circulation files are searched for a charge record. Each due date and special category of the circulation files, such as overdues, renewals, and bindery, must be searched until the charges for all copies are located. A metal signal is usually then placed on each card to designate that it is reserved (fig. 16); the due date is noted on the reserve-request card, which is then filed in the reserve file. In smaller libraries, the reserve card may be clipped to the charge card, or a note with the patron request information may be clipped to the charge. The reserve file is kept in the order most used by the library, usually by either title or author.

In transaction systems, there are no circulation files to search. Instead, the reserve-request information must be added to the reserve list, which is checked as materials are discharged or before they are shelved.

With computer circulation systems, the reserve request and patron information can be entered into the circulation records by means of the

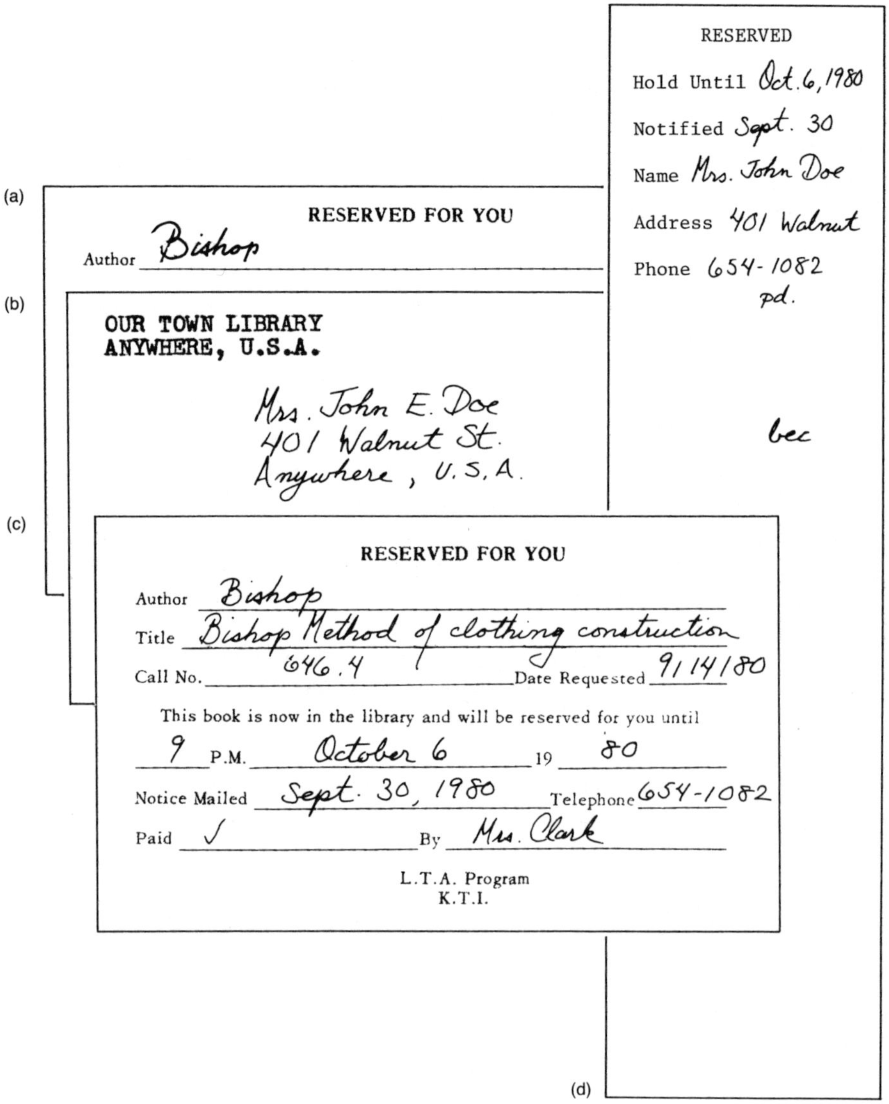

(a)

RESERVED FOR YOU

Author _Bishop_

(b)

OUR TOWN LIBRARY
ANYWHERE, U.S.A.

Mrs. John E. Doe
401 Walnut St.
Anywhere, U.S.A.

RESERVED

Hold Until _Oct. 6, 1980_

Notified _Sept. 30_

Name _Mrs. John Doe_

Address _401 Walnut_

Phone _654-1082_

_pd._

bec

(c)

RESERVED FOR YOU

Author _Bishop_
Title _Bishop Method of clothing construction_
Call No. _646.4_   Date Requested _9/14/80_

This book is now in the library and will be reserved for you until

_9_ P.M. _October 6_   19 _80_

Notice Mailed _Sept. 30, 1980_   Telephone _654-1082_

Paid _✓_   By _Mrs. Clark_

L.T.A. Program
K.T.I.

(d)

Fig. 15.   Reserve request records.
(a) and (b) Reserve request filled out by patron; (c) Reserve notice sent to patron by library; (d) Reserve slip placed in book.

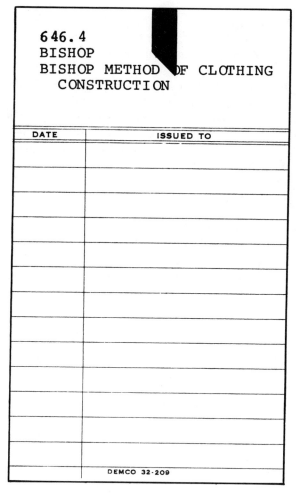

Fig. 16.   Reserve flag on book card.

computer terminal. When the requested item is returned and discharged, the computer system will alert the discharge clerk that the item is reserved.

Some libraries have instituted search procedures for items that are not found by the methods just described. The call number, author, and title of an item are noted on a search form and are regularly searched in all records and locations. Such a search usually includes all shelf areas, items waiting to be shelved, snags, repair shelves, circulation records, materials waiting to be bound, the catalog department, and the shelflist. The latter may contain helpful information such as that the item was lost at the time of last inventory. If items are not found after several such systematic searches, usually done weekly, the information about the missing material should be turned over to the librarian for replacement or interlibrary loan.

When the material is returned and discharged in a Newark system, the metal signal on the charge card designates that the item is reserved and may not be renewed. If a borrower wishes to renew an item whose charge has a signal, the reserve-request file should be consulted. If the file no longer has a reserve request, the signal should be removed. After a reserve material has been discharged, it is placed in a special area for reserve materials. Usually, all reserve items received in a day are processed at one time, but urgently needed items may be processed immediately.

When a reserved material is returned, the reserve request is pulled from the reserve file and filled out correctly. The patron is notified (fig. 15c-d). The notification may be by phone or by mail. The patron should be told how long the reserve material will be held. The reserve period varies from three to seven days and begins with the day after the patron is notified and counts only the days the library is open. Enough time should be given so that the patron has time to pick up the materials. A reserve slip with the material reserve date and borrower information is then placed in the item and the reserve material shelved within easy access of the circulation desk.

When the patron comes to pick up a reserve item, it is checked out according to the library rules. If the material has other reserve requests, the patron should be told that the item has been reserved again and cannot be renewed. If the material is not picked up by the reserve date, it is then reserved for the next person who requested it. If reserve materials become overdue or need to be recalled, the assistant may notify the present borrower and ask that they be returned as soon as possible.

Telephone reserves

Many patrons telephone the library to request information, and they deserve service as courteous as if they had come to the library in person. The employee should answer the telephone politely and ask the patron what information is wanted. The question may be a ready-reference question easily answered from a general reference book. At other times, a patron may just want to find out what hours the library is open.

Patrons often want information about particular books. The assistant should write down the correct author and title and find out as much as possible about what the patron wants to know. The patron should be asked to wait while the information is checked. If the library is busy, the patron's name and phone number should be taken and the patron promised a return phone call in a certain amount of time. The assistant should be sure to make the call within the stated length of time. If locating the information takes longer than expected, the patron should still be called on time and told of the progress and the need for more time.

The staff member should go to the card catalog to verify the information given by the patron and find out if the library has the item. The shelves should be checked to see if the book is in because most of the time the patron wants to come in and charge out the item. The assistant should notice adjacent items to see if they might satisfy the patron and write down authors and titles or take them to the phone. The patron should be told if the library has the material and whether or not it is in. If the item is in and the patron wants to come in for it, he or she should be told how long it will be held and where it can be picked up. A reserve slip should be put in the book with the patron's name and the reserve date, and the staff member should initial the slip. Telephone reserve requests are often given the same length of reserve period as other reserve requests. If the item is out, the patron should be asked if he or she wants to reserve it and the reserve policies should be explained. Also, the patron can be told of other materials that might be of interest. If the library does not have the requested item but can borrow it from another branch or library, the patron should be told about this service.

A patron who wants to reserve materials on a broad subject, such as the U.S. Constitution, is often asked to come in. Assistance will be available at the library to help locate the needed information. This policy is followed (except by special libraries) because students and their parents sometimes are willing to have library staff members do their homework for them. Special libraries, however, provide information on subject requests as well as on requests for individual items. These libraries provide subject searches because it is cheaper for trained library personnel to search for this information than for other personnel to do so.

Reserve materials collections

School and academic libraries provide collections of materials that students are required to study. Ideally, the teacher will notify the library of the materials to be placed on reserve before the assignment is given to the students. These materials are then pulled off the shelves or recalled from circulation and charged out to the reserve collection. The material charge often includes the teacher's name, the date the material is put on reserve, and possibly the date it should come off reserve.

The teacher may designate the length of time of the reserve period, which may vary from two hours to three weeks. Many problems may be avoided if the teacher is consulted about this time period when the reserve request is first made.

A reserve charge card is put in the material for the student to sign. This card contains the call number, perhaps the teacher's name, the author, title, space for the student to sign his or her name, and space for the date and time the material is due (fig. 17a). The materials are usually shelved in a restricted-access area and closely supervised because of the heavy demand for them.

Students must usually request reserve items from the staff attendant and write their names on the reserve card. The student or the attendant should write the time and the date the material is due on this card as well as in the material (fig. 17b). The student should be told when the item is due so that he or she will be aware of the restricted loan period. To encourage prompt return of the material, the fines for overdue reserve books are very high and usually have no maximum. Also, libraries may immediately make telephone calls when these materials become overdue.

These reserve procedures support a library's objectives and provide an important service for library patrons. Reserve collections in school and academic libraries contribute directly to the curricular needs of the students.

However, the patron's individual needs should not be overlooked. Students need materials for individual as well as group assignments, and a school or academic library should develop reserve procedures to satisfy these needs as well. Public and special libraries have procedures to provide requested materials to an individual patron. Public libraries sometimes also have reserve materials collections for holiday materials that are in great demand.

However, if materials are placed on reserve shelves because of their questionable subject matter, their monetary value, or their propensity for being stolen, this is a misuse of the reserve shelves. Policies that provide for such use should be reevaluated. Instead, reserve policies should contribute to a patron's access to the collection.

Interlibrary Loans

Libraries have always been dependent upon each other to supplement their library resources. For this reason, interlibrary cooperation has been in existence for many years. Libraries contact each other for many different purposes. A library system consisting of a main library and branch libraries will communicate daily to exchange materials, identify borrower and overdue information, and handle reference questions. A small library may borrow materials from a larger library, or a public library may borrow materials from an academic or special library.

In recent years, libraries have been forced by the rising cost of library

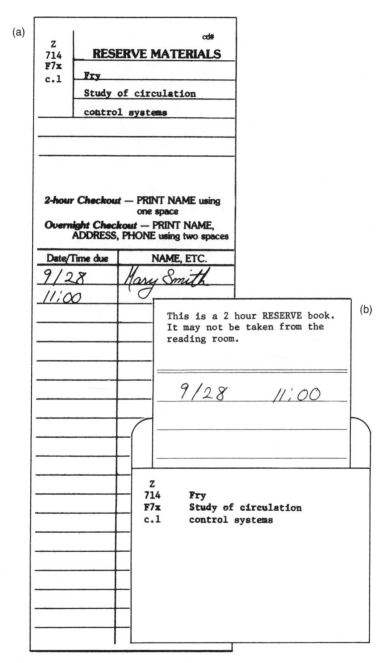

Fig. 17.   Reserve book collection circulation charge.

(a) Reserve charge card signed by patron; (b) Due date and time recorded on date card in book pocket.

materials to buy less and share more of their resources with other libraries. Now, instead of every agency within a library system or every library within a geographic region purchasing copies of specialized items, library purchases are more selective and made available for loan to other libraries in the area. This trend has encouraged libraries to develop lending policies and procedures within their systems and with nearby libraries of all types. It is important that all circulation staff members understand these new policies and procedures so that they can correctly inform patrons about borrowing materials on interlibrary loan. However, the actual procedures for such loans will usually be assigned to one interlibrary loan (ILL) assistant.

A policy that staff members must know is based on the 1978 copyright law and the limitations it places on the reproduction of copyrighted materials. In the 1960s and 1970s, libraries took advantage of the advent of inexpensive photocopying machines (and the feasibility of copying audio and video materials) to copy their materials for loan to other libraries. The revised copyright law attempted to protect the owners of copyrighted materials from losing revenues because of this practice by libraries and others.

The revised law allows libraries to copy materials, but this copying must be based upon the principle of fair use. In effect, fair use means that libraries can make single copies of magazine articles or parts of books to fill individual requests made through interlibrary loan. However, they can no longer make multiple copies of such articles, copy an entire book or audiovisual material, or place such materials in their regular or reserve materials collections. The responsibility for any violations of the copyright law has been placed on the person or library that requests such copying. Libraries that request magazine articles must now keep detailed records of these interlibrary loan requests; this is to ensure that they follow the guidelines on interlibrary lending developed under the aegis of the National Commission on New Technological Uses of Copyrighted Works (CONTU). Libraries also usually post copyright warnings at all copying machines and stamp materials with copyright warning disclaimers. If patrons ask about these warnings, the staff member should explain them or turn the patron over to someone who can.

Interlibrary or interagency loan procedures are usually followed when a library does not have the material that a patron wants. This may be because the library does not own the item, or it may be that the item is lost or long overdue and is now needed urgently by another patron. In any case, the staff member should follow the library's policy in requesting materials from other library agencies. This usually involves checking with all agencies within an individual system first. If the item is not owned by these agencies, the library may check with libraries in the local area. Libraries at the regional or state level may then be checked to find the needed item. However, no matter which library an item is requested from, the requesting library should remember that these loans are courtesy privileges extended by one library to another. If a library staff abuses these privileges, it may soon find that its loan requests are not filled by other libraries.

Although libraries try to fill all interlibrary loan requests, there are usually particular types of materials that may be loaned. Libraries in the past preferred not to loan reference materials, genealogical materials, and new fiction. Magazines themselves are often not loaned, but photocopies of magazine articles are made (sometimes free of charge) and sent to the requesting library. Audiovisual materials, especially motion picture films, are requested from and loaned to other libraries more often than other materials because they are so expensive to purchase. Libraries also loan nonfiction books, older fiction, and children's materials. However, the primary consideration involved in the loan of any of these materials from one library to another is usually whether or not the loan will deprive the patrons of the lending library.

Interlibrary loans among libraries became more flexible and important in the 1970s as libraries looked for new ways to provide materials to satisfy their patrons' needs. The *National Interlibrary Loan Code* of 1968 had limited loans between libraries to materials needed for research by scholars. This meant, for example, that academic libraries could not usually borrow materials for undergraduates and that public libraries were discouraged from borrowing items to satisfy the various interests of their patrons. To fill all of their patrons' needs, libraries began to organize cooperatives called networks, consortia, and systems to borrow and share library materials within local geographic regions. These cooperative networks not only allowed libraries to borrow materials through interlibrary loan, but many of them also permitted patrons of other libraries to use their facilities in person and charge out materials. Some agreements enabled libraries to cooperatively plan their purchases so that limited dollars could buy a variety of materials. Networks also enabled libraries to tap all the resources in a local area so that many requests could be filled locally that had previously been sent outside the area.

When a patron requests an item that a library does not have, the staff member should follow the library's procedures for such a loan. If the library belongs to a system, the staff member should check the library catalog or contact the headquarters library to see if another library or branch owns the item. If the material is owned by another library, the staff member usually will call that library to see if the item is available for loan. The staff member should identify him or herself, the library's name, and the request, and be sure to give the information completely, distinctly, and accurately. If the item is available, the patron may wish to pick it up or have it sent to the requesting library. In either case, the staff member should give clear instructions to the lending library so that the library's staff will know whether it should hold the item, send it, or reserve it.

If the library and its system together do not own the material, most libraries will then request the item from the library network to which they belong. This procedure is usually performed by an ILL assistant and involves completing an interlibrary loan request form. The assistant should give as much information about the item as possible including, for a book, the author, title, publisher, date and edition; for an article, the article title and author, name of periodical, and page numbers should also be given. The staff member should not take the patron's word for the correct title or spelling of the author's name. Instead, the bibliographic information for the material should be verified in appropriate catalogs or bibliographies, or by a search in a computerized data base; this information is recorded on the request form. If the information cannot be located and verified, this should also be noted on the request form. Finally, the borrower information and requesting library information should also be included (fig. 18). Usually, all the information is given on this request form in the format that will be needed if the request is sent to a library outside of the network. This ensures that the assistant has included all the needed information and eliminates the need for any backtracking to pick up missing data.

If the network libraries cannot provide the needed material, ILL materials requests are usually sent to research libraries or libraries outside the network. Because these libraries are now being used as backup resources rather than front-line resources, many of them are willing to broaden their services to include providing materials for "serious study" as well as for "research." Also, they may now loan materials in this category to libraries regardless of the status of the patron.

When the ILL assistants request materials from such libraries, they should know all interlibrary loan regulations and follow the *Interlibrary Loan Code* and its *Procedures Manual* exactly. (These are both published by the American Library Association.) Usually the assistant will fill out national interlibrary loan forms, state or regional forms, or computerized forms such as those used by OCLC, Inc. (Online Computer Library Center). These forms usually require the title, author or artist, publisher or producer, date, and the number of pages. The latter is needed since, if only a portion of an item is wanted, the lending library may wish to send a photocopy rather than the entire item. It is very important that the forms be filled out correctly and include all pertinent information (fig. 19). For photocopy requests, this may also include noting that the request conforms to the copyright law or guidelines.

Next, the ILL assistant checks in union catalogs or serial lists (which list the collection holdings of many libraries) to locate a library that owns

Date of Request _____

GTI — LRC INTERCAMPUS/INTERLIBRARY LOAN REQUEST FORM

CALL NO.	FOR BOOKS & A-V MATERIALS
	Author _____
	Title _____
	_____

(For I.L.L. Only)
Publisher, Place _____

Date & Edition _____

Source of Citation _____

FOR MAGAZINE ARTICLES

Title of Mag. *America*

Vol./Date *133 Aug. 16, 1975*

Author of Article
J. F. Donceel

Title of Article *Why is Abortion Wrong?*

Pages *65 - 7*

(For I.L.L. Only)
Source of Citation *RG 3/75 - 2/76 p.4*

Material not needed after this Date _____

Borrowed from ☐ Kenosha   ☐ Racine
☐ Elkhorn   ☑ Other _____

Date Needed *Oct. 15, 1980*

Date Due Back _____

Date Returned _____

For   ☐ Circulation   ☐ Reserve

Request Taken by: *JP*

PATRON
Name *Jane Doe*

Address *401 Walnut St.*

Phone *654-1082*

Fig. 18.   Interlibrary loan request form.

DEMCO
Madison, Wis.
Fresno, Calif.
NO. 65-250

A REQUEST

BORROWING LIBRARY

FILL IN LEFT
HALF OF FORM
INCLUDING
BOTH LIBRARY
ADDRESSES
IN FULL

Date of request 10/15/80   Not needed after:

Requester's order no.

CALL NO.

GATEWAY TECHNICAL INSTITUTE
LEARNING RESOURCES CENTER
3520 30TH AVENUE
KENOSHA, WI 53141
ATTN: INTERLIBRARY LOAN DEPT.

FOLD HERE

For use of   Jane Doe   Status Student   Dept. Soc. Sci.

Book author. OR periodical title, vol. and date

America.   v. 133,   Aug. 16, 1975

SEND SHEETS
A, B AND C
TO LENDING
LIBRARY, AND
ENCLOSE
SHIPPING
LABEL

Book Title, edition, place, year series: OR periodical article author, title, pages.   ☐ This edition only

Donceel, J.F.   Why is abortion wrong?   p. 65-7.

Verified in: OR: item cited in   RG   3/75-2/76   p.4

ISBN, OR ISSN, or LC card, or OCLC, or other number if known
If non-circulating, & cost does not exceed $ 1.00 ___, please supply ☐ Microfilm ☐ Hard copy

LENDING LIBRARY

FILL IN PER-
TINENT ITEMS
UNDER
REPORTS,
RETURN SHEETS
B AND C TO
BORROWING
LIBRARY

UW-Parkside
Library-Learning Center
Kenosha, WI 53141
ATT: Interlibrary Loan

REV 6/77

Request complies with
☒ 108(g)(2) Guidelines (CCG)
☐ other provisions of copyright law (CCL)

AUTHORIZED BY: (full name) Barbara Jones
TITLE ILL   LMTA

Request for ☐ **LOAN** or ☐ **PHOTOCOPY**
According to the A.L.A. Interlibrary Loan Code

REPORTS: Checked by
SENT BY: ☐   Library rate ☐
Charges $ _____   Insured for $ _____
Date sent
DUE

RESTRICTIONS: ☐ For use in library only
☐ Copying not permitted ☐

NOT SENT BECAUSE: ☐ In use
☐ Non Circulating   ☐ Not Owned
☐ Request of

Estimated Cost of: ☐ Microfilm
☐ Hard copy

BORROWING LIBRARY RECORD:
Date received
Date returned
By ☐   Library rate ☐
Postage
enclosed $ _____   Insured for $ _____
RENEWALS: ☐ No renewals
Requested on
Renewed to _____   (or period of renewal)

Note the receiving library assumes responsibility for notification of non receipt

Fig. 19.   National interlibrary loan form.

the needed material. These union catalogs may be book- or computer-based listings of libraries on a regional, state, or national basis. An ILL request should not be sent to a library that does not own an item unless that library is serving as a clearinghouse for such requests. Having identified libraries that own a particular item, the ILL assistant should send the request to the nearest library or perhaps to one that is closest in size to the requesting library so that the largest libraries are not burdened with all the ILL sharing.

When a lending library receives an ILL request, it should locate the material and send it out as soon as possible. The ILL assistant should pay attention to dates on which the materials are wanted so that he or she can satisfy the patron's needs. If the material is not in, the requester should be notified, told when it will be in (if that can be determined), and asked whether or not the material should be reserved. If the material is in, it is usually charged out to the requesting library and the material charge filed in the circulation or interlibrary loan files. The due date should be indicated in the material so that the receiving library knows when the material is due back at the lending library.

When the requesting library receives the material, it should check to ensure that the correct materials have been received in good condition. The patron should be notified and told how long the book will be held. Using a temporary charge card, the book is charged out to the patron so that it will be due back in the requesting library in time for the book to be returned to the lending library. The patron should be told that the material cannot be renewed and should not be kept past the due date. If a longer time period is needed, the lending library can be asked if the material may be renewed. Materials should be returned promptly and accurate records kept of the material's loan, receipt, and return. This is very important because the requesting library is responsible for the material and all insurance and transportation costs. Also, in some states the loaning libraries may charge a fee for each loan. Thus, accurate records are vital ingredients of good interlibrary loan service.

Circulation Desk Routines and Priorities

The various procedures discussed in this chapter often take place at the circulation desk. Many times a staff member is involved in more than one of these procedures at the same time, perhaps for more than one patron. The performance of procedures will be easier if the staff member understands what routines and priorities should be followed.

Staff members should also understand that the circulation desk duties are primarily clerical in nature. For this reason, most of the personnel at the desk will be clerks, aides, and students. These personnel should handle all routine circulation procedures. However, if problems or questions arise, they should be turned over to the clerk's supervisor, who is usually a more trained or experienced assistant or LMTA. This ensures that the circulation desk is covered at all times; a clerk should not be tied up with any one patron for a long period of time. The supervisor will handle routine complaints, problems, and questions and may assist at the desk if more staff help is needed. If complaints or problems become involved or complicated, the supervising LMTA should turn these over to the librarian. This chain of command enables problems to be handled at their appropriate level by trained personnel.

Daily routines are often called "setting up the desk." This refers to readying the circulation desk in the morning for a new day's circulation activities. The first routine should be to change the due dates for the loan periods if this is necessary. Next, stamp predated due-date cards if they are used so that the first patron will not have to wait. The changed dates must be checked against a calendar to ensure their accuracy. It is discouraging to discover at 10:00 A.M. that the hundred items just charged out will be due on Labor Day when the library is closed. Next, money from the previous day's fines should be counted and recorded. In Newark systems, the daily circulation may need to be counted, statistics recorded, and charge cards arranged in order and filed in the circulation file. The material return box should be emptied and all materials discharged. Perhaps other daily routines such as housekeeping for the library are necessary. These daily routines may be performed by one or more persons, but several staff members should be scheduled after weekends or holidays if the circulation is high or the library is large.

Continuous routines should be performed by every staff member at the desk as time permits. These include maintaining all the library supplies at the circulation desk. If predated due-date or transaction cards are used, they should be dated during slow periods so that the library is ready for peak periods. Returned materials should be cleared from the circulation desk so that patrons cannot take them before they are discharged. All materials should be discharged as soon as possible so that they can then be reshelved and made available to patrons.

The circulation desk should be designed for the most efficient use of staff time and energy. Attention paid to the placement of cards, slips, files, pencils, etc., can result in substantial savings in time. The desk should have sufficient space. A poorly designed desk that provides no space to discharge books comfortably is a handicap to efficiency and service. Chairs or stools should be the proper height for the desk and be on rollers so that they are easy to move and use. Attention should also be paid to the physical effects of lifting items from book return boxes, reaching, and walking. A circulation desk should be arranged so that one person can handle all the activities at a slow period. This would include making the phone accessible to the charging area and circulation files. A typewriter in registration procedures is useful at the circulation desk but may be too noisy to be used there for other procedures. Finally, the circulation desk should be placed so that it may be overseen from the library workroom or office and so that, in a small library, one circulation attendant can supervise the entire library.

A duty which often falls to those at the circulation desk is that of housekeeping in the library. This should not include the actual dusting and cleaning, because the library should hire a custodial staff for this. However, the staff can tell the custodians when light bulbs need replacing or chairs repairing. The circulation attendants can straighten the material on the shelves and reshelve reference materials no longer in use. This routine is more useful as a reference service than as a housekeeping chore. Many times, the needed reference book has been left on a table by a patron. Displays should be kept in good order by replacing fallen book jackets or restocking the book-display racks. If there are any racks that hold library brochures, these should be kept well supplied. When staff members perform these simple routines, they help make the library's resources better available to its patrons.

Staff members may perform many routines and procedures at the circulation desk, but the procedure that has top priority is that of helping a patron. When a patron approaches, the staff member should interrupt other duties and wait on the patron as soon as possible. The staff member should not be so engrossed in a task that the patron apologizes for interrupting the work. The staff member should explain that helping patrons is most important.

A patron in the library will take precedence over a telephone request. However, a staff member on duty alone should give a polite excuse to the patron and answer the phone. It might be wise for the staff member to listen for a moment, for the caller may only want to know the library's hours. If the call involves more than this, however, the caller should be asked to wait or asked if the call can be returned; the staff member should then return to the patron. If a second patron comes to the desk when the attendant is helping someone, the new patron should be asked if he or she can be helped. Again, the patron may just want to borrow the phone book or ask directions. The guidelines to follow in helping patrons are courtesy, awareness, and friendliness. A smile can quickly acknowledge to a patron that help will be available in a moment. Giving prompt attention to a person and his or her needs can reward a library with satisfied patrons. Learning to juggle one's attention in a cheerful way is a very important aspect of library service. It may also provide information for future library purchases and needs or alert the staff to potential problems.

Because of the importance of helping patrons, the staff at the circulation desk should be scheduled so that the desk is covered at all times. Enough attendants should be at the desk during busy periods so that patrons will not have to wait very long for assistance. This staff should be in addition to the staff available to assist patrons with reference questions. If possible, additional aides and clerks should be scheduled for shelving after busy discharge periods. Finally, staff members should be made aware that their responsibility is to assist all patrons as efficiently and quickly as possible.

When several attendants work at the desk, the duties may be divided up. Sometimes, each attendant may be responsible for one complete procedure, e.g., charging books or discharging books. Sometimes, the attendants may cooperate and organize a routine so that one sets up books to be discharged and the other discharges the books. The most important aspect of scheduling desk routines is that the entire staff work together to perform the procedures or get a job done. If the only staff member scheduled to be at the circulation desk is suddenly swamped by patrons, the rest of the staff must understand that their most important job at that moment is to help serve the patrons. Desk schedules should be flexible, not ironclad.

Conclusion

Libraries in recent years have been forced by economics to reevaluate the effectiveness and efficiency of their library systems and procedures in relation to their objectives. In doing so, many libraries have not only adopted more efficient circulation systems but have been streamlining their circulation procedures as well. This chapter has presented these basic circulation procedures, routines, and variations that are often carried out by different types of libraries or with different circulation systems. It has also discussed the changing concepts of library circulation Procedures and presented any recommended policies and practices.

These procedures and suggested routines or practices may be used to review and compare those in use in a particular library. The procedures presented here may not be satisfactory in every instance. If they cause someone to stop and think about why a procedure is performed a certain way or wonder how could it be performed better, then the chapter will have achieved its objectives. The guidelines described in "Instituting a Procedure" should be applied to all procedures a staff member performs. In this way, an analytical approach to problems will develop, as will good judgment. In completing the student work unit at the end of this chapter, these guidelines should be used.

Student Work Unit

The following sample library will be used by the student in this work unit:

A small public library is open Monday–Friday, 2:00–9:00 P.M. with its busy period from 3:00 to 9:00 P.M.. It uses the Newark charging system with numerical borrowers' cards issued for three years. Books are charged out for four weeks for regular materials and two weeks for magazines and new books. The date is hand stamped on the book card; the borrower's card number is written below the date. Predated due-date cards are placed in the book pockets. A daily count of the circulation is recorded according to the class and type of material. The circulation is then filed as fiction, magazines, and nonfiction behind their respective due dates. Fiction is filed first by author and then title; magazines by title and then date of issue; and nonfiction by call number, then author, and then title. All renewals and overdues are kept separate in the circulation files. Overdue fines are five cents per day for every day the library is open, with a maximum two-dollar fine. Overdue postcard notices are sent out every Friday for the previous week's overdues. Requests for reserve books carry a ten-cent charge and are held for the patron for five library working days after the notice is sent.

The student will need to understand chapter 3 thoroughly and refer to the above policies often in order to perform the work unit well. The student should be sure to consider all the factors involved in each procedure.

Based on chapters 1–3, and according to the policies described above, the student will be able to correctly and accurately solve the following exercises. Use appendix D to determine the 1980 dates needed in these procedures.

1. Use fig. 9 as a guideline and issue the next borrower's card to Mr. John E. Doe. Fill out the registration forms in fig. 20 correctly and completely. Assume Mr. Doe is registering right after Mary Jane Doe.
2. Use fig. 1 to charge out the book *Birds* by Zim to Mr. Doe. The due date should be determined from the date on which the student charges out the book. Stamp the due-date card and the book card and write the borrower information on fig. 1.
3. On fig. 1, record a renewal of this book for Mr. Doe. Be sure to record on the due-date card the information he should be asked to note.
4. Count the daily circulation for October 4, 1980, listed below and record it on the daily record sheet (fig. 21). Use fig. 13

No._____

Expires_____

_____
DO NOT WRITE ABOVE THIS LINE

    I apply for the right to use the Library and promise to comply with all its rules, to pay promptly fines or damages charged to me, and to give immediate notice of change in my address.

Sign Full Name_____

Address_____Phone_____

Occupation_____Business Address_____

Reference_____

Address_____

Age_____   Parent's
IF UNDER 14 YEARS   Signature_____

GAYLORD 175   PRINTED IN U.S.A.

No._____ EXPIRES_____

_____

_____
IS ENTITLED TO DRAW BOOKS FROM

AND IS RESPONSIBLE FOR ALL BOOKS TAKEN ON THIS CARD

No._____   Expires_____

Name_____

Address_____

Phone No._____

Fig. 20.   Student work unit registration forms.

as a guide in completing the form accurately. Make a list by due date of the charges as they should be filed in the circulation files.

301.3	598	818
MUMFORD	PETERSON	SANDBURG
	FIELD GUIDE	
	TO THE BIRDS	
598	582	817
PETERSON	RICKETT	SKINNER
FIELD GUIDE		
TO WESTERN		
BIRDS		
769	598	McCALL'S
REMBRANDT	ZIM	Jan., 1971
817	WOLFE, TOM	WHITE, T.H.
ROSTEN	KOOL-AID . . .	ONCE AND
		FUTURE . . .
590	TIME	WOLFE, THOMAS
ORR	July 26, 1971	THE MOUNTAIN
301.41	769	
DUVALL	SACHS	

5. Use fig. 12 (renewal files) and problem 4 above to discharge the following book that has just been returned but for which there is no book card in the October 4, 1980, circulation files.

    598

       PETERSON, ROGER TORY   due Oct. 4, 1980
       A FIELD GUIDE TO THE BIRDS

Describe the steps necessary to locate the book charge and explain what may have happened.

6. Describe how to handle the following situation:

    On October 13, 1980, a patron returned the book *A Field Guide to Western Birds*. The due date in the book was October 4, 1980, so he was charged an overdue fine of forty-five cents. He objected to the fine because he said he had renewed the book until November 1, 1980. As circulation desk supervisor, you are called upon to handle the situation and talk with the patron.

7. Determine the correct overdue fine for a book due on October 4, 1980, and returned on October 13, 1980. Write an explanation for a library clerk as to why the overdue fine charged in problem 6 was incorrect.

```
┌─────────────────────────────────────────────┐
│              DAILY RECORD                     │
│  Date_____      │
├──────────────────────┬──────────┬───────────┤
│  BOOK CIRCULATION     │  ADULT   │ JUVENILE  │
├──────────────────────┼──────────┼───────────┤
```

BOOK CIRCULATION		ADULT	JUVENILE
General Works	000		
Philosophy	100		
Religion	200		
Social Sciences	300		
Language	400		
Pure Science	500		
Technology	600		
The Arts	700		
Literature	800		
History	900-909 930-999		
Geography, Travels	910-919		
Biography	B-920		
Periodicals			
Pamphlets			
Total Non-Fiction			
Fiction			
Rental Collection			
Foreign Books			
Total Book Circulation			

(Over)   Signature_____

Fig. 21. Student work unit daily circulation record.

8. Send one of the postcard overdue notices in fig. 22 to Mr. Doe for the book charged out to him.

> 598
> ZIM, HERBERT   due date: the renewal date
> BIRDS   from work unit problem 3

Include all the information listed below on the overdue notice so that it is arranged well for clarity and efficiency (refer to fig. 14).

The borrower's name and address
Borrower's card number

Our records show you have the following overdue
materials:

        <u>TITLE</u>   <u>DATE DUE</u>

Please return at any of the campus libraries to
avoid being charged for ⬭ lost materials.

A REMINDER   Date

Please return the following overdue books
charged out to card number

Author   Title   Date Due

Overdue Assistant   Our Town Library
                             Anywhere, U.S.A.

Fig. 22.   Student work unit overdue notice.

Book information—could include author, title,
   or call number
Date the book is due
Date of the overdue notice
Name and address or phone number of the library
Initials or name of overdue assistant
Any other pertinent information

9. Reserve the following book for Mr. Doe on fig. 23.

598
   PETERSON, ROGER TORY
   FIELD GUIDE TO WESTERN BIRDS

Fill out the initial reserve request and note the date the book
is due according to work unit problem 4. Fill out the rest of
the reserve card and the slip that goes into the book based
on the return of the book on October 13, 1980.
10. Fill out the national interlibrary loan form on fig. 25 to request the materials listed on fig. 24.
11. Draw up a work schedule for two part-time employees who
have been hired to work twenty hours each to assist the one
full-time employee.

Teaching Unit

The teacher may wish to use the following class assignments
with this chapter. The teacher should establish the individual
library policies and procedures that the class should follow.

1. Have each student type a book card for five books according to a sample book card. Library books should be available for students to choose from and to copy the book card
information from the book pocket. These books and cards
can then be used in practice circulation procedures.
2. Have members of the class register each other as new
library borrowers. One after the other, the students would
assign the numbered borrower's card beginning with number one, complete the registration card, and type a numerical card. To give an example of another type of numerical
record, the information could also be recorded in numerical order on a sheet of paper. These records can be added
to every year and also provide excellent files for practicing
the overdue procedures.
3. Practice charging and discharging procedures in a laboratory situation. Students set up the due dates, charge out

RESERVED

Hold Until

Notified

Name

Address

Phone

OUR TOWN LIBRARY
ANYWHERE, U.S.A.

RESERVED FOR YOU

Author_____

Title_____

Call No. _____ Date Requested_____

This book is now in the library and will be reserved for you until

_____ P.M. _____ 19 _____

Notice Mailed_____ Telephone_____

Paid_____ By _____

L.T.A. Program
K.T.I.

Fig. 23.   Student work unit reserve request forms.

Date of Request _____

GTI — LRC INTERCAMPUS/INTERLIBRARY LOAN REQUEST FORM

CALL NO.	FOR BOOKS & A-V MATERIALS
	Author _____
	Title _____
	_____

(For I.L.L. Only)
Publisher, Place _____

Date & Edition _____

Source of Citation _____

FOR MAGAZINE ARTICLES

Title of Mag. *School Science + Math.*

Vol./Date *76, March, '76*

Author of Article

C. Neatrour

Title of Article *Teaching Mathematic via Learning Centers*

Pages *183 - 8*

(For I.L.L. Only)
Source of Citation *Education Index*

Material not needed after this Date *6/76*

Borrowed from ☐ Kenosha   ☐ Racine
☐ Elkhorn   ☑ Other _____

Date Needed _____

Date Due Back _____

Date Returned _____

For ☐ Circulation   ☐ Reserve

Request Taken by: _____

PATRON
Name *Robert Black - student*
Address *536 Oak St.*
Phone *654-3874*

Fig. 24.   Student work unit interlibrary loan request form.

A REQUEST

Request for ☐ **LOAN** or ☐ **PHOTOCOPY**
According to the A.L.A. Interlibrary Loan Code

REPORTS: Checked by
SENT BY: ☐   Library rate ☐
Charges $_____ Insured for $
Date sent
DUE
RESTRICTIONS: ☐ For use in library only
☐ Copying not permitted ☐

NOT SENT BECAUSE: ☐ In use
☐ Not Owned
☐ Non Circulating
☐ Request of

Estimated Cost of: ☐ Microfilm
☐ Hard copy

BORROWING LIBRARY RECORD:
Date received
Date returned
By ☐ Library rate ☐
Postage
enclosed $_____ Insured for $
RENEWALS: ☐ No renewals
Requested on
Renewed to _____ (or period of renewal)

Note the receiving library assumes responsibility for notification of non-receipt

DEMCO
Madison, Wis.
Fresno, Calif.
NO. 65-250

BORROWING
LIBRARY

FILL IN LEFT
HALF OF FORM
INCLUDING
BOTH LIBRARY
ADDRESSES
IN FULL

FOLD
HERE

SEND SHEETS
A, B AND C
TO LENDING
LIBRARY AND
ENCLOSE
SHIPPING
LABEL

LENDING
LIBRARY

FILL IN PER-
TINENT ITEMS
UNDER
REPORTS,
RETURN SHEETS
B AND C TO
BORROWING
LIBRARY

REV 6/77

Date of request   Not needed after.   Requester's order no.

CALL NO.

**GATEWAY TECHNICAL INSTITUTE
LEARNING RESOURCES CENTER
3520 30TH AVENUE
KENOSHA, WI 53141
ATTN: INTERLIBRARY LOAN DEPT.**

For use of   Status   Dept.

Book author: OR periodical title, vol. and date

Book Title, edition, place, year series: OR periodical article author, title, pages.   ☐ This edition only

Verified in: OR: item cited in

ISBN, OR ISSN, or LC card, or OCLC, or other number if known _____
If non-circulating, & cost does not exceed $ _____ please supply ☐ Microfilm ☐ Hard copy

Request complies with   AUTHORIZED BY: (full name)
☐ 108(g)(2) Guidelines (CCG)   TITLE
☐ other provisions of copyright law (CCL)

Fig. 25. Student work unit national interlibrary loan form.

each other's books, practice good library service, and discuss problems that may arise. Also, a library's circulation desk could be used for practice, but this should be well supervised and directed.

4. Prepare a practice set of circulation charges that students count and arrange in order. Describe the best methods for sorting charges easily and quickly.

5. Prepare a group of overdue-book charges for which students send notices. The overdues could represent several different charging systems and even problems such as illegible borrower's numbers or due date.

6. Have students reserve books for each other, filling out the requests correctly and sending the notice to the patron.

7. Practice role playing in telephone requests from patrons and requests to and from other libraries.

8. Have several groups of students set up efficient circulation desks and then have these desk setups critiqued by the other students.

9. The students as a group could design a public library by choosing the type of library (preferably small), the days and hours it will be open, and any programs or periods of heavy use. The teacher could assign the number and type of regular staff members who would staff that library, e.g., one full-time librarian, one full-time LMTA, and two part-time clerks. Each student could then draw up work schedules for each of the employees so that the library would be staffed. These schedules, and their strengths and weaknesses, could be discussed in class.

4 Shelving and Inventory

Unit Outline:

Shelving Arrangements
Arranging Materials on Shelves
Shelving Procedures
Shifting
Shelf-Reading
Inventory
Weeding
Conclusion
Student Work Unit
Teaching Unit

Unit Objectives:

Define the terms used in shelving operations.

Discuss the methods of arranging books and shelves.

Describe the correct methods for supervising and performing shelf-reading and shifting.

Identify the purposes and describe the procedures for taking and supervising inventory.

Describe the weeding policies and procedures and the assistant's role in this area.

Explain procedures followed and sources consulted in making preliminary decisions for weeding books.

The procedures involved in shelving and inventory are time-consuming but necessary for good library service. Library personnel should keep shelves neat and orderly, not so much for appearance's sake, but in order to make the materials accessible to the patrons. Materials that are out of order or falling over discourage patrons, who find it difficult to locate the items they want. The major objective of the shelving and inventory activities, therefore, is to make sure the materials are in their proper places and in usable condition.

Circulation personnel usually perform these procedures or supervise them. The actual procedures of paging materials, shelving them, shelf-reading, and shifting may be done by part-time assistants (in an academic library, these are usually students). However, everyone should know how to perform these procedures and should do so when the necessity arises. For example, every staff member should take a moment to straighten fallen books when he or she notices them rather than wait for the page to do it; the collection thereby becomes more accessible. Supervisors should know the best ways to perform all shelving and inventory procedures. They should stress the importance of accuracy and competence to all the personnel involved in such procedures.

Shelving Arrangements

Shelving is the arrangement of the library's materials on shelves, in drawers, or in other appropriate housing. Shelving should permit the most efficient and effective use of the collection by the library patrons. Libraries arrange their collections in various ways depending upon their type of library and their major objectives. Some common shelving arrangements will be discussed here. All personnel must realize, however, that they are often reexamined and changed to meet library conditions such as overcrowding or construction.

Bookshelves have a specific terminology. The library shelves that contain the library's collection are often called the "stacks." Stacks are usually a series of double-faced bookcases arranged in a room or area of a room to house the main collection of the library. The double-faced bookcases are called "ranges" and the ranges are made up of "sections" or tiers of shelves (fig. 26).

Many types and designs of bookshelves are available, either wood or metal, from which library personnel can choose to best suit their needs. Library personnel should choose durable shelving which will not warp or sag. The shelving should be a standard size so that it can be interchanged with that of other manufacturers. Shelves are usually 3 feet wide with a shelf depth of 8 to 9 inches. Sections are usually 3, 5, or 7½ feet high. The library stacks (as well as the floor of the building) should be strong enough to support the material weight. Librarians often visit other libraries and consult with other librarians to learn about bookshelves.

The physical environment provided for the books and other materials is also important. Books require a temperature range of sixty-five to seventy degrees Fahrenheit and humidity at 50 to 60 percent. Proper air and light should be provided to protect the books from mildew and so that people are comfortable.

The terms commonly used when speaking of patron access to library materials are "open stacks" and "closed stacks." Open-stack collections allow the patron complete access to the materials. Patrons may browse

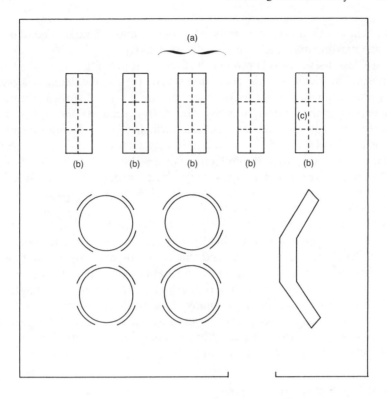

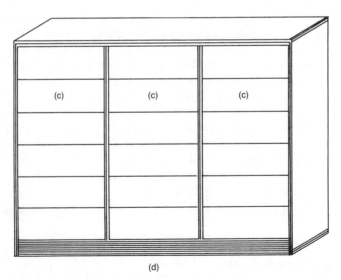

Fig. 26. Library book stacks.

(a) Stacks housing library collection; (b) Ranges of shelves; (c) Sections of shelves; (d) Front view of three sections of a range of shelves.

and choose their own materials. The shelves must be kept in good order since patrons may shelve materials improperly.

Closed-stack collections may be found in university, large public, and special libraries where the collection is valuable and the demand is great. In libraries with closed stacks, materials are "paged," or brought by an assistant to the patron. Usually, the patron requests the material by writing the call number on a "call slip" which is given to a staff member. The page will bring the item if it is in or return the call slip to the patron if it is out. In this system, the collection is accessible only to the library staff. Therefore, the shelves are generally in better order. Another advantage is that the stacks may have narrower aisles than open stacks, so the collection requires less floor space than open stacks. (The patron's convenience must be provided for.) University libraries that have closed stacks often allow access to faculty and graduate students for research.

The choice of open or closed stacks usually depends on the type of library. School, public, special, and smaller academic libraries usually have open stacks, in which materials are easily accessible to their patrons. Within the last twenty years, many large academic libraries have also built new facilities that provide open-stack access for all their patrons. This new open access to the library collections reflects the libraries' objectives of serving all their students.

Compact storage systems

Meanwhile, rising costs in material storage and maintenance encouraged other libraries to investigate new ways of arranging their collections to increase their book capacity. Several types of units called "compact storage systems" were installed by libraries. More than double the usual amount of materials could then be stored in the same amount of floor space. Some of these systems consist of movable ranges mounted on metal rails, so that one stack aisle serves a group of ranges. The inner ranges can be moved sideways on these rails so that an aisle is opened up between the desired ranges. The ranges usually move quietly and easily, and safety devices prevent them from closing on a person standing in the stack aisle. Compact systems may also consist of metal, drawerlike shelves that can hold two shelves of books per drawer. The drawers are then pulled out into the aisle when someone wants to gain access to the materials.

Closed access systems

Completely closed access systems, operated remotely by computers, have also been designed. These systems enable libraries to store their lesser-used or rare materials in climatically controlled, compact storage buildings or areas that are only accessible by mechanical means. Each book or item is assigned a fixed location number, in addition to its call number, and is stored in a specific metal box. The boxes are shelved in storage units. The books may be arranged in these storage boxes by general class number, so that similar books are kept together, or they may be assigned locater numbers and stored in the order in which they are received. The library staff "pages" these items by keying in the location number at a computer terminal. The computer activates a machine that moves up and down the stack aisles, picks up the desired metal box, and deposits it on a conveyor that delivers the box to the circulation attendant. The desired book or item is then removed from the box and the box returned to its location. The whole process for calling up an item may take less than half a minute. However, the speed of such systems is offset by the inability of library patrons and staff to browse in the library stacks.

Special collections

Sometimes, libraries with open stacks keep certain materials or collections in closed or separate stacks because of their demand, value, or likelihood of being stolen. Reserve-book collections, local history collections, and rare books are examples of such special collections. Special materials may be shelved in closed stacks because of their value or their physical shape. Magazines, newspapers, and maps are often shelved separately or stored in closed stacks because of their size or because they tend to be stolen more than books.

Special materials

Audiovisual media such as films, records, tapes, and microforms are sometimes shelved in closed stacks because their size may raise special storage problems. The shelving arrangements of these media will be further discussed in chapter 5.

Arranging Materials on Shelves

Libraries that shelve most of their collections in open stacks should exercise good judgment and imagination in placement of the stacks and arrangement of materials on the shelves. Stacks and ranges should be placed parallel to the lighting fixtures. Aisles should be wide enough to accommodate wheelchairs or enable several patrons to browse in the stacks at one time. The location and height of the stacks should suit the patrons' needs. Children need shorter stacks and ranges than adults. Patrons using reference books or atlases may need counter-height shelves. These can be interspersed with taller shelves or tables on which to place heavy volumes. Magazine shelves and shelves of new materials may need to be placed near lounge areas. Libraries have found that paying attention to such factors can increase usage of their collections.

In a small library, the reference collection is often near the circulation desk. In a large library, there is usually a separate reference room. Oversize materials that cannot fit upright on regular shelves may be shelved on a top or bottom shelf, or even in a separate section, to better utilize the shelf space. Such large, separately shelved books may be marked "oversize" or have a Q or F (for "quarto" or "folio") added to their call numbers. Sometimes materials are placed temporarily in such special collections; these may include new books, display books, or holiday materials.

However, libraries should not divide their materials into too many special collections, or there will be too many places to look for a particular item. If any materials are shelved separately from the regular collection, all the records for them should be clearly marked so that the staff and patrons can easily locate them. Also, keeping a list of the books that are on display can be very useful and save much time in looking for a requested item.

Shelf arrangement is also influenced by the size and shape of the library building. A library, especially a new one, may have enough space to shelve its collections in a block arrangement (see fig. 27a) so that all materials will be in order by classification number. To allow for expansion, the materials may be spread out so that the shelves are only half to two-thirds full, or the top and bottom shelves of each section may be left empty. More crowded libraries that prefer a block arrangement may be forced to shelve some blocks of classification numbers—e.g., biographies, science books, or mysteries—as separate collections in order to use every available nook and cranny. Such libraries should identify these separate collections well and try to keep them in some logical sequence.

Ribbon arrangement is another method. This arrangement places different types of material on the upper, middle, and lower shelves of a section or range (see fig. 27b). For example, a small library or bookmobile might want to shelve adult items in the upper and lower shelves and juvenile in the middle so that patrons have more physical space in which to move and browse. Another library might use a ribbon arrangement of fiction and nonfiction to encourage patrons to browse more in nonfiction than they might ordinarily do.

Imagination may play an important role when more shelf space is needed in a library. One librarian who did not wish to sacrifice the inviting atmosphere of her small branch library to seven-foot-high bookshelves shelved the mystery and western collections on book trucks. The

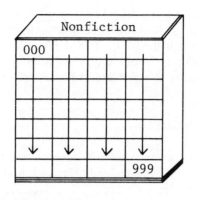

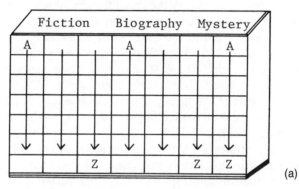

(a)

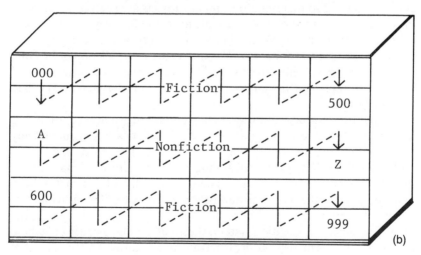

(b)

Fig. 27. *Arrangement of books on shelves.*
(a) Block arrangement; (b) Ribbon arrangement.

patrons did not mind having these books on nonstandard shelfs. Instead, they seemed to enjoy pulling the trucks over to a table so that they could sit and browse through the titles. This is just one example of how the supervisor of shelving can be on the alert for ways in which the books may be rearranged to make the best use of library space.

Shelving Procedures

For staff members to page or shelve materials correctly, they must know how to locate them in a particular library. Each staff member should spend some time in a new library looking over the shelves to become familiar with the filing order, the classification system, and where any special collections may be housed. This examination may also raise questions to be directed to the librarian or supervisor.

In all libraries, materials are shelved from the top shelf to the bottom and from left to right. There should be a book support, such as a bookend, on each shelf. To preserve their spines or backs, the books should not be shelved too tightly. Books are also usually aligned evenly with the front of the shelf so that they are more accessible and so that their titles are more legible.

Books are arranged on the shelves according to call numbers or groups of numbers and letters that are usually written on their spines. These call numbers usually represent the subject classification of an item and are assigned so that items on similar subjects are shelved together in the collection. Nonfiction books usually have numbers representing their subjects on their spines. Fiction books may not be assigned any number or may be assigned a capital *F* or *JF* to indicate they are fiction or juvenile fiction books. Some libraries also add a code composed of letters and numbers to represent the author and subject. This designation is called the "author number."

In public and school libraries, fiction books are usually shelved either alphabetically by the author's last name or alphabetically and numerically by the author number on the spine of the book. The books under each author are then filed by title. All authors with the same name may be filed in one alphabetical order (e.g., Erskine Caldwell and Taylor Caldwell may be filed together) or each author's works may be filed individually.

Nonfiction books are filed by the call numbers on their spines. In the Dewey decimal classification system, these call numbers consist of whole numbers and decimals and are shelved numerically. This means that 629.13 would be shelved before 629.2 (fig. 28). The Library of Congress classification system is based upon groups or units of letters and numbers (fig. 29). The first unit of the call number consists of letters and is shelved alphabetically; the next unit consists of whole numbers and is shelved

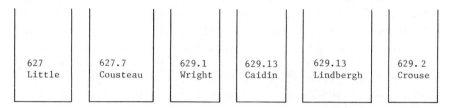

Fig. 28. Dewey decimal call numbers as books would be arranged on the shelves.

numerically. A period may separate the unit of whole numbers from the next units which consist of both letters and numbers (as in QA 4.C22). These further units usually represent the author or the special subject of the book. They are filed first by the letter and then by the number, but the numbers in these units are considered decimals rather than whole numbers. Thus, QA 4. would be filed before QA 39., but QA 39.L345 would be filed before QA 39.L35. Any dates in call numbers, however, are filed chronologically as with the sequence QA 39 1975, QA 39 1981.

    If the library has an individual biography section, books are arranged either by subject classification or by the biographee, the person about whom the book was written, and then by the author's last name or by author number. Other special collections of books are arranged accord-

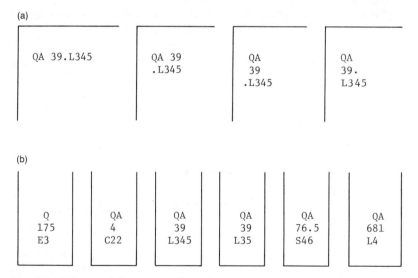

Fig. 29. Library of Congress call numbers.

(a) Various ways call numbers are arranged on catalog cards; (b) Order of call numbers as books would be arranged on the shelves.

ing to the general rules which would apply in the major library collection. Special letter designations such as *M*, *W*, or *SF* (for mystery, western, and science fiction) may be added to the call numbers to show that the books are shelved in a separate collection. Magazines and newspapers may be filed in flat piles with the latest issue on top and the oldest on the bottom, or upright in boxes on shelves with the oldest issue at the beginning on the left and the latest at the end on the right. Labels on the boxes show which magazines and issues are in each box.

Paging is a formal job in closed stack libraries. A paging request from a patron or librarian takes precedence over all other shelf duties. It consists of locating the correct material by taking the call slip to the stacks. Pages in large libraries may be stationed on a stack floor or in a periodicals room. The page should check the author and title on the call slip as well as the call number, because the number on the item may be illegible or the item out of place on the shelves. If the item is not in its correct place, the page should check to see if it is improperly shelved nearby or if there is another copy or edition of the title. If unavailable, the page should check if there is a book on the same subject that might interest the patron. (This is like suggesting alternatives in responding to a telephone request.) If the item is found, the page should take it to the patron or book station. The page should return the call slip if the item is not found. If the material cannot be found and there is no record of it being charged out, the library's search procedures should be initiated. If the page notices that shelves are out of order in the search area, the materials should be reshelved. Needless to say, the stacks should always be left in correct order to make them most usable.

In most academic libraries with closed stacks, the page is a student assistant who pages and shelves materials and performs other routine work. In a public library with open stacks, the page's main function is to shelve materials. If the page pays attention to the subject matter and the call numbers of the material being shelved, he or she will come to know the collection and will find that books can be shelved more easily and quickly. This attentiveness can make the job more interesting and make it easier to find irregularities in shelving or other book processing.

Since shelving takes up most of the page's time, he or she should devise routines that will make it speedy. In some libraries, other staff members place returned material on book trucks in call number order. However, if they do not, the page should not arrange all books to be shelved in complete shelving order. The page should separate the items by major categories such as adult, juvenile, fiction, and nonfiction and group them generally by call number. Then, when the page takes the item to the shelves, he or she can easily locate the area where the group of items belongs and shelve the returned material quickly on the shelf. This is the fastest method of shelving and trains the page to recognize call numbers, locate their place on the shelves quickly, and spot improperly shelved materials.

The shelver's job includes quickly checking the returned materials for any needed repairs not spotted during discharging and setting damaged books aside. This can be done as the books are separated into categories. If the circulation system uses permanent charge cards, the shelver must check every card against its pocket to verify that the call number, author, and title or accession number are correct; this is most easily done at the time the book is shelved. When the shelver places a book in its proper place on the shelf, he or she should straighten all the books on the shelf. If the shelf is too tight to hold the item, the materials on this shelf and the surrounding shelves should be shifted until they are loose enough that the book bindings or containers will not be damaged. The shelver should also correctly shelve any misplaced items, even if it takes a while. The object of the job is not to shelve books in the shortest time possible but to make the collection usable by the patrons and staff.

In order to ensure that pages perform their jobs well, the shelving supervisor should instruct them in the most efficient procedures and check their work as they learn. This can be done in two ways. The page can either shelve the books with their spine up or make a list of the call numbers of the books being shelved and of those on either side. The supervisor must check the page's work not only to ensure accuracy, but also to impress upon the page how important the job is. This also emphasizes the bad effect a poor job will have on the library's objectives.

The supervisor should set up schedules so that books are shelved as soon as possible after peak-discharge periods and so that pages are available during peak-circulation periods. The schedule should provide for books to be shelved on a regular basis. It should allow for items in great demand to be shelved immediately. Schedules should be used as guidelines and pages should understand that they should perform their jobs efficiently and well rather than just meet a schedule deadline. If the supervisor suspects that a page is taking too long at a shelving task, he or she should observe the page's work rather than jump to the conclusion that the page is slow or lazy. The supervisor might find that the page had to shift a section, or even a major part of a collection, in order to shelve some books.

In addition to training and supervising the shelving staff, the shelving supervisor is responsible for the general arrangement and appearance of the library's collection. With the librarian, the supervisor may design a pleasant furniture arrangement to provide for the best utilization of the collection. He or she may help decorate the library and supervise its housekeeping to give it an inviting and attractive appearance. This supervisor usually plans and directs any major shifts or moves of the collection and supervises and plans the inventory.

Shifting

Because a library's collection is never static, materials must be shifted from time to time to make room for new materials or returned items. The library should shift materials on a continuous basis rather than wait until the shelves are full. If it is done in an organized and efficient manner, shifting books can be accomplished easily and swiftly. Otherwise, it can take many staff hours.

Books should be shifted on the shelves as one shelf becomes tight or crowded. Shelves may be considered full when only three-fourths of their capacity is reached. If equal end space is kept on each shelf in a section, the shelves look neater and the shelving and paging of books is much easier (fig. 30). Shifting within a section is easy for a page or shelver to do. He or she should just visually estimate the number of books that should be moved on each shelf to approximately provide this equal end space. As the books are moved from one shelf to another, the shelver should be certain that they are moved in correct call-number order. Shifted books should be aligned at the front of the shelf. Books and bookends should be pushed to the left. If the shelves in one section are too crowded, the shelver should shift books in the nearby sections until a balance is reached.

Sometimes the shelves become so crowded that a major shift or move in the book collection is required. The shelving supervisor should organize this with the help of the staff and the approval of the librarian. In major shifts, there should be enough shelves for new books. The move should not produce a lot of empty shelves all at the end of the collection.

Major shifts are big projects that should not be frequently repeated. They should therefore be carefully planned. There are many books available to advise a supervisor in major shifts or in moving a library. However, several rules of thumb can be mentioned here. Space for the current collection, planned expansion, and materials currently charged out should be considered. The stacks in a new library should be designed to hold two or more times the number of books presently in the collection; if the collection is already crowded, the original count should be increased by one-quarter to one-third before being doubled. In an older library, both rearranging the shelves to make room for new ones and improving the use of existing shelves are possible. A floor plan and scale models of stacks and furniture can be used to determine rearrangements of the shelves. Sometimes, just rearranging special collections can provide several shelves of much-needed space.

Several methods can be used to determine how much shelf space is needed when shifting books. One way is to measure the shelf length presently used for the items to be shifted; divide this number by the total shelf length available to find out how full each shelf should be. For

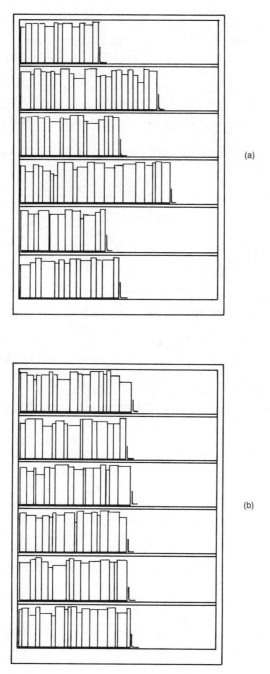

Fig. 30.   Shifting books.

(a) Shelves which need to have books shifted; (b) Above shelves after books have
been shifted.

example, if a library has ten shelves of books and adds five shelves, divide the ten by fifteen and determine that each of the fifteen shelves should be filled 67 percent or two-thirds full. Another way is to measure the shelflist cards, estimating 100 books for every inch of cards. Approximately 100 books can be held in a standard 3 × 7½ foot section; allowing 10 percent free space, every inch of cards represents about one section of shelving.

If possible, each shelf should be filled only half to two-thirds full in order to provide for expansion.

The book shift itself should be designed and carried out efficiently. The supervisor should be certain that all involved personnel understand their jobs and the order in which items should be placed on the shelves. Before and after any major shifting, the items should be shelf-read to catch any errors in the shifting process.

Shelf-Reading

Shelf-reading is a process of checking the shelves to make sure that each item is in its proper place. The library collection should be regularly shelf-read in some areas so that the entire collection is shelf-read every week, two weeks, or month. The shelving staff is usually responsible for this procedure, each staff member being responsible for his or her section of shelf-reading. The supervisor should divide the collection into parts of equal difficulty for shelf reading; for example, in a Dewey system, 000-299 gets out of order less than 600-799. Every person should be given the opportunity to do a good job; shelf-reading for more than an hour or so at a time is fatiguing and reduces a person's efficiency. Each staff member should understand that the efficiency and public image of the library depend upon maintenance of the collection in correct order.

To shelf-read, the staff member compares the call number of each item to the call numbers of the items shelved on each side of it to ensure that it is in the correct place. However, the shelf-reader needs only to compare the parts of call numbers that are dissimilar; he or she should compare each call number to the previous one line by line until it differs (refer to figs. 28 and 29). As the shelves are read, the reader should shift any materials on crowded shelves.

Items should be checked for any needed mending or processing at the same time. The shelf-reader (as well as the shelver) should open every misplaced book to see that it contains the correct charge card. Shelf-reading may turn up lost or long-overdue items which were inadvertently shelved by the staff or the patron.

The shelving supervisor should instruct the staff in correct shelf-reading procedures and check periodically to see that the shelves are being read. In training a new staff member, the supervisor can either shelf-read or spot check the shelves immediately after the assistant has read them. If desired, the supervisor can preshelve designated books incorrectly and check them when the assistant has finished.

Inventory

The purpose of an inventory of a library's collection is similar to the purpose of any other inventory. The library wants to compare its records with the materials it actually has and find out what condition these materials are in. The staff taking an inventory should not only confirm that the library has a given book, but should also verify that it matches the library's shelflist information and that the material is not outdated or in need of repair or replacement.

An inventory also familiarizes the staff with the total collection of the library. It may indicate items that should be discarded or subject areas that should be built up. During an inventory, lost items may be located. Discrepancies in cataloging or processing may be discovered.

Since the inventory is the major process by which the library verifies its official records, the requirement for accuracy and thoroughness cannot be overstated. Staff members' attitudes can make the difference between a well-done inventory taken in a short time and one that is a burdensome chore.

Inventory procedures can be involved and expensive, especially in large library collections. Because of this, some libraries do not take detailed inventories. Other libraries take inventories of their collections on a regular basis, especially if their losses are great or if books are often out of order. Libraries may inventory their total collections on a continuous basis over a span of three to five years by using a rotating schedule. Other libraries, such as school libraries, inventory their total collections in a few days or weeks at the end of each school year.

A library's ability to take inventories is strongly affected by the type of circulation system it uses. Newark and computer circulation systems provide the most complete records for inventory. Computer records and Newark permanent charge cards may give detailed histories of the circulation of each item and enable libraries to locate the charge record for every item not on the shelves during the inventory. Systems that use temporary charge records have charges located in their circulation files for items not on their shelves.

Transaction systems make the inventory process very cumbersome. Once an inventory has been taken of the material in the library, all returned materials must be checked against the list of missing materials for one or two loan periods.

To begin an inventory, the materials should be shelf-read and any materials that had been temporarily shelved in another place (such as display collections) should be reshelved in their proper shelflist or call number order. The inventory should be taken bit by bit in small enough sections that each section can be checked in two to three hours. This time limit is recommended so that patrons will not be too inconvenienced. (While an inventory is being taken, no books should be removed from or shelved in that section.) The time limit is also useful because inventory procedures tend to become tedious, and assistants can become tired and make mistakes.

Usually, two assistants take inventory together, one working with the materials and the other with the shelflist. The shelflist is the official record of the library's collection. It consists of catalog cards (see fig. 31a) arranged in the same order as the materials are arranged on the shelves and contains the record of all copies of every item that the library has.

The assistants take the shelflist drawer to the shelves. There, one assistant reads aloud from the book the call number, author, and title and the unique number given to an item when it was added to the collection, usually a copy number or accession number (see fig. 31b). The other assistant verifies the information against the shelflist record. As each item is verified, some notation (such as a checkmark) may be placed on the charge card or the book to indicate that it was inventoried (fig. 31c). The absence of such a checkmark on a book from an inventoried category that is later found will alert the staff to set it aside to be inventoried. If some or all copies of an item are missing from the shelf, checks are placed on the shelflist card next to the information for any copies that are found. For missing items, the shelflist card is upended or clipped with a metal signal or paper clip. In computer systems, the bar code label or item number can be read by a light pen or entered into the computer. The computer can then print out a list of items that were not entered and not checked out.

Notes are made on slips of paper for any problem materials such as those missing charge cards, needing repairs, or bearing false information. The note and problem material are set aside. The inventory team or technical processing staff will take care of them later.

When the section of materials to be inventoried has been completely checked against the shelflist, all the circulation records must be carefully searched for missing items. In computer systems, the computer can be queried by item number or title code to locate the item. In Newark and double-record systems, the circulation charge must be located in the circulation file. When the charge is found, the check on the shelflist card is erased, the clip is removed, and a check is placed on the charge card. If the charge is not found or the computer indicates the book should be on the shelf, other areas of the library may be searched such as mending, snags, or even staff members' desks.

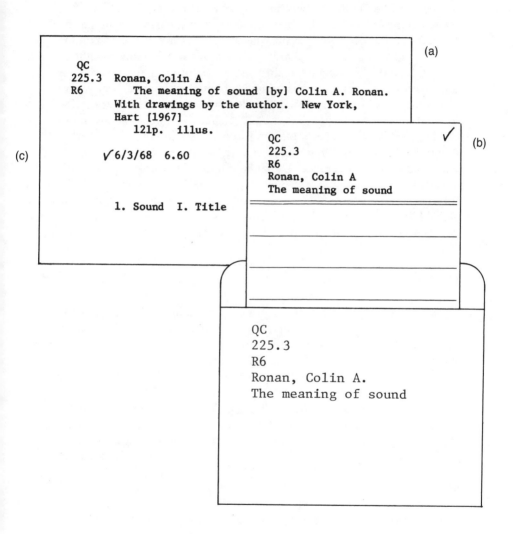

Fig. 31.   Library records that have been checked for inventory.
(a) Shelflist card; (b) Book card; (c) Inventory notation.

After the shelves and all the circulation files have been checked against the shelflist, the shelflist cards that are left standing or have signals or clips on them represent the materials seemingly missing from inventory. A list of these items giving the call number, author, and title should be typed and frequently checked against returned books, the shelves, and records in the first few weeks. In computer systems, missing items may be charged out to "inventory" so that the computer traps any action on the item such as charging or discharging. In transaction systems, each item discharged must be checked against the list before it is reshelved. This search often turns up materials originally missed in the inventory procedure. Materials with charge cards that do not have the inventory notation on them may also turn up; they should be checked against the inventory list. The list should be checked every three or four months to see if other materials can be found, but after a year the items on this list are usually considered lost in inventory. Depending upon the library's policy, the records may then be marked "lost in inventory" or "withdrawn." The librarian should be notified so that needed replacements can be ordered. If a withdrawn item is the library's only copy and it is not to be replaced, the catalog cards for it should also be withdrawn.

Weeding

Weeding a library's collection is just like weeding a garden. It is the process of removing worn-out and outdated materials and either replacing them with new copies or editions or making room for new or better materials. Since weeding is designed to help keep a library collection usable, up-to-date, and attractive, it is also an integral part of a library's collection development policy.

Libraries have established collection development policies for acquiring, storing, and removing materials from their collections for several important reasons. Due to phenomenal growth in publishing and limited physical space, many libraries have been forced to limit collection sizes and adopt various selection policies. Some libraries follow a no-growth policy, which means that a library collection has an equal number of discards and acquisitions. Other libraries allocate 50 to 70 percent of their budgets for replacement items for weeded materials and 30 to 50 percent for new materials. Acquisition for children's collections has traditionally been based on a ratio of two replacement items to one new item (sometimes the ratio is one to one).

The development of library systems and networks has also influenced collection development. Libraries in such systems and networks have been able to coordinate their collection development so that they avoid unnecessary duplications, yet provide material to meet their patrons' needs. These libraries select materials so that their collections complement other collections. They avoid purchasing little-used materials that are easily available elsewhere. Thus, libraries have been able to withdraw duplicate copies of former best-sellers, lesser-known works of famous writers, and materials of only slight value or interest to most of their patrons.

How does a library know what books to weed? Librarians spend many hours in library school learning how to judge the value of books and how to develop excellent library collections. Librarians write material selection policies. They also use various bibliographies of selected and recommended books as guidelines. Assistants often use these selective bibliographies, found in almost every library, to help in the preliminary steps of the weeding process. The staff should participate in the weeding process on a continual basis as it circulates materials, shelves items, and takes inventory. Each staff member should alert the supervisor to books that are older imprints not included in selective bibliographies, too outdated to provide accurate information, or too worn to repair.

The library's objectives and the needs of its public are the first considerations in weeding. They often determine whether little-used books should be kept or not. In actually judging books to be weeded, factors of physical condition and circulation are considered. The first decision to make about an item in poor physical condition is whether it should be repaired or discarded (see "Judging Books for Mending and Binding" in chapter 6).

If discarding is chosen, the next decision is whether it should be replaced or not. The assistant can check the standard bibliographies used in that library to see if the book title is included. If it is, the title of the bibliography and any special information (e.g., *Fiction Catalog*) should be recorded in the book, usually on the card or pocket. The assistant should then check in the latest volume of *Books in Print* (*BIP*) to see if a new copy can be ordered; if so, the assistant can write *in BIP* in the book. If not, *O BIP* or O.P. (out of print) can be written. If the information in *BIP* is different from that in the book in hand, the new information should be recorded, too. During the checking procedures, the assistant may discover that a new edition has been published or that more highly recommended books are available on the same subject. The assistant should note such information in the book card or pocket or write a note to be placed in the book. The librarian can then quickly review the information and make the final weeding decision.

Books that have not circulated very often are harder to judge in the weeding process. For such a title, the most important factor for the assistant is whether the book is included in one of the standard lists. If it is, the librarian and staff will know that this book is recommended for inclusion in a library's collection and should not be discarded. If the book is not included in any standard list and has had infrequent circulation (library policy usually determines what is meant by infrequent circulation), it can be recommended to the librarian for withdrawal.

No book should ever be discarded or withdrawn without the final approval of the librarian. This protects the assistant from costly errors and provides the librarian with an opportunity to keep books that may have some special place or value in the library's collection.

Each type of library uses different bibliographies as standard guidelines for collection development. The H.W. Wilson Company's Standard Catalog series is often used and includes, among others, the *Fiction Catalog, Public Library Catalog, Children's Catalog*, and *High School Library Catalog*. For reference books, Sheehy's *Guide to Reference Books* is often used, as is the American Library Association's *Reference Books for Small and Medium-sized Public Libraries*. An assistant should get to know the standard or selective bibliographies used by the library in order to make suggestions for weeding, replacements, or newer titles in subject areas in which the library has many requests. By doing this, the assistant can assist the librarian and help in developing a quality collection for the library's public.

Conclusion

The shelving and inventory functions make current, attractive, usable materials available to the library's public. The materials and their shelves should be arranged so that they can be most effectively used to fulfill the library's objectives. Materials should be shelved quickly and shelf-read constantly so that patrons or pages may locate them more easily. Inventories enable libraries to verify their records and maintain their collections. The weeding process provides libraries with an opportunity to withdraw or replace worn-out, outdated, or little-used materials.

Student Work Unit

Based on chapter 4 and the materials listed in the References, the student will be able to correctly and accurately:

1. Shelve a designated group of materials according to correct library procedures, placing the books with their spines upward so they can be checked by a supervisor.
2. Shelf-read a designated section of bookshelves, doing any necessary shifting and checking of misplaced books to ensure that they have been correctly discharged.
3. Take inventory with another student of one hundred designated books in 1½ to 2 hours, including checking all shelves

and files, giving problem books with notes to the supervisor, and giving a list of items missing in inventory to the supervisor.

Teaching Unit

The teacher may wish to use a library's collection as the laboratory for these procedures. If so, he or she should impress the need for accuracy upon the students and closely supervise their performance. The teacher should demonstrate correct shelving and shifting procedures.

1. Students can shelve returned materials with the spines upward to be checked by the supervisor. As they shelve, they should also shift and straighten shelves that need it.
2. The teacher shelf-reads one section of shelves for each student, either noting down all the call numbers of misplaced books or misplacing some books. The teacher can also mix up or remove the book cards from several books to verify that students are checking the book card against the book pocket. (This lab exercise also helps the library staff by performing part of their duties.)
3. The teacher assigns about one hundred of the library's shelflist cards to each pair of students (trying to pair novices with those who have taken inventory before). The library may suggest particular classification sections that they would like to have inventoried. The students should be spread throughout the book stacks so that they can work comfortably but not inconvenience patrons. Students should be provided with supplies and instructed in that library's inventory procedures. They should make missing-in-inventory lists and write notes about any problem books to give to the teacher. The teacher should be constantly available to answer questions. At the next class meeting, working pairs of students should discuss their problems in taking inventory. It would be good for a library staff member to be present to help answer any questions. The students must verify that the shelflist cards are in their correct order before they are returned to the library.
4. In chapter 6, students will learn to use bibliographic tools as they would in the weeding procedures.

5 Audiovisual Media and Equipment

Unit Outline:

Types of Media and Equipment
Shelving
Circulation
Booking Systems
Preview Materials
Film Rentals
Maintenance and Minor Repairs
Weeding
Conclusion
Teaching Unit

Unit Objectives:

Identify the characteristics of the major types of audiovisual media.

Discuss concepts in intershelving audiovisual media with books.

Describe the various kinds of circulation procedures that libraries follow for audiovisual materials and equipment.

Describe the basic procedures for audiovisual booking and film rental.

Identify maintenance procedures and minor repairs of audiovisual materials and equipment that media technicians can make.

Discuss the criteria used in weeding audiovisual materials.

In recent years, audiovisual materials and equipment have begun to take their rightful places among print material in library collections. Many libraries have recognized that some of their patrons' needs in a media-oriented society can best be satisfied by audiovisual materials. They recognize that the advent of film, television, and electronics technologies has challenged the supremacy of print media for the attention and interest of their patrons. Audiovisual materials have enabled libraries to help provide for the entertainment, relaxation, aesthetic appreciation, information, and education of their patrons. Together with print media, audiovisual media have allowed libraries to satisfy their patrons'

112

individual interests, abilities, and needs in terms of the content of the material, in a variety of formats.

Although audiovisual media are added to a library's collection because of their content value, their special formats often present collection or logistics problems for libraries. The many media forms come in all shapes and sizes, from one-inch rolls of filmstrip to sixteen-inch-diameter cans of motion-picture film and art reproductions measuring two by three feet. It is this very variety that causes many library staff members to dislike working with audiovisual media.

The basic types of audiovisual materials and equipment as well as their circulation, shelving, and maintenance procedures will be discussed in this chapter. If staff members understand this information, they will feel less frustrated when problems arise.

Types of Media and Equipment

Many types of audiovisual media and equipment are found in libraries today. There are sound (or audio) media such as records and tapes, visual media such as art prints and sculpture, and media that are both auditory and visual, such as videotapes and motion-picture films. The audiovisual (AV) media most commonly found in libraries until recently were records, tapes, and films. However, many libraries now provide a greater range of media including microforms and minicomputers.

Film in all its variety has been included in library collections for many years. Types include motion-picture films, filmstrips of sixty to eighty pictures, or frames, to be projected one by one. Single-picture slides may be mounted in individual cardboard, metal, or plastic sleeves. Short films whose ends are joined together are called filmloops; they are usually contained in cartridges. Filmloops are designed for continuous showing of a short subject or single concept. The various film media are shown in figure 32.

In addition to being produced in these varying formats, films also have other identifying characteristics. Films may be photographed in either color or black and white, and they may be silent or include sound.

Films are differentiated by their width measured in millimeters; typical film is thirty-five, sixteen, or eight millimeters. Feature-length films in commercial theaters are thirty-five millimeters wide, sometimes seventy, and usually an hour per reel to project. Most libraries stock sixteen-millimeter films that are shown in classrooms. They run from fifteen to thirty minutes per reel. Another type is eight-millimeter film (often used in home movies); it is kept in library collections for eight- to ten-minute showings or as eight-millimeter filmloops. These films and filmloops are further identified as "standard 8" or "super 8." This indicates how much of the film contains the image to be projected and how

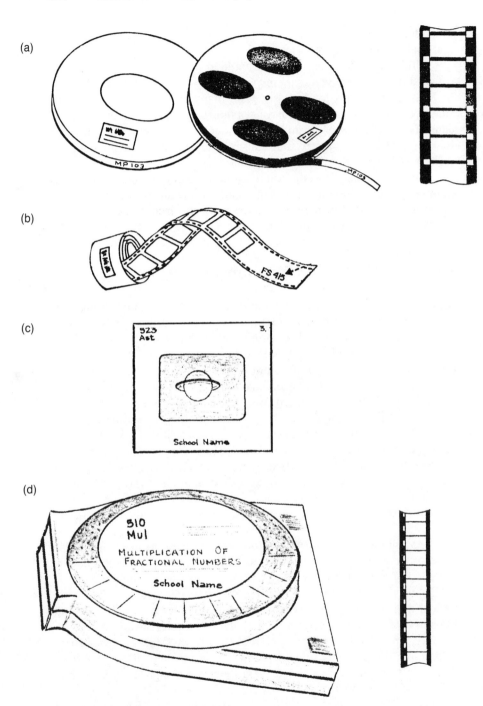

Fig. 32. Film media.
(a) Film; (b) Filmstrip; (c) Slide; (d) Filmloop.

much is used to hold the film on the sprockets of the projector (super 8 has a bigger image).

Filmstrips and slides are usually photographed on thirty-five millimeter film. They can either be projected onto large screens for classroom use or viewed by individuals on small viewers or individual projectors with built-in screens. Sometimes, filmstrips and slides are accompanied with sound from phonograph records or cassette audio tapes.

All of these varied formats and characteristics require that a library have the proper equipment to project the images. Each medium requires its own type of equipment, although some projection equipment can be used for both sixteen-millimeter and eight-millimeter films, and other projectors handle both filmstrips and slides. Some projection equipment is so specialized that it cannot even be used for all film of the same width. For example, super 8 filmloops cannot be projected on standard eight-millimeter filmloop projectors (filmloops in general must be projected on equipment manufactured by the same company that produced the film). In this case, staff members must be certain that they match AV materials to the correct equipment.

Phonograph records are also often included in library collections. In recent years, however, records are being replaced more and more by cassette tapes. Library phonograph records are usually recorded at 33⅓ RPM (revolutions per minute) and are ten to twelve inches in diameter. Their size and susceptibility to damage often require libraries to house them differently from other AV media. Because records can be easily scratched or warped, and because many patrons own cassette recorders, many libraries have begun to transfer the contents of their records onto cassettes; the cassettes, not the records, are then made available for circulation to their patrons. The records are stored as masters.

Cassettes have grown in popularity in the last decade, especially because of better recording quality, greater durability, and increased playing time per cassette. Cassettes contain many types of literature as well as music; libraries have been quick to add cassettes to their collections. Cassette tapes usually have playback periods of 15, 30, 60, 90, or 120 minutes.

Sometimes, libraries have older, reel-to-reel tapes. In using a reel-to-reel tape, one must pay attention to the playback speed, noted in inches per second (i.p.s.). If libraries have reel-to-reel audio tapes, they usually record their contents on cassettes and retain the reels as master tapes.

Videotapes have also become very popular in some libraries. The older videotapes stored on reels have generally been replaced by cassettes or cartridges that fit into cassette players. These players are then plugged into television sets so that the pictures are shown on the screens. The videotape industry has not become as standardized as other media industries, so libraries are faced with a multitude of videotape sizes and cartridges. Videotapes are produced on 2-, 1-, ¾-, and ½-inch magnetic tapes that come in cartridges of different sizes and shapes. Even videotapes of the same width may have been prepared with different technology, so videotape cassettes usually are not interchangeable from one manufacturer to another. In the future, videotapes as well as films may be replaced by video discs, similar in shape to phonograph records.

Microforms are another form of media included in library collections. Some microforms are similar to other film media in that they contain images that have been photographed on film. However, these images are very small and need equipment with powerful magnifying lenses and self-contained projectors and screens in order to be viewed. If the images are produced on sixteen-millimeter or thirty-five-millimeter rolls, they are called microfilm. If they are produced on sheets of film, usually four by six inches, they are called microfiche. Aperture cards (another microform) contain a small piece of film in a window opening. Opaque Microcards also contain images; these, too, need magnification but are not used in film projectors.

Microforms contain a variety of information. Back issues of serials are often kept on microfilm since one year or half a year of a serial may be recorded on one reel (see chapter 7). Microfiche may contain copies of technical reports, research documents, college catalogs, or other reports. Each microfiche can easily contain 100–120 pages of information. Aperture cards may be used to store blueprints and other single pieces of data. Microcards contain information similar to that contained on microfiche.

The variety of microform media means that libraries need a variety of equipment for viewing. Occasionally, microfilm readers have microfiche attachments, but each type of microform usually needs its own equipment. In addition to readers, libraries provide reader-printers for microforms so that paper copies can be made from the images. Because most microform equipment is fairly large, it is permanently housed in the library. Libraries often house microforms in special areas near the microform equipment. Because microforms are small and easily lost, libraries rarely circulate them.

Libraries also include many other types of AV media in their collections. Graphic materials such as pictures, art prints, and maps are housed in special collections by some libraries, while other libraries may include such materials in their pamphlet files (see chapter 9). Framed art reproductions and reproductions of sculpture are loaned to patrons by many libraries. These media as well as films, tapes, and microforms present storage problems for libraries. Some libraries even keep collections of realia, or real objects, such as models, toys, puzzles, games, home and yard tools, and even pet animals. Storing realia tests a library's ingenuity.

School media centers also usually include two special types of media that they tend to use more than other libraries do. Transparencies on translucent plastic or film are primarily designed for group or classroom presentations. They are usually 8½ by 11 inches in size and contain printed or graphic information that can be projected onto a screen. They can be used individually or as a series and may be purchased or produced in-house. Multimedia kits combine media such as filmstrips, records, and student workbooks. They may also contain such items as eight-millimeter film, cassette tapes, and realia such as Indian artifacts. Both multimedia kits and transparencies are designed to enrich classroom presentations and assignments.

Audiovisual media are usually stored in sturdy cardboard or plastic containers, especially when they are to be circulated. Their classification and processing aims to keep all parts of a particular title easily identified and together. Each AV item and its container must be carefully labeled, since it is very difficult to identify the titles of a cassette tape or a slide just by looking at it. Libraries place the call number or item identification number on each part of an AV item (see fig. 32). This information can either be printed on the item or typed on a label which is placed on it. Each slide in a series, each filmstrip in a set, or each tape or record in an album will thus include such a number. In addition, each piece should also include ownership identification, labeled or stamped on, in case it gets separated from its container or from the rest of the AV title. Each container should include the call number, identification number, title, and any author. Both the container and the card pocket should also show the number of pieces included in the title (e.g., "4 filmstrips, 2 tapes, 1 guide").

Some libraries code their labels or items using colors to help in the quick identification or visual inspection of some of their media. For example, libraries might run a colored marker across the top edges of slides or microfiche that are correctly placed in their trays or folders. Any slides or fiche that later became misplaced would easily stand out because the colored edge would be missing or out of sequence. Other libraries with several departments or agencies code their identifying labels with departmental colors so that misplaced media can be easily recognized by the department that finds them and easily returned to the correct department. Attention to such details will make it easier for both patrons and staff to keep the media items together and in their correct order.

Libraries that hold a variety of audiovisual media (often called software) usually provide the equipment (or hardware) to play or project them. Equipment may be available for use outside as well as inside the library. Libraries have projectors for films, filmloops, filmstrips, and slides; equipment for filmstrip and slide sets with sound is also available (see fig. 33). Overhead projectors that project transparencies and opaque projectors that project print materials are also included in school collections. Even to use one type of media, one may have to use any of several pieces of equipment, each operated differently and each from a different

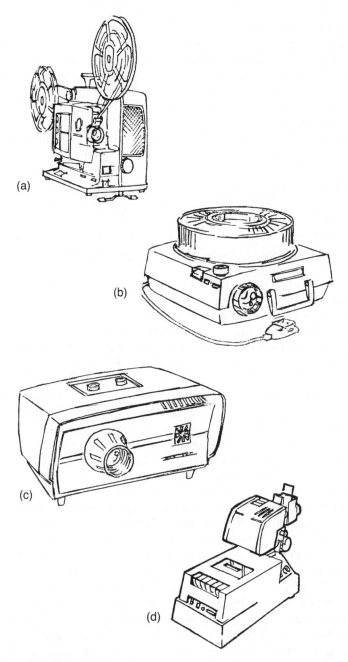

Fig. 33. Projection equipment.
(a) 16mm projector; (b) Slide projector; (c) Filmloop projector; (d) Sound filmstrip projector.

manufacturer. Film projectors are available with either manual or automatic film threading. Sometimes, libraries prefer to make only tape playback units available (rather than tape recorders) so that the library's tapes cannot be erased. They also may make headsets available so that patrons using sound materials will not disturb other people. Other equipment includes viewers, screens, tape recorders (both audio and video), record players, computer terminals, and television sets. If libraries produce their own media, video cameras, microphones, speakers, television monitors, tape decks, and photographic and graphic equipment are also included. Finally, in order to maintain and repair their many media forms, libraries have splicers, inspection machines, and cleaning machines.

Since the variety of AV media and equipment can be bewildering to staff and patrons alike, libraries have standardized the names for the materials and equipment in their individual libraries. Thus, phonograph records may be called "records" by one library and "phono-discs" by another, but within a library system the chosen term will always be used to refer to that particular medium or piece of equipment. Such terms (called by catalogers "general material designations") should follow the title wherever it is written—in a bibliography, on a catalog card, or on a circulation charge card. This practice identifies AV materials and equipment quickly so that staff members know they should carry out appropriate policies and procedures.

Shelving

When libraries first added audiovisual materials to their collections, they often restricted their patrons' access to them by separating the AV materials from the book collection and shelving them in controlled-access areas. Films and filmstrips were usually kept in closed cabinets, often locked. AV materials of one type were kept together and arranged by accession number. If patrons wanted these materials, they often had to request them by accession number. However, as AV media became more important in fulfilling libraries' objectives, libraries began to recognize that their contents were more important than their formats. Many libraries began to classify AV media by subject rather than form. Some libraries continued to shelve classified AV materials separately by type of media, but others began to intershelve them with the books in the stacks.

In order to intershelve these materials, libraries first had to devise new shelving and audiovisual containers. Filmstrips, slides, cassette tapes, videotapes, kits, and even films were stored in specially developed containers similar in size and shape to books (fig. 34). Although some of these containers took up much more room than the items they contained

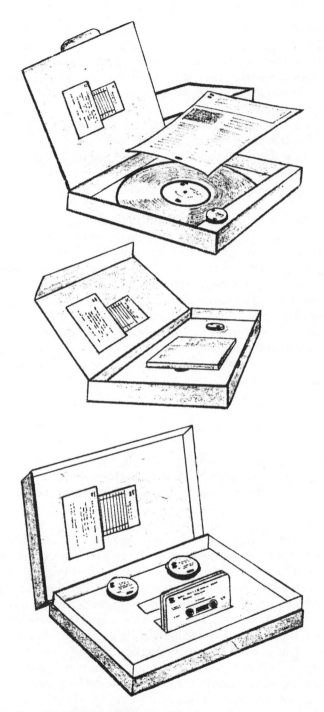

Fig. 34.   Example filmstrip media containers.

would have, the ability to shelve all media together by subject classification number offset the inconvenience.

Audiovisual materials arranged by classification number should be intershelved with books having the same classification number. Sometimes, because of space requirements, the AV materials are shelved in areas adjacent to the books. When this is done, the classification order should be maintained and the shelves clearly marked so that the patron does not miss important materials.

When AV materials are arranged according to media form and accession number, the staff must take particular care that materials are not misfiled. Because there is no subject relationship to accession numbers, an item one number away from its proper place can be hard to find or even considered lost.

Libraries continue to shelve several major forms of media separately. Unusual formats such as realia, toys, and tools often require specially designed shelf units. Records and large sixteen-millimeter films are also too large to fit on the regular bookshelves. If a library has a section for large or oversize books, larger AV materials can be shelved with the books. Otherwise, films are often shelved in a film rack and records in a record bin. Record bins are often near a lounge or listening area to encourage browsing. Some libraries also place their cassette tapes on carousel units for easier browsing and access. In some libraries, records and audio tapes have been stolen so frequently that they are removed from their containers and kept at the circulation desk. When a patron wishes to charge one out, he or she brings the container to the desk, and the attendant gets the actual item.

Microforms are almost always shelved separately from the book collection. They are usually kept near the microform readers and reader-printers. Microforms can be kept in a variety of storage units such as cabinets, bins, and boxes. Microfilms are usually kept in protective cardboard boxes and microfiche in paper envelopes, although envelopes for microfiche can require up to three times the filing space needed for the fiche themselves. When such microforms are reshelved after they have been used, the staff must ensure that each microform has been replaced in its correct container and its correct location. Microforms require temperatures below seventy degrees Fahrenheit and humidity levels below 40 percent and are therefore kept under climatically controlled conditions. Extreme fluctuations in temperature or humidity damage the microforms. Some libraries have special microform rooms staffed by library assistants. Even libraries without separate microform rooms have staff available to assist patrons and to service the microform equipment when it malfunctions.

Libraries may have separate AV areas for other types of equipment. Record players and audio tape decks are often available in lounge or study areas. Videotape players and television sets as well as filmstrip, slide, and filmloop equipment may be kept in electrically wired carrels, or study cubicles. Film projectors may be housed in soundproof preview rooms or in storage areas. However, no matter where the AV equipment is kept, it should be readily accessible when the patrons need it and there should be a convenient and comfortable place for patrons to use it.

Circulation

Because of the cost of audiovisual materials, libraries in the past were often reluctant to circulate them outside the library's walls. Records, tapes, and films were used in the library or loaned only for short periods. Sometimes only certain types of patrons, such as adults or teachers, could use them.

However, as AV media became an accepted part of library collections, libraries began to reevaluate these restrictive loan practices.

Libraries began to base loan periods on demand rather than type of media. Thus, libraries that had heavy use of small collections of records, films, tapes, and other media might limit their use more than would libraries that had larger collections. The limitations varied from restrictions on the number of items that a patron could charge out at one time, to loan periods of from twenty-four hours to three weeks, to heavy fines for overdue AV materials. Some AV media such as films, videotapes, and kits were wanted so often that libraries developed procedures for reserving, or "booking," items for their patrons to use on specific dates. These booking procedures will be discussed below.

Once libraries began to classify their AV materials and intershelve them with books, it seemed reasonable to charge them out just like print materials. Thus, libraries began to charge out all types of AV media such as records, videotapes, sculpture, art prints, games, and toys for the same loan periods as books (fig. 35). Also, many libraries ended restrictions on who could borrow AV media. To the surprise of many staff members and librarians, children proved that they could be just as responsible with these items as they were with books.

One major difference that still exists between the circulation of AV media and print media, however, is the very careful inspection that must be made of such materials when they are charged or discharged. When the staff member charges out AV materials, it is imperative that they be checked; all the correct items must be included. Patrons can get rather frustrated when scripts are missing for filmstrips or the pieces of a game are incomplete. When audiovisual materials are returned to the library, the circulation charge should not be cleared until the materials have been inspected.

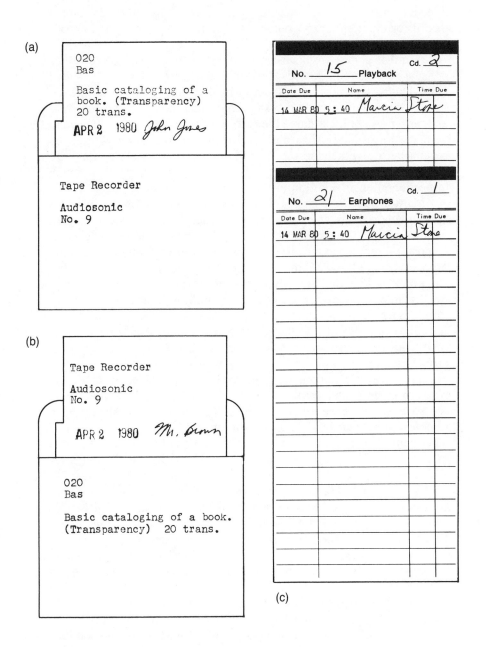

Fig. 35. Audiovisual charge cards.
(a) Materials; (b) Equipment; (c) Equipment on reserve.

Staff members should check each AV container to ensure that everything is in order. Many times, patrons have mistakenly returned personal records or tapes in library containers or left some parts of the library's material at home.

A quick glance from an assistant's trained eye can often notice unusual scratches on records, broken audio tapes, or torn or twisted films. Unless these damages seem to be deliberate or have totally destroyed the material, the library should consider them to be normal wear and tear. Few libraries charge the patron for the repairs that will have to be made for ordinary wear and tear. However, they do make needed repairs before reshelving the item. Films and filmstrips, as they are discharged, are usually put aside to be cleaned and get a more thorough inspection later, in addition to the quick initial inspection.

Many libraries also circulate audiovisual equipment for the materials they circulate. This equipment is often charged out for shorter loan periods, ranging from one to three days, because it is in great demand. Deposits or rental fees may be charged to help ensure prompt return and proper usage of the equipment and to defray the cost of maintenance.

Libraries that circulate AV equipment recommend that it be identified with permanent, nonremovable identification and that it be insured. Each piece of equipment should also have clear operating instructions prominently displayed on it. All knobs should be labeled. Instructions can also include directions for solving common operating problems.

Every piece of equipment should be issued with all needed accessories. For example, film projectors should have large take-up reels, tape recorders should have microphones, and slide projectors should have remote control switches. All projectors should have spare bulbs issued with them, and the correct bulb identification number should be posted on the machine for easy replacement. All equipment should have heavy-duty extension cords and two-prong adapters. "First aid" kits containing spare needles, extra batteries, extension cords for microphones, remote control switches, and items needed for quick repairs can also be issued. An operation manual should also be circulated with the equipment. Libraries can label the equipment with a phone number for operation assistance or emergency instructions. Some libraries even offer training sessions that patrons must attend before they are allowed to charge out equipment.

Procedures for charging out AV equipment may differ according to the type of equipment. Small equipment such as audio tape recorders or playback units, headsets, calculators, or slide, filmstrip, or filmloop projectors that are designed for individual use may be charged out following procedures similar to those for AV materials (see fig. 35b-c). Larger equipment meant for group use or in heavy demand may be charged out for shorter loan periods and require a deposit or fee. Some libraries ask patrons to sign a statement accepting responsibility for expensive equipment such as film projectors, video cassette recorders, or television sets.

Libraries with heavy demand for equipment may place the charge slips in visible scheduling racks or boards. These may be arranged by the type of equipment so that the staff can quickly see which pieces of equipment are charged out. The racks or boards may also be arranged by the day of the week so that the staff can see which items are charged out or reserved for use on a particular day. Sometimes the boards are arranged by both the day and the type of equipment.

A library may use temporary charge slips, permanent charge cards, or both for AV equipment. The charge slips include the type of equipment, its identification number, dates in use, and user information including a location or address and a telephone number. One useful system involves a permanent charge card that indicates the user and the dates on which the item was issued and returned. The charge slip can provide a record of accessories issued, such as take-up reels, microphones, and so forth (see fig. 36). When the item is charged out, the user information should be noted and the charge card placed in the correct place on the scheduling rack or board. At the same time, a temporary charge card can be placed in the card pocket on the equipment, on which the borrower can later indicate any equipment malfunctions or needed repairs.

When the equipment is returned, the temporary charge card should be removed. The staff member discharging the equipment should remove the permanent card from the scheduling board and check it to see that all items charged out have been returned. If the user has indicated any needed repairs, the equipment can be set aside for service by a media technician. Otherwise, the permanent card can be returned to the card pocket on the piece of equipment and the temporary card thrown away or saved for statistical purposes.

When any piece of equipment is returned, the assistant should quickly examine it for signs of wear and tear. If any signs are detected, the equipment should be repaired before it is charged out again. This inspection step is very important in maintaining the usability of the AV equipment and the reliability of the library. Nothing is more frustrating to patrons, particularly to teachers who use the equipment often, than to charge out equipment that is malfunctioning or has necessary components missing.

Booking Systems

Some types of audiovisual media are in such great demand that libraries design special reserve procedures to ensure that they are equitably shared. Further, because patrons usually want to use AV materials on specific dates for classes or programs, libraries have designed "booking systems" to control distribution carefully.

	USER'S NAME	Date/Time Issued	Date/Time Returned	Hrs. Used	Mtl. Isd.				Oper. Ch. Out				
					Mike	Pwr Cd	Case	Remote	Phy Cond	Sound	All OPS	Remarks	
1	BROWN	9/15	9/19			✓	✓		✓	✓	✓	OK	
2													
3													
4													
5													
6													
7													
8													
9													
10													

GTI No. Equipment Type — D1 Filmstrip Proj.

GTI No.
Date/Time Rcvd. 9/15 D/T Rtrn. 9/19
Use Location Rm.330 Hrs. Used

The undersigned assumes complete responsibility for above eqmt. and accessories while checked out.

User Analysis – Rate as Good/Fair/Poor
Check out procedures Good
Instructions Rcvd. Good
Operational Quality OK

Comments and/or problems encountered None

Signature John Brown

Fig. 36. Audiovisual equipment charges.
(a) Permanent equipment charge card; (b) Temporary user charge.

Booking systems enable libraries to reserve the use of a film, videotape, multimedia kit, or other medium for particular individuals and particular days or times. Usually, the items are booked on a first-come-first-served basis—the item is reserved for a particular day for the first person to request it. However, this simple principle can become complicated to act on when two people try to reserve it at the same time or if time for the item to be sent from one library or school to another must be allowed. Because of this, most libraries request patrons to indicate several alternative dates for the use of the material requested. Even then, libraries often cannot fill all of their patrons' requests if the demand for an item is great. When this occurs, the staff member dealing with bookings should inform the librarian so that a second copy of the item can be purchased.

Specific staff members usually carry out all the booking procedures, so that one or two people are aware of items in great demand, can identify items that have not been returned on time, and locate items that need to be delivered for use at other agencies. Attention to detail is necessary so that patrons can be assured that the item will be available for them on the days they expect to use it.

To keep track of all these requests, libraries have established several basic procedures. First, the borrower may request the item on a request card or reserve slip that indicates the item and the desired dates (fig. 37a). Then this information is compared with permanent records that note the dates on which the item is already reserved and the names of the persons who have reserved it (fig. 37b). If any of the desired dates are open, the requester's name will be filled in on the permanent card and the date confirmed on the request card. Multicopy request forms are particularly useful for this step because one copy can be returned to the requester as a confirmation and the other copy can be kept in a file arranged by reservation dates.

As the reserve date approaches, a staff member should check the items against the request slips to be sure that all items are available for the patrons. Materials should be inspected once more to be sure that they are complete and in good working condition. They can then be set aside to be picked up by the patron or mailed to the school or library that requested them.

When the materials are picked up, the staff member should point out any restrictions in their use, the date they are due back, and the structure of overdue fines if different from that for other fines.

Some libraries ask the user to complete a form after using the material. The form may ask the user to indicate if there were problems with the material or equipment. This form often contains questions about the number of people who viewed or used the material, the type of presentation (i.e., individual, class, or club program) for which the

(a)

INSTRUCTIONAL MEDIA CENTER
REQUEST FOR MATERIALS
LOAN RECORD

SCHOOL. . . *Lance* . . . .

Teacher. . *Smith* . . . .

CATALOG NUMBER: | *F-6147* |

Title. *The Shopping Bag Lady (Film)*

Delivery Date. . *Sept. 15* . . . .

   2nd Choice . . . *Sept. 22* . .

   3rd Choice . . . *Sept. 29* . . .

Loans delivered Monday, collected Friday.
Please have material in school's office by
3:30 o'clock, Thurs. No reservations for
alternate dates will be made unless 2nd and
3rd choices are indicated.

KENOSHA UNIFIED SCHOOLS

(b)

F -6147

TITLE   The SHOPPING BAG LADY   (FILM)

SOURCE

		1979-80			1980-81
	SEPT. 3	*Butler*	SEPT. 1	*Butler*	
	10	*Lance*	8	*Lincoln*	
	17	*Lincoln Jr.*	15	*Lance*	
	24	*Washington*	22		
			29	*Tremper*	
	OCT. 1	*Tremper*	OCT. 6		
	8	*Bradford*	13	*Reuther*	
	15	*McKinley*	20	*McKinley*	
	22	*Reuther*	27		
	29	*Wilson*			

Fig. 37. Booking records.
(a) Teacher reserve request; (b) Permanent booking record.

material was used, and whether or not the item met the users' needs. This information is saved for statistical purposes.

There are potential problem areas in booking procedures. Booking records must be kept absolutely accurate so that an item is not booked for two people on the same day. Also, requests may have to be juggled so that materials are shared among several agencies or schools rather than sent to one school because that request letter was opened first. Libraries usually give preference to their own patrons over outside users. Finally, sometimes the staff will have to track down missing or overdue items needed for another booking. In order for the staff to solve such problems, they must be tactful, organized, and vigilant.

Preview Materials

Libraries may request copies of audiovisual materials from producers and distributors for preview or arrange to purchase them on approval. These preview or approval copies are not to be shown to an audience but are only to be viewed or listened to by a librarian, teacher, or other appropriate person to determine if the material is suitable. The staff members should stress this principle, because if preview or approval materials are shown to an audience, there is a copyright infringement and the library and patron could face a lawsuit. Under no circumstances should video or audio copies be made of these materials without prior written approval.

Film Rentals

Many libraries, especially school media centers, cannot afford to purchase all the films their borrowers and teachers need. Instead, they rent large numbers of films from commercial rental sources. These sources include commercial film rental companies, governmental agencies, nonprofit organizations, business and industrial firms, and film producers. They also include such large university audiovisual departments as those at Indiana University and the University of Wisconsin. The rental fees charged by these sources are usually very small in relation to the purchase price. Some films may even be free.

Library audiovisual departments usually collect as many rental catalogs as they can. They also use AV bibliographic sources such as the *NICEM Index to 16mm Motion Pictures* or the *Educational Film Locator* to find out what films are available, especially for rental. Patrons or teachers usually select the films, and the library staff will then send for them.

Procedures similar to film bookings are followed for rental films. The library will choose a likely source and request the film for specific showing dates (giving alternates). If the film is available, the library will receive confirmation from the rental source. The library then notifies the re-quester. When the film is received, the requesting teacher or patron is notified of its arrival and informed of its return date. These films must be returned to their source within the stated time period or the library's future requests to the lender might be refused. If the film is not available from one rental source and there is enough time, the library can try another. If the film cannot be booked at all, the requester should be notified.

There are several problem areas in handling rental films. Often, teachers or patrons do not allow enough time between their request dates and showing dates for the library to rent the films. Libraries should especially encourage teachers to place orders in the spring for films needed the following school year. Another common problem occurs when several teachers at a school request the same film several weeks apart. To alleviate this, some libraries publish a list of rental films that will be at a school during a specific time period and encourage other teachers to use these films while they are available. If several teachers in a school or school system order the same film every year, it may be cost effective to purchase the film instead of renting it every year.

A final problem involves tracking down and returning rental films on their due dates. The library should not let one or two teachers who are constantly delinquent jeopardize the borrowing privileges of the rest of the school. On the other hand, library staff members should be sure that teachers have used the films before they are returned. A film should not be returned in the morning mail if the teacher plans to use it in a noon class. A good film assistant learns the usage patterns of frequent borrow-ers of film and works with the librarian to be sure that rental-film policies are understood by the library's users.

Maintenance and Minor Repairs

Preventive maintenance of AV media and equipment is the best policy for libraries to follow. Every staff member should be taught to use and care for AV materials and equipment. Only if the staff understands how to handle them properly can they instruct a patron in using an AV item or help diagnose a problem with equipment. This knowledge can be gained in "hands on" in-service workshops or training sessions conducted by the media technician or LMTA. Such workshops can also be held for li-brary patrons or teachers and aides who will be using the materials and equipment.

Libraries can improve their media services by carefully evaluating materials and equipment, and purchasing those that have proven to be serviceable. The *Library Technology Reports* published bimonthly by the

ALA provide very useful evaluations. The need for replacement parts should also be evaluated and examined; equipment that costs less to purchase may require more service time and replacement parts. For example, some film projectors use automotive-type projection lamps that last 250–300 hours and cost less than a dollar. Other film projectors may use lamps that last only an average of fifty hours and cost five or six times as much. Some film projectors cannot take the largest film reel. The alert library staff should find out such information before they purchase AV equipment rather than afterwards.

Libraries should consider the abilities and knowledge of their users before making purchases. If inexperienced people are going to use the equipment and if it will be circulated, the library should purchase equipment that is easy to operate. For example, projectors that thread film automatically rather than manually may be purchased. Libraries may purchase audio-tape playback units rather than recorders if the recording capability is not needed. Because audio tapes contained on reels can be erased easily or become tangled, libraries may transcribe these tapes onto cassette tapes. To prevent damage to both the materials and equipment, libraries may transcribe from records onto audio cassettes. Motion-picture films may have extra-long leaders (blank film placed at the beginning) to prevent damage from incorrect threading; the leader should then have the film title written on it for easier identification. Such precautions lower the cost of maintenance.

Maintenance procedures for audiovisual materials and equipment should be a continuous process. As each item is inspected after its use or discharge, any needed repairs should be noted on a maintenance card, the card attached to the item, and the item sent to the proper area for repair. If AV equipment is examined only briefly after each use, a schedule should be set up so that each piece of equipment is cleaned and thoroughly examined after a specific time period or number of uses (for example, film projectors every week or after three uses, slide and filmstrip projectors weekly or after five uses). If AV materials such as records, filmstrips, or microforms are not cleaned after every use, they should be cleaned on a regular basis.

Once repair needs have been identified, they should be made as quickly and skillfully as possible. The library may need to buy mechanical equipment (such as a film splicer) and commercial supplies to make the repair easier and more professional if material is frequently broken and outside repairs are expensive. When using such equipment, the staff member should read and understand the directions given in the instruction manual. There may be a filmloop or videotape produced at the library showing how to use the equipment correctly. The staff members can practice repairs on material no longer in use before making repairs on current items. The media technician should oversee this learning process and determine when the person is sufficiently skilled.

The media most often in need of repairs are slides, films, filmstrips, and tapes. Because they are heavily used, they often require emergency repairs (sometimes in the middle of a film program) that must be made by hand.

Slides often come loose from their mounts and can be placed in new cardboard mounts and sealed with a hot iron.

To repair or splice a film, the two sides of the break should be butted together as perfectly as possible (fig. 38). Transparent tape should then be placed across the film on one side of the break and on the other side, keeping the sides of the film parallel. The tape should be rubbed smooth to remove any air bubbles. Next, cuts should be made very carefully on each side of the film cutting slightly into the film and cutting off the excess tape. (This helps keep the projector from being jammed by gum from the tape.) Finally, the film should be pressed firmly down on a thumb tack to make a new sprocket hole to replace the torn one. Film repair tape with sprocket holes can also be used. The film is lined up on a holder, and the repair tape goes down with the film and sprocket holes lined up.

Filmstrips can be repaired in the same manner as films. In a filmstrip,

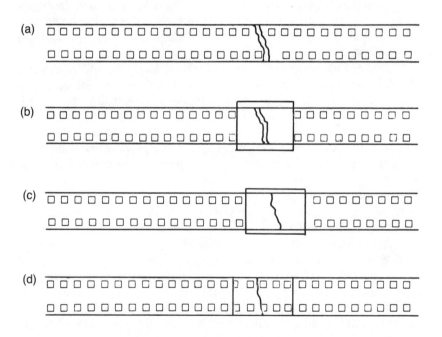

Fig. 38.   Repair of torn film.

(a) Abut broken ends of film; (b) Place tape over tear and press down; (c) Trim tape; (d) Press holes through tape.

it is very important to match the ends of the film exactly because each frame of a filmstrip is important. For this reason and because sprocket holes of filmstrips are easily destroyed by projectors, filmstrip repairs are usually stopgap measures. Libraries usually order replacement filmstrips, and most companies have established reasonable replacement policies for them.

Audio tapes and videotapes are repaired in the following way. The broken ends of the tape are overlapped. One diagonal cut is made across both pieces of tape. The ends are then placed on a smooth, dry surface and butted together. (It can be tricky to keep the tape straight instead of curled up.) A piece of special splicing tape is placed across only the unrecorded side. As with films, the tape should then be rubbed and cut off. This repair process works better on shorter audio tapes than it does on longer ones. (Manufacturers have also developed reasonable replacement policies for longer tapes.)

Maintenance procedures for AV equipment primarily involve inspecting, cleaning, and testing the operating parts. A media technician or trained media aide does this maintenance. Usually, the media technician tests the equipment by using it to see that the visual and audio components work correctly. All knobs and controls are tested. Replacement parts such as new projector lamps, record needles, and tape-recorder batteries are installed. Electric cords and cables are checked for broken housing or wires. With the power cord unplugged, the equipment can be cleaned with soft brushes, compressed-air syringes, or soapy-water solutions. Parts can be oiled, lenses cleaned, and other maintenance procedures followed that are recommended by the manufacturer. If a thorough inspection uncovers any need for repairs, those that can be done in the library should be done immediately.

Media staff should also know what kind of repairs they should not make. The media technician should be able to locate and define a problem and identify some probable causes for it. If remedying these causes is within the skill and knowledge of the technician, he or she should attempt to solve the problem. However, if these attempts fail or if the causes involve mechanical, electrical, or circuitry problems for which diagnosis and repair are complex, the equipment should be sent to the manufacturer's service department. In making these decisions, the technician should use the manufacturer's equipment manual as a guide and should be careful not to attempt any repairs that might void a warranty.

Weeding

Audiovisual materials should be weeded from library collections on a regular basis just as books are. However, libraries may consider different criteria for retaining AV materials in their collections. Primarily, audiovisual materials usually become outdated more quickly than books. Pictures of outdated dress styles or old automobiles and audio soundtracks using outdated slang tend to distract viewers and listeners from the message of the presentation. Older audiovisual materials sometimes presented stereotyped characters or simplistic explanations for concepts now seen as complicated. For these reasons, libraries should not automatically purchase new copies of damaged or worn-out materials but instead reevaluate each item before replacing it.

AV materials being considered for replacement should be compared with up-to-date materials on the same subject. Review sources such as *Booklist, Media and Methods*, and *Library Journal* should be consulted for reviews of new materials. The NICEM (National Information Center for Educational Media) indexes to each type of audiovisual material may also be used to identify newer materials that can be ordered for preview. The librarian may also review school curricula and patrons' comments that have been made on audiovisual users' forms to determine if the material still meets library needs. Then a library can determine whether it should reorder a worn-out AV item.

Conclusion

Libraries offer a variety of audiovisual media to help satisfy their patrons' needs. Media such as films, slides, filmstrips, filmloops, records, audio tapes and videotapes, media kits, games, toys, and so forth can be found in many of today's libraries. Microform collections of periodicals, reports, and documents are also usually included. Although this variety of media (and the equipment to use them) often require special care, handling, and procedures, libraries have found that AV media can fit very well into their regular library collections.

Many libraries now process AV materials based on content and usage patterns rather than on their formats. AV media are often classified, shelved, and circulated just as books are. AV equipment for these media is also circulated, so that use outside the library is possible. AV media that cannot easily fit on library shelves, such as microforms and toys, may be kept in special collections or shelf areas. Media such as films, videotapes, and media kits, which receive heavy usage, may require special reserve, or booking, procedures. As with books, the library will maintain, repair, and weed the AV materials and equipment, but these procedures for care of AV materials may require different skills and knowledge than those needed to repair print materials.

Teaching Unit

Students could practice operating various pieces of audiovisual equipment. The teacher could set up typical user problems, such as burned-out lamps, and broken tapes, beforehand.

The teacher should select audiovisual materials and equipment that need simple maintenance and repairs. The teacher should demonstrate the correct methods for repairing AV materials and equipment. Each student could then be given the same number of audiovisual materials needing representative repairs. The students could repair these AV materials following correct work habits.

Students could also clean and inspect AV equipment and make recommendations concerning needs for repairs they discover.

6 Mending and Binding

Unit Objectives:

Discuss the care and preventive maintenance that should be used in handling books.

Identify the guidelines and criteria that should be followed when inspecting and separating materials for mending, binding, or discarding.

Define bookbinding terms.

Describe typical mending repairs made in libraries.

Describe the decisions made in binding and the procedures followed in preparing materials for binding.

The decision-making process is the most important function of mending and binding. The actual procedures for mending or binding should be carried out only after guidelines have been applied to each material being handled. Mending and binding may be performed by a formal library department or informally by various support staff members under the librarian's direction. In either case, similar functions will be carried out. The librarian is always the final authority. No material should be discarded, extensively mended, or bound without his or her approval. This will prevent expensive and irreparable errors as well as inefficiency in the use of staff time.

The librarian or head of the activity chooses a reputable library binder and consults with that firm concerning the library's binding needs. The librarian also consults with other library departments concerning binding schedules for their materials, makes recommendations concerning the feasibility of mending or binding certain materials, and instructs library staff members in the care and repair of library materials. Under the librarian's direction, the mending and binding staff will perform these procedures according to the guidelines established by library policy.

Book Care and Preventive Maintenance

Preventive maintenance is the backbone of the mending and binding activities, and the entire staff is responsible for it. Normal care must be exercised every time materials are handled from the very first time they enter the library. This does not mean that staff members should be fanatical about protecting the books, but it does mean that they should practice good maintenance habits themselves.

Several maintenance habits that prolong the lives of books can be suggested to library staff members and patrons when they are observed practicing harmful habits. Instead of placing an open book face down on a flat surface, a reader should place a piece of paper in the book to mark his or her place. It is amazing to discover the materials used as bookmarks by some readers. Items such as paper clips, pencils and pens, notebooks, and other bulky items are often used to mark a place in a closed book. These items can easily break the spine of the book and should never be used. Another harmful habit that is practiced by some readers and that should be discouraged is that of eating while reading a book. Food stains often cannot be removed from a book page, and spilled liquids often warp the pages and spine if they are not properly sponged and pressed.

The best method of protecting a new book is to open it correctly. This once was a normal part of the acquisitions procedures, but because of the large number of books handled in libraries today, acquisitions departments seldom have time to open each book properly before it is shelved. It therefore has become the responsibility of every staff member to be alert to new books and to open them properly the first time they are used. To open a new book correctly, place it on its spine on a flat surface, holding the book upright by one hand. Firmly but gently press open first one book cover and then the other along the inner margins of the book. Then alternately press open a few pages at a time from the front and the back until the center of the book has been reached (fig. 39a-c). This helps to prevent the spine from breaking and ensures longer life of the book.

Another procedure that protects a book's spine is not to pull it off the shelf by the top of its spine. Instead, the neighboring books should be pushed back a little until the desired book can be grasped firmly on both sides and removed from the shelf. Some libraries further protect their books by placing plastic jackets on them to protect the book covers from damage as well as to attract the reader's attention. Libraries can also buy books in sturdy library bindings that can quadruple the life of a book.

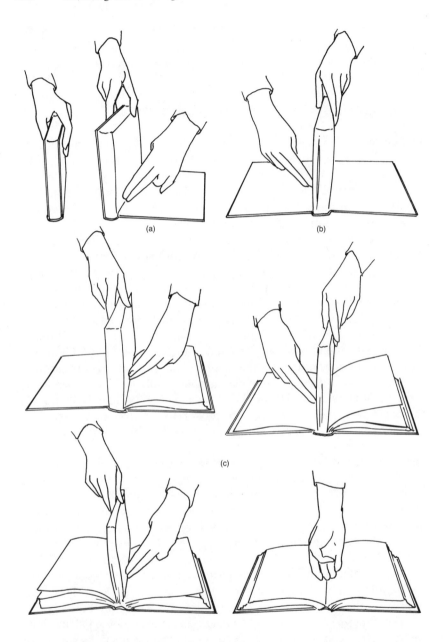

Fig. 39. *Correct method for opening a new book.*

(a) Place the book on its spine on a flat surface, holding it upright by one hand; (b) Firmly but gently press open each book cover along the inner margins of the book; (c) Alternately press open a few pages at a time from the front and the back until the center of the book is reached.

The life of a book can be increased by practicing preventive maintenance during the normal course of charging and discharging routines.
When torn pages are noticed, they can easily and quickly be mended with
transparent mending tape. Do not use cellophane or regular Scotch tape!
Plastic jackets coming loose should be secured; if they are torn, they
should be replaced. If more involved mending is needed, a note to this
effect should be placed in the book at the spot needing the mending; the
book should then be set aside so that the correct mending decisions can be
made for them.

Preventive maintenance and watchfulness by the entire library staff
are the only means for truly protecting and preserving the library's
collection. The library's guidelines for mending and binding its materials
should be known by all staff members and applied whenever a judgment
has to be made about the condition of a book. At the time of charging and
discharging as well as during shelf-reading, inventory, and weeding, the
guidelines for mending, binding, and discarding books are most important. Otherwise, by the time a book is set aside for mending and binding,
it may be in such poor condition that it cannot be saved.

Judging Books for Mending and Binding

Many considerations affect a library's mending and binding policies.

Libraries used to mend and bind most of their books, but library
economics have changed dramatically. Libraries must weigh the personnel costs for repairing and rebinding books against the rapidly rising costs
of new books. In making these decisions, many libraries have adopted a
rule of thumb that a book should not be mended if it will take more than
fifteen minutes of a staff member's time. This was adopted because of the
rising cost of personnel. Even a fifteen-minute mending job would cost a
library a minimum of seventy-five cents since the minimum wage has
risen above three dollars an hour.

A library's objectives also strongly influence its mending and binding
policies. If a library's major objective is to encourage use of its materials
by its patrons, it often finds that the public prefers a bright new copy of a
title to a mended copy of the same title. (This is especially true of
children.) A library may serve its patrons better by either withdrawing
and replacing its worn-out copies or by rebinding them in bright library
bindings.

Libraries will usually consider three factors in making their mending
and binding decisions. These factors are: (1) How much will the material
be used? (2) Can it be easily and reasonably replaced? (3) What is the
value of this particular copy? If a material is not too worn and will not be
used very much, it may not be worth using staff time to mend it. If the

contents of a book are in good condition and its use will be moderate to heavy, the book may be worth rebinding in an attractive library binding. If a book can be easily replaced and will be used a great deal, the cost of a replacement may be worth the added circulation obtained from a fresh copy. If it cannot be replaced, it may be bound or mended so that it will be preserved. Materials valuable because of their age, interest to local historians, or some other important feature are usually not mended or rebound because their value may be decreased if their original condition is altered in any way.

With these factors in mind, a library can establish a policy for mending or binding books for library assistants to follow. Books with firm bindings but torn or loose pages, loose hinges and covers, or worn spines are usually repaired. Titles in too great a demand to go to the bindery (this sometimes takes from four to eight weeks), adult titles of temporary value that are not to be rebound, rebound items needing minor adjustments, and little-used materials retained for specific reasons are usually mended at the library. If books of value are mended, great care should be taken not to destroy the value.

A far more important consideration can be knowing when not to mend a book. Books that will be bound later should not have their spines mended because books with mended spines cannot be rebound. Books to be discarded or replaced should not be mended because staff time is too costly. Other books to be discarded rather than mended are those with a large number of missing pages, extremely soiled pages, or yellow and brittle pages. Brittleness is determined by folding back a corner of a page to see if the paper breaks or leaves a heavy crease. Old editions that have been revised, books of doubtful or little value, and outdated books are others that should not be mended but should be recommended for withdrawal.

Some books should be rebound rather than mended, especially if the decision can be made before they become too damaged to rebind. Books can only be rebound if the pages are intact and clean and if the margins are at least one-half inch at the center of the book. The one-half inch must be left at the center to allow for binding and trimming. A book is usually bound if the sewing or glue has loosened or if the cover is loose and shabby. However, books should not be bound that can be replaced for approximately the cost of rebinding. Books that receive continuous hard use, fiction and nonfiction of permanent value in the collection, and expensive items are usually rebound. Periodicals are often rebound so that they will be in good condition and intact.

These guidelines can be used by assistants to make the preliminary decisions concerning mending, binding, or discarding library materials. However, a knowledge of the steps of the weeding process (see chapter 4) is also needed. An assistant cannot decide whether an adult fiction book is of only temporary value and should be mended or is of permanent value and should be bound unless he or she checks the library's selective bibliographies to see if it is included. The assistant should also check the selective bibliographies to see if an old book has been replaced by new editions. *Books in Print* should be checked to ensure that the book can be replaced. Notations of all the information found should be placed on the book card or pocket of each book. Books can then be separated (according to the library's policy) into piles for mending, binding, or discarding and are then ready for the librarian's final decisions.

Bookbinding

Although bookbinding is an ancient craft, the quality of commercial binding varies tremendously; there are in fact, different types of binding. It is important for librarians and their staffs to know the differences among various book bindings. Only then will they be able to analyze, evaluate, and select the proper bindings and editions to suit their libraries' needs.

In order to understand the differences among various editions and bindings, it is necessary to know something about how books are made. Each page of a book is not printed individually, but sixteen pages are printed at one time on each side of a large sheet of paper. This paper is then folded so that a "signature," or booklet, of thirty-two regular-size pages is obtained. The book is made by sewing all these signatures together. Sometimes, each signature has a lowercase letter on the bottom of its first page that helps the printer to assemble the book in its correct order.

Signatures can be sewn together in several ways (fig. 40). A book of only one signature (for example, a magazine) is usually "saddle-stitched" so that the stitching goes through the fold of the open signature from inside to outside (fig. 40a). If the signature is held together with two or three staples, rather than thread, it is called "saddle wire stitching." "Side-sewing" produces a stronger binding; thread or wire goes through the pages of the closed signatures from front to back approximately one-quarter inch from the fold (fig. 40b). The pages in such books will not open all the way, so thicker books cannot be side-sewn. Some books are "Smyth-sewn," which means that each signature is saddle-sewn and then joined to its neighbors by the same threads (fig. 40c). The pages open flat, but the inner pages of the signatures sometimes tend to pull loose. "Over-sewing" is used in library bindings and rebinding (fig. 40d). Here, the signatures are progressively side-sewn together with a specially curved needle. Books sewn in this manner do not open completely flat but are more flexible than if they had been side-sewn.

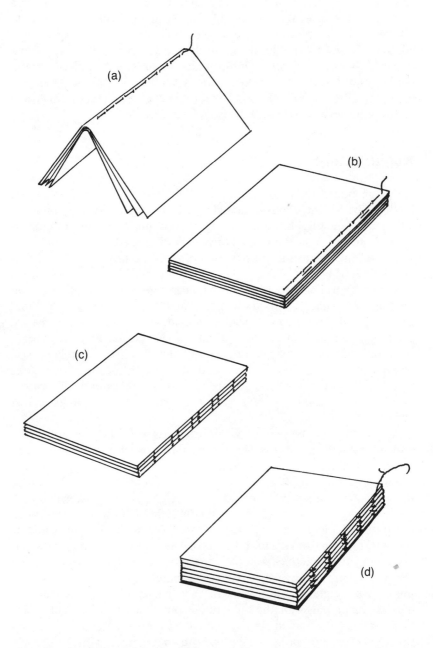

Fig. 40. Sewing methods used in library binding.
(a) Saddle-sewing; (b) Side-sewing; (c) Smyth-sewing; (d) Over-sewing.

In recent years, glued bindings, usually called "perfect bindings," have proven to be sturdier in testing than many sewn bindings and are used extensively. With glued bindings, the folded backs of the gathered signatures are trimmed off, thus exposing the back of each leaf. Glue is applied to the inside of the spine of the cover, and the cover is then fitted to the pages. All the leaves of the book are held equally strongly and the book can open flat.

Once the signatures are sewn or glued together, the pages are fitted to their cover. (A perfect-bound, paperback book has already received its cover.) Much of the strength of a binding depends upon how well this is done. Covers can be of many materials, but the best and strongest is buckram, a stiff cloth. Regular cloth can be coated to protect it from soil, but some cheaper books have cloth coated with starch and are susceptible to stains. Cloth substitutes can be suitable and are definitely superior to the paper-over-board covers often used on trade-edition picture books. Sometimes, covers consisting of hard-rolled binder's boards with buckram spines are used for bindings that will not receive heavy usage. These bindings fit the LUMSPECS (Little Used Materials Specifications) of the Library Binding Institute.

Books may be published in many different bindings depending upon the needs of the publisher and the consumer market. The majority of books published today are called "trade" editions because they are printed and supplied by the publisher to the booksellers, or "book trade." Since cost is a major factor in their production, trade editions are bound in the most economical way. Children's picture books are usually either saddle-sewn or side-sewn with paper-over-board or cloth-substitute covers. Libraries prefer not to buy these editions because their sewing falls apart quickly and they are costly to repair. Trade editions of older children's books and adult books usually have glued bindings or are Smyth-sewn. They generally have cloth covers, but only rarely would this cloth be buckram. If libraries do not expect heavy usage of a book, they will usually buy it in a trade edition.

An important binding for libraries is the "standard library binding," or "class A binding." This binding is regulated by standards set by the Library Binding Institute (LBI), a trade association of commercial binders. Because these bindings are oversewn with buckram covers, they are more durable than trade bindings and can withstand severe library use. Studies have shown that library bindings can average 100 circulations while trade editions average only 15–30 circulations. Although tests have been conducted on new materials by the LBI's book binding laboratory, they have shown that none of the new materials or methods will produce a volume as strong as a class A–bound volume.

Originally, standards for class A bindings were only used for rebound materials. However, for economic reasons, many libraries began to demand this same quality in many of their original purchases. Commercial binders began to purchase trade editions, rebind them, and sell them to libraries as prebound books. Eventually, most publishers also began to make their publications (particularly children's books) available in library-binding editions as well as trade editions. However, publishers also set up new pricing practices for these editions. Rather than charge a discounted list price as they did for trade editions, publishers quoted the actual price the library would pay. These were called "net prices" and were lower than list prices but higher than discounted prices.

Other hardcover editions are also published. "Textbook" editions are books intended for students. They often have summaries and review questions added. The bindings of these editions are similar to trade-edition bindings, but the list prices of textbook editions can be cheaper. Libraries usually prefer to order trade editions because they ordinarily get 20 to 40 percent discounts on trade editions and only a 10 percent discount on text editions.

Publishers often bind books in special types of bindings for book clubs. These editions are often cheaper than trade editions but they may not prove as sturdy. The paper may also be poorer quality than that used in trade editions and may age more quickly.

Many publishers now publish trade and text editions in paperback form. Other publishers may publish exclusively in paperback. Because the quality of paper and bindings of paperbacks has improved dramatically over the years, libraries have found that they hold up very well under library usage. For this reason, libraries often buy paperbacks as duplicate copies of best-sellers and heavily used books.

Mending Books

Once staff members understand the basics of bookbinding, they should be able to mend books properly. Mending a book poorly is a waste of time and materials, and its poor looks give library patrons the impression that the library does not care about its holdings. Therefore, the mending assistant should work carefully and follow good mending procedures. In order to mend books well, a person should be interested in doing a careful job. He or she should understand the guidelines behind the mending decisions and should understand the purpose of each type of mending operation. By following these guidelines, he or she should be able to repair library materials easily and quickly within the recommended fifteen-minute time limit for such repairs.

In order for the staff to mend materials efficiently, they should have a work area with enough clean, dry space to house the mending supplies and provide suitable working conditions. A plentiful stock of basic library supplies should include opaque tape for mending that becomes clear when placed on a book page. Cellophane or clear tape should not be used on book pages because it will eventually become discolored and stain the page. Other supplies usually necessary are Mylar tape for albums and jackets, cloth adhesive tapes in many widths and colors, white plastic adhesive or glue, single- and double-stitched binder cloth in several widths, and perhaps some nylon binder's cord for book spines. Basic tools include scissors, glue brushes, and art-gum erasers as well as steel erasers, different weights of mending papers, and perhaps a library stylus or electrically heated pencil. Although some libraries have more extensive mending supplies, these generally satisfy a library's mending needs.

Libraries have found that extensive, in-house library repairs can cost more in staff time than they save in book costs. Thus, libraries usually do not sew books any more or make new book covers. Instead, the more typical library repairs are mending torn pages, tipping in and replacing loose pages, replacing plastic jackets, and mending and replacing spines. If a cover becomes worn, a library might get more value for its money by re-covering it with an attractive jacket, rebinding it in a brightly illustrated bindery cover, or replacing it with a new copy than by mending the worn cover.

The mending job most typical in libraries is probably the mending of torn pages with transparent mending tape. (Such tape usually looks frosty on the roll but mends transparently.) However, even here the library staff should not get carried away with mending small tears on almost every page. The staff should quickly mend a sizable tear when it is first noticed, not wait for tears to accumulate. To mend a torn page, the staff member should smooth out the edges of the tear and overlap the edges so that the tear cannot be seen (fig. 41). Then, transparent mending tape should be

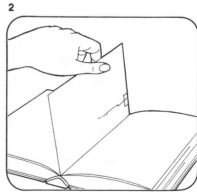

Fig. 41.   Mending a torn page.
(Courtesy of Gaylord Bros., Inc.)

carefully placed on the tear. If the tear ends at the edge of a page, the tape should be cut longer than the tear so that it can be carefully folded over the edge to cover part of the tear on the opposite side. Staff members should be sure to use only transparent mending tape; cellophane tape will eventually discolor the page.

Other common library mending jobs involve problems with the pages themselves. Loose pages can be tipped in by applying a little adhesive to the inner edge of the loose page and carefully inserting this edge into its proper place in the book (fig. 42). Any excess glue should be wiped off,

loose pages

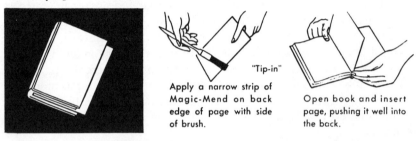

"Tip-in"

Apply a narrow strip of Magic-Mend on back edge of page with side of brush.

Open book and insert page, pushing it well into the back.

Fig. 42.   Tipping in a loose page.
(Courtesy of Gaylord Bros., Inc.)

and pieces of wax paper may be placed inside the book on either side of the page tipped in to prevent it from becoming glued shut to the other pages. If a few pages are completely missing, libraries usually photocopy the missing pages from another copy of the book and tip these into their proper places. However, if many pages are missing, a new copy should be purchased.

The last in-house type of book repair involves the book spines and book hinges that hold the book contents to their covers. Several common problems can be solved easily if repairs are started as soon as the problem starts. Books tend to show their first signs of wear at the hinges, where the contents are joined to the book cover. In fact, this is often the major repair needed for library bindings. To mend the book, open it in an upright position so that the cloth back or spine separates from the body of the book (fig. 43). Then apply adhesive carefully with a brush inside the spine to the loose hinge or other weak spots. Sometimes glue can be carefully dribbled down the inside of the loose hinge. The glue should be applied first to one end of the book and then to the other end. If it seeps through the hinge to the inside cover, the extra glue should be wiped off and wax paper placed against the hinge inside the cover. After the glue has been applied, the book should be pressed well into its cover, weighted

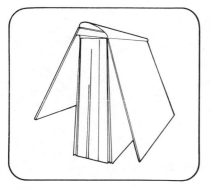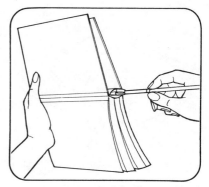

Fig. 43. Repairing a loose spine.
(Courtesy of Gaylord Bros., Inc.)

down with another book, and set aside until it is dry. This repair takes only a few minutes but adds circulation life to a book.

Sometimes, the book hinges become so loose that they are actually torn. When this occurs, cut a strip of hinged binder tape to fit the exact length of the hinge (figs. 44 and 45). Either single-stitched or double-stitched tape would be used depending upon whether one hinge or two had been torn. This preglued tape should be moistened on one side and attached to the back edge of the book contents. The other side should then be moistened, and the book spine and cover should be carefully closed and pressed down well so that the glue of the binder tape sticks to the cover and forms a new hinge. One should never use cellophane tape to form a hinge! It is not cheaper to use this tape, and the tape is not strong enough to serve as a hinge for very long.

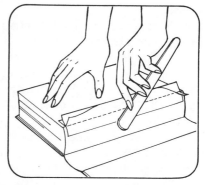

Fig. 44. Repairing one loose hinge using hinge tape.
(Courtesy of Gaylord Bros., Inc.)

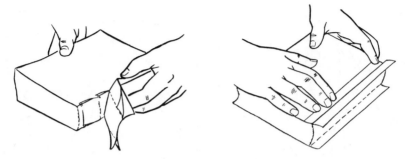

Fig. 45.   Repairing loose hinges using double-stitched binder's tape.
(Courtesy of Gaylord Bros., Inc.)

Another common mending problem involves torn or loose book spines. Rather than glue or mend these strips of cloth, one would do better to peel off the cloth spines and replace them with spines of cloth adhesive tape. If the entire cover is so loose that removing the spine will also remove the cover, double-stitched binder's tape may be attached to the book contents and the covers before the cloth tape is attached to make a new spine. After the original cloth spine is removed, the back of the book and the edges of the covers should be trimmed so that they are smooth and so that wrinkles will not show. Next, a piece of cloth adhesive tape should be cut to match the book in color and size (fig. 46). This tape should be about 1½ inches wider than the back of the book and an inch longer at each end. After the tape is pulled off the roll, its smooth side can be stretched across the book to measure it without sticking to the book. After cutting the tape, place it with the sticky side up on a flat, smooth surface. Sometimes, a piece of paper may be centered on this tape strip to form a slightly smoother spine than the adhesive tape alone would provide.

Next, grasp the book contents firmly, holding the spine approximately one inch above the tape strip, center it over the tape, and lower it carefully onto the tape. Great care should be taken at this step because this tape is usually so sticky that it cannot be peeled off the book without taking some cover with it. After placing the book on the new tape spine, check the book cover and contents to see that the contents do not stick out from the covers. Then roll the book over onto one of its sides, roll it carefully onto its spine, and lay it down on the other side. This method allows the tape to form a natural spine that has normal flexibility and is not stretched so tightly that it will pull back the book covers.

The final steps in this mending process serve to attach the tape securely to the covers. Make two cuts in the tape at each end of the book; the cuts go from the edge of the tape to the book cover and are made at the edge of the spine. The result at each end of the book is three tabs, one for each cover and one for the spine. Cut two pieces of binder's cord as long as the width of the spine and place them at the top and bottom of the spine on the sticky side of the tape. Then, working with one end of the book at a time, gently peel the tape back from the book enough to fold the center tab down over the piece of cord so that it is tucked between the book contents and the tape on the spine. The tape should be repressed against the book and the tabs smoothly folded into final position to form a smooth line at the top and bottom of the book covers.

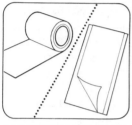  

1. Cut Cloth Tape to length desired or strip backing sheet off tape strip.

2. Center the back of the book on strip with equal space on all four sides.

3. Roll to the left.

4. Roll to right, smooth with Folder.

5. Cut the overlap at the top and bottom of the book, as shown.

6. The two outside flaps are brought over on the inside of each cover board.

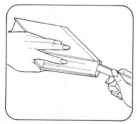 

7. The middle part of the overlap folds into the spine.

8. Close book, crease the hinge with a Folder, rub down thoroughly.

Fig. 46.   Replacing a worn spine.
(Courtesy of Gaylord Bros., Inc.)

Once library personnel have replaced the spine of a book, they usually type the call number on a label placed on the spine of the book. The label may be pressed with a sealing iron and the finished spine sprayed or coated with a thin layer of plastic. The plastic is allowed to dry, and the book is then returned to the shelves.

Besides repairing library materials, the staff must often clean soiled book pages which have ink and crayon marks or other stains and particles on them. However, care should be taken; the cleaning materials and process should not erase the printing or damage the paper. Ink, crayon marks, and mud stains can sometimes be erased with art-gum erasers. Steel erasers can often scrape off heavier crayon marks or stains such as candy, eggs, mud, and so forth. Sometimes, if the marks or stains appear on the inside covers or on extra pages at the front or back of the book, clean white paper can be glued over them or the pages can be removed altogether.

However, if books do have ink or crayon marks that cannot be removed, they should probably be withdrawn and replaced. This is especially true for children's books. Small children get upset when their favorite library books have marks in them, and some children might get the impression that making marks in books is acceptable.

Sometimes, libraries find things that cannot be repaired very easily. Books chewed by puppies or children should be replaced rather than extensively repaired. Books warped by moisture can sometimes be pressed smooth in book presses. However, if the pressing fails or if books get a moldy odor, they should be replaced. Although books caught in floods have sometimes been freeze-dried to remove moisture, this process is outside the capabilities or needs of the local library confronted with a damp and moldy book. Instead, libraries usually replace such books, because one moldy book can spread its odor to nearby books.

The major repairs that have been discussed here are not the only ones which arise in libraries, but they are the most common. If instructions and information on other mending repairs are needed, they can be found in a number of books written specifically about the preservation of library materials. Using this written information, the staff member should be able to learn how to make such repairs. However, it takes a great deal of patience, fortitude, and practice for a mending assistant to be able to mend books quickly, easily, and well. Only after an assistant has mastered both the principles of mending and the actual mending processes should he or she attempt to teach other assistants how to mend.

Binding Procedures

In recent years, libraries have begun to bind their own materials using small available machines. Some libraries use heat-binding machines to repair glued bindings or to reinforce paperback bindings. Other libraries use small binding machines to staple loose library materials such as a volume of periodical issues.

However, most of today's binding is still done by professional bindery firms. To utilize their services effectively, the librarian (or binding supervisor with the librarian) decides what binding policies the library will follow. These will be influenced by the library's acquisitions policies and the changing needs of the library. For instance, a library may decide to purchase its periodicals on microfilm rather than continue binding them. It might become more reasonable to purchase prebound books than to spend the money on bindery personnel and equipment. A library's policies will be affected if it receives many pamphlets or government documents that need to be bound.

The librarian is also responsible for choosing the binder. The binder should belong to the Library Binding Institute because membership certifies that the binder maintains clearly defined standards, including a warranty about the quality of binding (it must meet "class A" standards), and has been recommended by librarians. Binders in the LBI must show proof that they are responsible business firms, insure their customer's property, and be subject to periodic quality-control inspections. A binding company that meets these rigorous criteria can be trusted to bind materials to the library's satisfaction.

Because the prices charged by members of the Library Binding Institute are usually comparable, the librarian may consider other factors in choosing a binder. If transportation is an important factor, a library may choose a binder who picks up and delivers books on a regular basis. The length of time a binder will keep materials or the company's ability to handle large quantities of work at one time may be important to a library. The financial responsibility of the binder should be considered. (Accidents can happen—one large university library reportedly lost a large portion of its wartime European periodical collection when a truck caught on fire on the way to the bindery.) Auxiliary services offered by a binder may also influence the choice.

If one binder cannot handle all of a library's binding, a library may use two binders. If so, it would be wise to send all material of one type (e.g., periodicals) to one binder and all of another type (e.g., books) to another. No matter what binding company is chosen, the librarian should choose one that provides quality workmanship and should give the company proper instructions for the library's binding.

The librarian should schedule binding so that no backlog is accumulated. Materials should be sent to the binder on a regular schedule based upon the library's needs. Public libraries usually bind their materials throughout the year. They may wish to avoid the summer months, when schools and colleges ordinarily send in their binding so it will be returned in time for the new school year. A library should be aware of its patrons' needs and should not send in items at a time when they might be needed, such as during term-paper season. Planning may also eliminate the need for sending many materials marked "rush" to the bindery (there may be an additional charge for rush jobs). Periodicals are often sent as soon as the volume is completed.

Once the bindery schedule is set up, the binding staff can decide what should be sent to the bindery. Using the guidelines for judging books for mending that were discussed earlier, the assistant should be able to make the preliminary binding decisions. In addition, the assistant should follow guidelines for determining what type of binding a material should receive. These guidelines are established by the librarian and binding supervisor. The assistant should know the types of bindings available and choose those that fit the "end use" requirement of a material.

Materials that receive the heaviest use (and those that are used less but are of particular value to the collection) will usually receive class A or standard library bindings. Heavily used periodicals and expensive periodicals of long-term value often receive class A bindings. Class A binding is usually synonymous with oversewing. However, materials less than one-half inch thick may be side-sewn, while valuable materials that have brittle pages and no margins may require hand sewing. Class A binding requires the covers and advertisements of periodicals to be removed and all the pages collated. Buckram covers are also part of class A binding standards.

Libraries may bind archival or storage materials in other types of bindings. Little-used materials that do not need durable class A bindings can be bound according to LUMSPECS. Some libraries use small binding machines in-house for periodicals and lesser-used materials. These bindings may or may not have covers. They may be bound with cleats or by drilling holes in the material and holding it together with steel brads or rods.

In determining what bindings should go on each type of material, libraries should be certain not to bind rare or fragile materials and should avoid the costly tendency to overbind. The end use of the material is an essential element in setting definite standards concerning what and how materials will be bound.

When materials are ready to go to the bindery, several procedures should be followed. The binder may have standing written instructions covering the library's binding decisions. Otherwise, instructions have to be submitted with each item to be bound. Usually, when a book is to be bound, the title and author that the library wishes printed on the new spine are indicated on the title page. Usually a line is drawn under the first initial of the author's last name, and two short strokes or dots are marked under the first word of the title. The call number should also be written on the title page or its verso so that the binder gets the correct information. The book pages should be collated (counted, or verified) to be sure that the book is complete. If a few pages are missing, they can be photocopied from another copy and inserted in their correct places. The book card and pocket can be removed from the book and filed in the library's binding record. Also, the book can be charged out to binding so that there is a record of its location in the circulation system. Binding instructions for an individual item should be prepared, if necessary. The books and binding slips should be prepared according to the binder's specifications. When materials are returned from the bindery, they should be checked for completeness and accuracy and all bindery records cleared.

Many libraries bind their periodicals or magazines so that individual issues cannot be lost and because bound volumes are easier to handle and take up less shelf space than unbound periodicals. Although this practice has become less common with the availability of periodicals on microfilm and microfiche, binding is still done for a variety of reasons. Periodicals that have many colored illustrations are usually too expensive to buy in color microfilm. Larger periodicals are often microfilmed at nonstandard reduction ratios, so their microfilms may require lenses different from those the library has in order to be viewed. Finally, many patrons and staff members do not like to use microform equipment and prefer reading the actual periodical. For these reasons and because specialized serials may not be available on microfilm, many libraries continue to bind some of their periodicals. This may even be the major function of the binding activity. For each periodical, the library's binding instructions include a record of the color of the binding and a pattern sheet for the spine. Libraries usually choose different colors for bound volumes of different periodicals that might be shelved near each other, to reduce the incidence of misplacing periodical volumes.

Some libraries have begun to bind their periodicals with standardized library bindings rather than with class A bindings. With standardized bindings, only the issue sequence is collated, and the advertisements and covers are left in the volumes. Also, the lettering on the spine and the color of a periodical's binding are determined and standardized by the binder. These bindings are cheaper than bindings in which the covers and advertisements have been removed. Libraries may use them if they have room to store larger volumes. They may also use them for periodicals that will not get heavy use.

It is most important to be sure that a periodical volume is complete before it is sent to the binder. Missing pages may be photocopied and tipped in, but missing issues must be replaced by the library before the volume is bound. If the periodical provides a separate title page and index for the volume, they should be bound into it. Large volumes, such as those for weekly periodicals, may be split at reasonable points (e.g., January–June, July–December) and bound in several volumes so that they will be easier to handle.

Conclusion

Preservation of a library's collection depends upon the efforts of every staff member. Each person should adopt preventive maintenance habits and follow the guidelines for judging when books should be mended, bound, discarded or replaced. Bookbinding terms should be understood by staff so that they can intelligently make decisions for mending library materials. Procedures should be followed for common mending problems such as torn or loose pages and torn or loose spines and hinges. Finally, the importance of the binding activity and its procedures in relation to the library's overall preservation policy should be understood by every staff member.

Student Work Unit

Based on chapter 6, the student will be able to:

1. Correctly open a new book.
2. Use proper book care and maintenance habits when handling books.
3. Identify five typical mending problems found in library books and describe how each problem would be solved.
4. Based on the guidelines libraries usually follow to determine which books should be mended, discarded, replaced, or rebound, make separate lists of the types of books that would be: (a) mended, (b) not mended, (c) bound, (d) not bound, and (e) discarded.
5. Follow the weeding procedures in chapter 4 and guidelines given by the teacher to correctly inspect and separate five to ten books needing repairs into groups that should be mended, rebound, discarded, or replaced by newer editions or other recommended books. Look up each book in the library's designated selective bibliographies and correctly record this information in each book. Look up each book in *Books in Print* and record the necessary information, choosing the edition that the library would be most likely to order. Place a note in each book explaining the decision concerning it and give the books to the teacher for the final decision.
6. Under a teacher's guidance, mend books and periodicals using correct mending techniques.
7. According to directions given by the teacher, correctly prepare books and periodicals for the bindery. This will include correctly marking the title page, collating the material, and preparing bindery records.

Teaching Unit

The teacher should provide detailed instructions on how to make typical mending repairs and provide practice for the students in making these repairs. Nearby libraries may be willing to provide books in need of mending for this instructional purpose.

The teacher could give each student five to ten books to inspect and make preliminary mending and binding decisions for. The teacher should give the students guidelines for inspecting materials such as what selective bibliographies to use; what types of books to mend, discard, or replace; and what editions to order.

The teacher could establish binding procedures and, if possible, require each student to prepare one book and one periodical volume for the bindery.

7 Serials

Unit Objectives:

Define serials and explain their importance in different types of libraries.

Identify typical frequencies of serials.

Identify sources and procedures used in locating and verifying serial bibliographic information and locations of serials.

Describe the various ways a library acquires serial publications.

Discuss the uses of serial microforms in libraries.

Describe typical procedures for checking in and claiming serials.

Explain why and how a library would route its serials.

Of all the activities discussed in this book, the serials activity is probably the one that will most often have its own staff. This activity may be a separate unit in the acquisitions, cataloging, or reference department, or it may be a separate department. The special problems involved in handling serials and the special needs serials fulfill in the library's collection call for this kind of administration.

What Are Serials?

Serials have been defined as publications that are issued at regular intervals for an indefinite period of time. This collective term applies to a large variety of publications—periodicals or magazines (serials that contain articles by several contributors), newspapers, annual reports, and yearbooks.

Serials have been called the backbone of the research collection because information concerning recent developments and results of scientific research are published in serials long before they are published in book form. Many times, this information is never published in book form, so serials contain the only written record. Such information is extremely important for special and academic libraries that must serve the researcher. School libraries find that serials provide up-to-date information on current topics being discussed in the classroom. Public libraries provide current issues of general-interest periodicals as a service to their readers; medium-sized and large public libraries also have business and technical serials to serve the research needs of their patrons.

The types of serials that libraries most commonly receive are periodicals and newspapers. Periodicals or magazines (the terms are synonymous) may also be defined as publications that are published in successive parts and are issued at regular intervals. These intervals can be weekly, biweekly, semimonthly, monthly, bimonthly, quarterly, or even somewhat irregular. Some periodicals that are published on a seemingly regular basis change their frequency for the summer months. For example, the *Wilson Library Bulletin* is published monthly from September to May, and the *Library Journal* is a semimonthly except that in July and August it is published monthly.

Usually, each year's cumulation of a periodical is called a volume. Since the first issue of a periodical is usually termed volume 1, number 1, the first issue of each volume of a periodical is entirely dependent upon the month in which it began publication. Thus, periodical volumes may begin in any month of the year. This also means that the annual index to a volume, often included in the last issue of the year, may also appear in any month of the year. For example, the index for *Choice* magazine appears in the February issue, while semiannual indexes for *Booklist* appear in the February 15 and August issues.

Newspapers are also published at differing intervals. Many newspapers are published daily, but they may be published in several editions per day or may only be published Monday–Saturday. Other newspapers are published on a weekly basis. Many newspapers publish large Sunday editions which contain special feature magazines, such as *The New York Times Magazine* and *The New York Times Book Review*; libraries may separate these from the newspaper and file them in the periodical collection. Some libraries add newspapers to their permanent collections by replacing the paper copies when microform copies are received. Other libraries discard national or regional newspapers after a specific period of time, such as a month or two. Most public libraries keep local newspapers either in their original form or on microfilm.

Other serials such as yearbooks, proceedings, and annual reports are also useful in libraries. However, once they have been checked in, these serials are more likely to be either cataloged or placed in the pamphlet file than maintained with periodicals.

Because of the emphasis and importance placed on the current information provided in serials, they should be received in a library and made available to patrons as soon after publication as possible. When an issue is late or is not received, the library patron is deprived of access to information that may be needed right away, and the library's collection may develop gaps that can never be filled. Because many serial issues go out of print quickly and cannot be replaced even a short time after their publication date, library staff members must be alert to such problems and follow procedures that will remedy them as soon as possible.

Serial publications present many problems in acquisitions. Large amounts of staff time are required simply to check in serials and post the records. In addition, the amount of time needed to claim late and missing issues and to prepare the materials for the shelves and bindery leads to a large work load for any library serials unit. It is imperative, therefore, that each assistant perform required procedures accurately, efficiently, and quickly! If serials are the backbone of the research collection, the backbone can be broken by an inefficient staff.

Acquisition of Serials

Which serials a library will order and receive involves major decisions based on a library's objectives and policies. Small school and public libraries may receive only fifty to seventy-five serials; university libraries may receive thousands. Considering the thousands of serials that are published from which libraries must choose, the selection process is most important.

Before deciding which serials it will receive, a library considers factors important in serials acquisition. A serial is not like a book because, once a serial has been subscribed to, it will normally continue to be received as long as it is published. A library needs to evaluate each serial and its contribution to the library's collection before it commits its acquisition, bindery, and microfilm budget and shelf space indefinitely to a particular serial. It should also review its serials policy and subscriptions every few years to ensure that it is satisfying its major objectives.

Libraries try to develop basic serial collections that they hope will satisfy most patrons' needs. These basic collections are developed with the help of standard lists for various types of libraries. Periodical index guides are also used as standard guidelines in ordering periodicals. Such index guides and services as *Readers' Guide to Periodical Literature,*

Business Periodicals Index, Humanities Index, Social Sciences Index, Applied Science and Technology Index, Biological Abstracts, and Chemical Abstracts index the articles in serial publications that subscribers consider most useful or that are considered representative of the knowledge in a particular field. These indexes enable librarians and researchers to retrieve the wealth of information that would otherwise be buried in the serial publications. If a staff member wishes to know if a particular serial is indexed by any indexing service, this information can be found listed under the serial title in a bibliography such as *Ulrich's International Periodicals Directory*. If a serial is not indexed, a library may not want to purchase or keep it, because access to its contents will be more difficult. If a serial is indexed, a library may want to know if it is available in microform. Most libraries prefer to also add back volumes (if there are any) of a periodical upon subscription. Catalogs from companies such as University Microfilms indicate the availability of back volumes.

A librarian who wants to find further information about a serial or what serials are available on a particular subject can consult the various periodical directories, such as *Ulrich's International Periodicals Directory, Ayer Directory of Publications, Standard Periodical Directory*, and *Magazines for Libraries*. These will give bibliographic information for older serials. *New Serial Titles*, published by the Library of Congress monthly, gives the date of first publication, frequency, and price and tells which of about seven hundred important libraries receive them. Reviews of new serials may be found in *Library Journal* or other professional publications. Usually, a sample copy of a serial can be requested from the publisher for review by the library staff.

After the librarian has learned whether or not a serial is indexed, available in microform, and recommended by any standard list, he or she must determine whether the serial has sufficient value for the particular library's collection. Faculty members and patrons of special libraries are often consulted in making such decisions. If the use of a serial will be limited, the librarian must consider its value in relation to the total serials budget.

In the past, serials subscriptions were not as carefully evaluated as they are today. In the 1970s, serial subscription prices rose so drastically that they wrought havoc on library budgets. Many serials doubled and tripled their prices, while others kept their subscription prices down by breaking one serial up into several titles that had to be purchased separately. These price increases forced many libraries to reevaluate and curtail their serials subscriptions or to sacrifice their book budgets to increase their serials budgets.

When libraries reevaluted their serial collections, duplicate subscriptions were the first to be cancelled. Some libraries had purchased duplicate copies when there was a great demand for a serial or when copies were needed for several service points such as a main library and branches. Special and academic libraries often needed several copies so that one could be used for current consultation in the library and the other could be routed to interested individuals. Since duplicate copies were seldom bound, libraries began to eliminate them. They also began to study whether duplicate serials were really needed at branch or department libraries as well as at a main library. Many libraries cancelled such duplicate subscriptions.

Libraries have looked for other ways to stretch their serials budgets. Some pooled their funds to cooperatively buy serials, which were housed in common "periodicals banks." Many libraries joined together in cooperatives that shared serials through interlibrary loan (ILL). This process was spurred on by such national programs as the National Library of Medicine's regional medical libraries and by the CONSER (Conservation of Serials) Project to build a U.S. and Canadian serials data bank. The OCLC data bank developed a serials subsystem that enabled libraries not only to find out which library had a serial but also to make requests for an interlibrary loan of articles. Union lists of serials, which indicate the volumes of the serials owned by particular libraries, have been published on national, regional, and local levels. These lists are not used only for ILL but even for selection and weeding tools as serials collections are evaluated (there is less need to purchase a title if it is available from a nearby library).

In addition to sharing their serials collections, libraries found that there are a number of ways to procure serials without paying for them. Some may be obtained from the publisher as a gift or a complimentary subscription. This is particularly true of "house organs," periodicals published by companies or industries for their employees and customers. Personal or institutional membership in an organization such as the American Library Association entitles a library to obtain some serials free or at reduced rates. Sometimes, libraries receive gift subscriptions, but a library should subject gifts to its selection policy concerning gift materials before accepting them. Subscriptions that come through memberships and gift subscriptions may require extra record keeping to ensure that the membership or gift is not allowed to lapse.

A library might give its duplicate copies of a serial to another library in exchange for a desired serial. If the library belongs to an organization that has a press or publishes a house periodical, it may use house publications for exchange with other libraries. The librarian should not overlook free subscriptions to serials published by state and federal governments. Sometimes, these serials must be supplied free to libraries according to state law. They may either be obtained by requesting them from the issuing agency or by contacting the appropriate government representative.

Libraries may order serials either from the publisher or from a periodical "jobber." Such jobbers receive orders from libraries for periodicals (they may handle other kinds of serial publications, too) and place them with the publishers. Because they are able to place subscriptions for many libraries at one time, jobbers often receive special discount rates, so they can offer libraries reduced subscription rates. In recent years, some jobbers have begun adding service fees to these reduced rates to cover their operating costs.

However, cost is not the most important reason that libraries use jobbers. They do so mainly because the jobber can set a common expiration date for a library's subscriptions, bill the library on one invoice, and eliminate a substantial amount of financial record keeping for the library. The jobber also provides services such as claiming missing issues from the publisher and corresponding with a publisher when a new subscription has failed to begin. Before choosing a jobber, a library should check the jobber's reputation with other libraries. The library should verify that the firm is reputable, is interested in handling the library's subscriptions and attendant problems, will place the library's subscriptions with the publisher quickly, and will take care of claims promptly. How well a jobber can perform these services and their cost to the library determine whether or not a library uses either a particular jobber or any jobber at all.

In choosing whether to order a serial from a jobber or a publisher, a library should compare the cost of ordering each serial directly from a publisher to the cost and service offered by the jobber. For example, small libraries with twenty-five to seventy-five subscriptions might not have large enough staffs to correspond with fifty publishers about their orders, claims, and renewals. For these libraries, it might be very economical and timesaving to use a jobber and pay one invoice. Other libraries that order serials from many different publishers and process all orders through a single business office can also eliminate a great deal of record keeping by using a jobber.

Libraries that order multiple copies of serials or order many serials from one publisher often subscribe directly from the publishers. Some publishers give special rates for multiple copies or for " 'til forbid" subscriptions, which are renewed automatically until the library stops them. Larger libraries with thousands of subscriptions may use several jobbers to handle different types of publications such as foreign periodicals, technical periodicals, and popular periodicals. These libraries often order a portion of their serials directly from publishers who do not sell through periodical jobbers.

Maintaining accurate records concerning the ordering and receipt of serials is an important function. This includes keeping track of the source of each subscription and its renewal date so that the library will not miss any issues.

When a serial order is placed, the library should record the bibliographic information about it that will be needed when the serial is received. The recorded information (fig. 47) includes the title, publisher, address, source of subscription, frequency of publication, price, number

(a)

Title	NATIONAL GEOGRAPHIC									Due	Monthly	
Year	Vol.	Jan.	Feb.	Mar.	Apr.	May	June	July	Aug.	Sept.	Oct.	Nov.,	Dec.

No. Copies 1   Location Library   Indexed in RG

(b)

Publisher   Address
   National Geographic Soc.   Wash., D.C. 20036
Expires 12/80   Bind Yes   Tp & I

Renewal Date Jan.   Price 7.50   Comments

Ordered From Membership   1/80
Ordered From
Ordered From
Ordered From
Ordered From

Issues Short   1st Notice   2nd Notice Sent   3rd Notice

GAYLORD 35Y   PRINTED IN U.S.A.

Fig. 47. Bibliographic information recorded on serial check-in card at time subscription is placed.

(a) Front of card; (b) Back of card.

of copies, availability on microfilm, and whether it is indexed in any periodical guides. The serial record should also include an ISSN (International Standard Serial Number) or similar standard number. Such standard numbers enable libraries, jobbers, and publishers to distinguish periodical titles easily and help to ensure a correct response. Some serials have the same title but different publishers. Other related information, such as previous titles of the serial or the call number and location the serial is to have, should be recorded. Binding instructions, microform copies, claim correspondence for missing issues, and other data can be recorded on this one record so that complete information is kept in one place.

Serials on Microform

Microform copies of serials may be added to library collections for a number of reasons. Libraries can save space by storing serials in microform rather than in bound volumes. They can also cut down on the theft and mutilation of serials that occur in paper copies or bound volumes of serials. Some materials, such as newspapers, can be better preserved in microform. Other materials may be out of print and only available in microform, especially back issues of serials that have been published for a long time.

In choosing which serials to order on microform, libraries consider patrons' preferences. Many patrons, particularly researchers in special and academic libraries, do not like to use microform materials. Therefore, libraries serving these patrons may limit their microform purchases. Others, such as users of newspaper collections, are perfectly satisfied with microform copies because they are far easier to handle than bulky newspaper volumes. If patrons can make copies from microforms conveniently, using microform reader-printers, they may not care whether the serials are in microform. They may appreciate the fact that the serials are available when they need them.

Libraries usually choose one type of microform for all their serials, and this type is most often microfilm. Microfilm often contains an entire year or volume (sometimes half a year) of a serial on one roll. Rolls are easier to file and find than microfiche. However, although microfiche contain only one periodical issue or serial number on each fiche, they do enable several patrons to use different issues of the same serial volume at one time. The major disadvantage of microfiche is that they can easily be misplaced.

Microfilm is often available in either 35-mm or 16-mm widths and can comprise either positive or negative images. A positive image will be projected as black letters on a white background, and a negative image will be projected as white letters on a black background. When copies are made, however, the images are reversed. Although most of the microfilm sold is positive-image film, some libraries prefer to purchase negative-image film; it enables readers to make notes on the white backgrounds of the printed copies and projects less glare on the viewing screen. However, whichever type of microfilm a library decides to order, it should try to order the same type in the future. A serials assistant must take great care in ordering microfilm (or microfiche) to be sure that the correct width and image of the film are ordered. A library may be required to maintain a current subscription to a periodical to purchase it in microform.

Although there are a number of microfilm publishers, most libraries still purchase their microfilm from University Microfilms. In choosing a microfilm publisher, the library should evaluate the product of each firm and check out its reliability with other libraries. For instance, some libraries in the past developed frustrating collection problems when a different-quality film was used to microfilm the *New York Times* and the storage boxes began to disintegrate on the libraries' shelves. Libraries should be as careful choosing their microform suppliers as they are choosing binders and jobbers.

Once an order for microform has been placed, the serials assistant should keep accurate and detailed records of receipt. Because serial volumes may begin at any time, microforms may be received at any time throughout the year. Microfiche may be received as soon as each issue has been published, while microfilm will usually be received after each serial volume has been completed. Larger or more-frequent serials may be filmed and received semiannually. For these reasons, the assistant should be certain to record the correct volume and date of each microform received on the serial check-in card. The assistant should also view each fiche or roll of film to ensure that it matches the box in which it has been packaged. Finally, paper issues of serials may be withdrawn after the microform has been received.

A final caution about serial microforms is that the assistant should note that the invoice that a library pays usually covers the microforms for the previous year's publications. Thus, an invoice paid in January, 1980, might pay for a microfilm for January–December, 1979, that was not received until March, 1980. However, if the microfilm is not received within three months after the completion of the volume, the library should claim it from the publisher.

Receipt of Serials

When serials are received in a library, they are usually checked in. The two main aspects of a good checking system are that the record reliably shows what the library has received and that the record facilitates a prompt and thorough follow-up for claiming missing and late issues. Its purpose is to provide a control for a library's serial holdings. It should show at a glance if the latest issue has been received or if a copy is a duplicate.

Libraries keep their control records in several different formats. Small libraries may use simple card files on which they record the receipt of the periodicals. Other libraries may have visible-record indexes that can be simple or complex. The simplest visible-record indexes are manually operated trays of cards. Complex files may consist of trays in motorized, rotary drums that are activated by keying in a location initial or code. Computerized check-in systems are also in use. The computerized systems provide closer controls for ILL and claim purposes. However, if a library has a need for closer control of its serial check-in procedures, it would probably do better to review its present procedures before automating its serial routines.

The most common type of control record is kept on cards that can be placed in a visible-record index (fig. 48). This enables the assistant to locate the check-in card for a serial with the least amount of effort. To make check-in easier, the cards should be filed by the titles that appear on the serials rather than by main entries assigned by catalogers. The cards should also contain all the information recorded when the serial was ordered.

The information for the issue received should be recorded by the assistant in the manner most useful for that particular serial. Some serials, such as daily newspapers, may not be checked in because it is quickly known whether the issue arrived and because newspapers may not be kept permanently. For other serials, a check mark may be placed in the appropriate column of the check-in record to designate that the issue has arrived, or two check marks may be entered for two copies. Sometimes, a library wants to know on what date an issue was received, so the date of receipt is noted in the column corresponding to the issue date (fig. 49). If a serial has a distinctive numbering or designating system for its issues, this may be recorded in the check-in column as no. 1, no. 2, Jan.–Feb., or Spring (fig. 50). Some serials, such as those published annually or irregularly, are received on a standing order basis, which means that when they are published, they will be sent to the library. Their receipt should be noted in the appropriate records.

When all the issues of a volume have been received, this may be noted in some way on the serial check-in record. This is particularly useful if the issue notation is confusing. Sufficient information should be included on the check-in records so that the holdings of the serial can be read and understood at a glance.

In organizing the work of checking in serials, the assistant may find the following procedures useful. First, remove the mailing cover from the

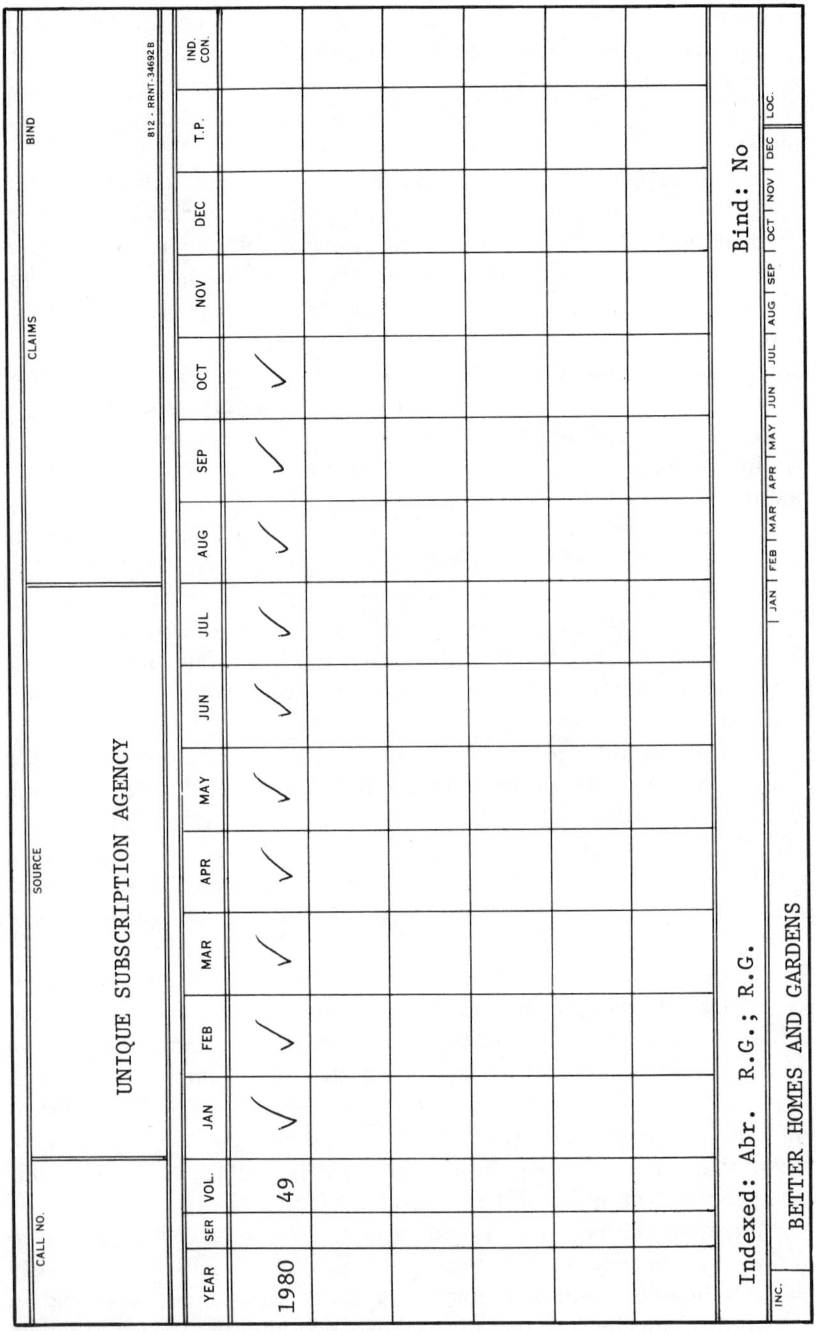

CALL NO.

SOURCE

UNIQUE SUBSCRIPTION AGENCY

CLAIMS

BIND

812 - RRNT.34692B

YEAR	SER	VOL.	JAN	FEB	MAR	APR	MAY	JUN	JUL	AUG	SEP	OCT	NOV	DEC	T.P.	IND. CON.
1980		49	✓	✓	✓	✓	✓	✓	✓	✓	✓	✓				

Bind: No

Indexed: Abr. R.G.; R.G.

BETTER HOMES AND GARDENS

INC.

JAN | FEB | MAR | APR | MAY | JUN | JUL | AUG | SEP | OCT | NOV | DEC | LOC.

Fig. 48. Serial check-in card for visible record index.
Received issues recorded by checks.

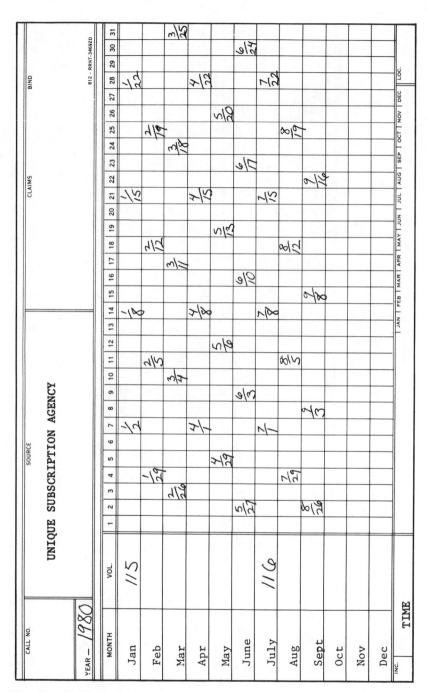

Fig. 49. Serial check-in card.

Received issues recorded by date received.

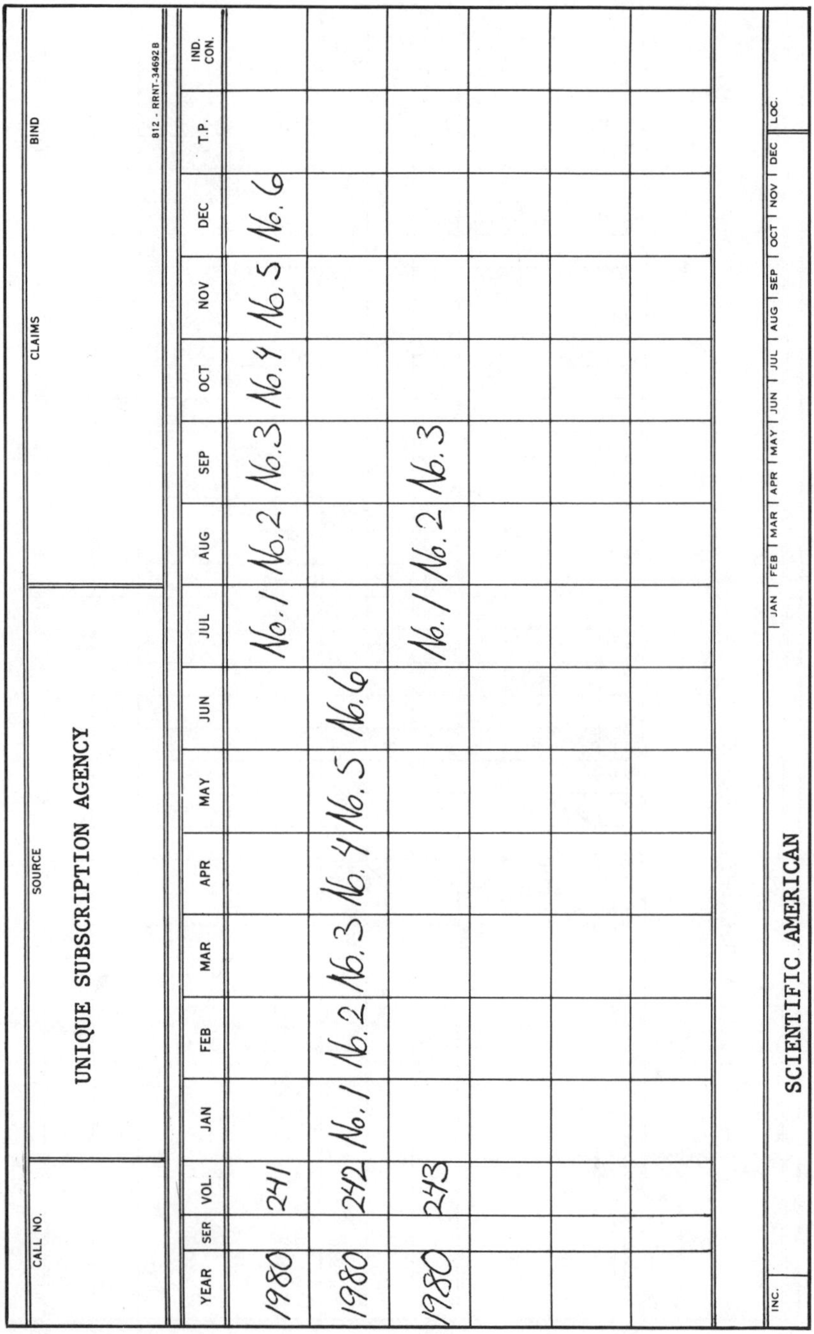

CALL NO. | SOURCE: UNIQUE SUBSCRIPTION AGENCY | CLAIMS | BIND

812 - RRNT-34692 B

YEAR	SER	VOL.	JAN	FEB	MAR	APR	MAY	JUN	JUL	AUG	SEP	OCT	NOV	DEC	T.P.	IND. CON.
1980		241							No. 1	No. 2	No. 3	No. 4	No. 5	No. 6		
1980		242	No. 1	No. 2	No. 3	No. 4	No. 5	No. 6								
1980		243							No. 1	No. 2	No. 3					

INC. SCIENTIFIC AMERICAN | JAN | FEB | MAR | APR | MAY | JUN | JUL | AUG | SEP | OCT | NOV | DEC | LOC.

Fig. 50. Serial check-in card.

Received issues recorded by issue number.

issue and place it inside the issue. This will provide the correct mailing address if there has been some error. Rush serials should be separated so that they may be checked in first. Next, the serials should be roughly alphabetized, then finely alphabetized if there are a large number. Each serial should be checked in with legible notations made on the record.

The assistant should look for any problems or variations and make a note of them. Typical problems might be a missing issue, a completed volume, or a change in title. The note should be placed in the serial issue and the serial put aside to be taken care of after the others have been checked in.

If an issue is to be routed, an individual's name can be placed in the issue or a note made of which routing slip to attach.

The serials are stamped with the library's ownership stamp after being checked in. (This is particularly important if other departments in the institution might also receive their own copies.) Sometimes the back of each issue is then reinforced with Mylar tape. Sometimes the date of the issue is lettered on its spine or prominently on its cover to help file it with the other issues of that title. Libraries may add a card and pocket or due date slip if the serial is to be circulated. Often, the latest issue of a serial is placed in a plastic jacket in a special shelf area. The previous issue is then removed and placed with the other back issues.

After all the serials have been checked in, the assistant should follow up on the problems that arose. Title changes, serial mergers or splits, and changes in format or frequency are common. Magazines sometimes cease publication without warning.

Serials that seem to be duplicates should be double-checked against the issues already received before they are treated as duplicates. The wrong periodical may have been checked in on the serial record card. The mailing labels should also be checked to determine if the addresses are correct. Sometimes subscriptions overlap and duplicates are sent for several months. In addition the jobber or publisher may send a second subscription to the wrong location. Duplicate issues should be carefully researched before they are made available for exchange or discarded as unwanted items. Most of the time, confusing duplicates have actually been ordered and paid for by the library.

Any changes, particularly title changes, should be noted on all records and reported to the librarian. Often, only the first issue bearing the new title will refer to the previous title.

If an issue completes a volume, the assistant may flag the check-in record so that when the next issue arrives, the completed volume may be prepared for the bindery. The assistant should be sure to record whether there are a separate title page and index for inclusion in a bound volume on the check-in card as well as on the bindery slip.

Missing issues are a major problem in libraries. If a missing issue is not discovered quickly and the publisher notified immediately, the publisher may be out of stock, and the library would then have to locate the issues through avenues for out-of-print periodicals. The process for retrieving missing issues from publishers is called "claiming" and can take a great deal of staff time if it is to be effective. Missing issues should not be discovered by libraries in a hit-and-miss fashion, such as when a patron asks for one. They should be detected as part of an organized claim process.

The claiming process begins when an issue is checked in. The serials check-in clerk should check to see that all previous issues have been received. If not, complete information for the serial is recorded on a claim slip, a mailing label or wrapper attached to it, and the slip turned over to the claims assistant. To expedite claims, some libraries place colored tabs at the bottom of file cards and move them along to indicate when the next issue is expected. It is then an easy matter for a check-in clerk to see if a serial is out of sequence with its tab. If so, this should be indicated on a claim slip. Weeklies, monthlies, quarterlies, and irregulars can be given tabs of different colors to indicate frequency. (Daily newspapers are usually noticed quickly if they are not received.)

As the tabs are moved along, a general pattern is developed for the receipt of each type of serial. Noting the pattern, the assistant can set up a systematic schedule for claiming. Weeklies can be claimed once a month, monthlies every other month, and quarterlies about three times a year. The claims assistant should not allow more than ninety days to elapse before a serial is claimed. Otherwise, the publisher might be out of stock.

In claiming serials, the assistant should be careful not to overclaim or underclaim. Careful checking is important in avoiding these problems. The assistant should be watchful of serials with similar titles that can be confused or checked in on the wrong cards. Also, he or she should watch for notes on serials records that indicate changes in the publishing frequency. (A monthly may suddenly become a bimonthly or quarterly.) Sometimes, missing issues that are outdated (last year's almanac) or superseded (an issue that has already been cumulated into a more comprehensive work) need not be claimed at all.

Claiming may proceed in several ways. If a library uses a jobber, the assistant may complete the jobber's claim form and mail it. The jobber will contact the publisher for the library but will not be able to directly supply the missing issue; the jobber is only an expediter of orders, not a wholesaler. If the publisher must be contacted directly, the assistant should provide the complete serial information, attach a mailing label if one is available, and write the publisher for the missing issue.

This claiming process becomes very involved in larger libraries. The assistant must first determine which source (jobber or publisher) supplies the serial. Then, if several copies have been ordered for several locations, the assistant should determine whether all copies should be claimed or perhaps only one. Sometimes, the assistant finds that all copies have been mistakenly sent to one location. If serial issues are checked in at more than one location, there should still be only one person responsible for claiming all serials in a library system. Other check-in clerks should notify this claims assistant of any missing issues. Only if such constant vigilance is practiced by all staff members involved will a library's serial collection remain complete and useful.

Some libraries, particularly special libraries, route periodicals to interested individuals. This can be done in several ways. The main consideration in choosing a method is to provide the most efficient service to the user at the lowest cost to the organization. A copy of a periodical may be displayed in the library with a distribution slip attached that interested persons may sign to receive it when it is routed. It is more common to have people indicate which serials they would like to receive and then compile a routing slip for each periodical that contains the names of all the people who want it. When the serial is ready to be routed, it can be checked out to the first person on the slip, returned to the library, then checked out to the next person, and so on. A simpler method is to attach a routing slip to the serial and have the issue returned to the library only after the last person on the list has seen it; in this case, the routing slip should be arranged so that the serial will move along the shortest route from person to person (fig. 51).

Rather than route a serial issue, some libraries send copies of the table of contents to interested individuals. These persons then indicate whether they wish to see an issue or a particular article, which is then sent to them. Libraries with computerized serials may have the capability to enter the interests of each individual and match them with the table of contents of each magazine. More sophisticated systems might even index each article and provide an individual with a list of articles on very specific aspects of a subject. If a large number of persons in a particular department wish to see a serial and if the funds are available, the library may order a duplicate copy that will be sent to that department when it is received. The library, however, should check in all serials, no matter what their final destination, in order to control serial receipts and claims.

The main responsibility of serials personnel is to accurately control the acquisition and receipt of the library's serials. This work can be carried on largely by nonprofessional staff members under the guidance of the librarian. The librarian will determine what serials will be ordered, renewed, bound, or purchased on microfilm. The serials assistants can handle the routines involved in ordering and receiving serials.

According to policies and procedures set by the librarian, the assist-

(a)

Fig. 51.   Serial routing slip.

(a) Library record copy kept in library files; (b) Copy attached to serial.

ant can locate serial bibliographic information, including where a serial is indexed or if it is microfilmed. He or she can locate reviews of the serials and request sample copies and price quotes from the publisher or jobber. This correspondence may be written on preprinted postcards or forms. Claims correspondence is often preprinted on blank forms, too. The assistant can submit purchase orders and requisitions to publishers and business offices and process invoices for subscriptions received. All the routines for checking in serials and preparing them for routing or the bindery can be performed by assistants.

In performing all these procedures in the serials department, the assistants must understand the importance of accurate record keeping and thorough follow-up correspondence and procedures. Only when attention is paid to these areas will the serials collection be kept up-to-date and complete so that it will be a vital part of the library's information collection.

Conclusion

Currency and immediacy, which provide the excitement of working with serials, can also become their downfall. Serials are constantly changing—their titles, their frequencies, their formats, and their content. Serials can begin publication, suspend publication, cease publication, or resume publication without any notice. Although libraries are hard pressed to keep up with their serial publications, they must do so if they are to serve their patrons' needs. Libraries must carefully evaluate new serials and add them to their collections judiciously. Serial check-in records must be accurately kept and constantly monitored for claims. Serials that are bound or received on microforms must be carefully controlled so that no gaps develop in these important research collections. Only then will libraries be sure that serials justify their expense and effort and fulfill their patrons' needs.

Student Work Unit

Based on Chapter 7, the student will be able to:

1. Write a hundred-word essay explaining the importance of serials in library collections.
2. Use fig. 47 as a guide to look up and record below (fig. 52) the information that should be recorded if an order were placed for the serial entitled *Library Journal*. Use the bibliographic sources described in chapter 7.
3. Record the receipt of the next issue of *Time* magazine on fig. 49 and *Scientific American* on fig. 50. (Use appendix D to estimate the probable date of receipt.)
4. Following the teacher's guidelines, accurately check in five serials from the time they are received in the mail by the library through their final processing for the shelves.

Teaching Unit

The teacher may set up a laboratory unit requiring students to locate and record the complete serial bibliographic information, reviews, and the library location for a particular serial. The teacher may provide serials that the students can check in according to specified guidelines. The students could also develop a complete check-in record for issues of a serial.

Title												Due	
Year	. Vol.	Jan.	Feb.	Mar.	Apr.	May	June	July	Aug.	Sept.	Oct.	Nov.	Dec.	T.P.&I.

No. Copies   Depts.   Indexed in

(OVER)

(Publisher's name)   (Publisher's address)

List price   Vols. begin   Bind

Ordered of......DIRECT......................Date................Expires................Cost................
Ordered of...Date................Expires................Cost................
Ordered of...Date................Expires................Cost................
Ordered of...Date................Expires................Cost................
Ordered of...Date................Expires................Cost................
Ordered of...Date................Expires................Cost................
Ordered of...Date................Expires................Cost................
Ordered of...Date................Expires................Cost................
Ordered of...Date................Expires................Cost................
Ordered of...Date................Expires................Cost................

Short   1st Notice sent   2nd Notice sent   3rd Notice sent

GAYLORD 35Y   PRINTED IN U.S.A.

Fig. 52. Serial check-in cards for student work unit.

8 Filing in Library Catalogs

Unit Objectives:

Describe the types and purposes of library catalogs.

Identify the information found on library catalog cards and describe the types of catalog cards.

Discuss the AACR2 (*Anglo-American Cataloguing Rules*, 2nd ed.) changes in personal and corporate headings.

Describe how shelflist cards are filed.

Explain the rules for filing catalog cards according to the *ALA Filing Rules*, 2nd. ed.

Present examples of these filing methods to demonstrate the rules.

Describe procedures for maintaining library catalogs.

Libraries gather materials and build collections so that they can satisfy the information needs of their patrons. In order to do this, they must provide some means of access to this vast store of knowledge. Library catalogs are a means of access, providing as much information as possible about the materials in the library collection in a manner that will be most useful for the library user. Library staff members must remember that this is the major purpose for which the library's catalogs should be designed and maintained.

Patrons use many different approaches to find information. Some patrons ask for books written by particular authors. Others ask for a particular book by its title. Sometimes a patron wants information on a broad or a specific subject. In addition, patrons may want information concerning the edition of a book, the translation of a work, what serials the library receives, or what volumes in a series a library has. To satisfy all these approaches, librarians have designed criteria for the information that should be included in a catalog and have formulated rules that facilitate the easy location of this information.

Library Catalogs

Library catalogs come in many different physical forms and arrangements, but the information included in them is basically the same. This information will be discussed in detail in a later section entitled "Library Catalog Cards."

The first library catalogs were sometimes called "indexes" and were lists of the manuscripts a library contained. Over the centuries, the indexes became more refined and useful. Besides just listing the manuscripts, they gave detailed physical descriptions of them in a list arranged by subject matter. The indexes, or catalogs, were kept in book form and were consulted by users and other libraries to determine what manuscripts a particular library had. Book catalogs had many disadvantages for libraries with rapidly growing collections, especially in that they could not be supplemented or updated easily.

The now-familiar card catalog grew out of the practice of recording new additions to a library on slips of paper that were interfiled in preparation for the next revision of the book catalog.

The card catalog had several advantages over the book catalog. It could be revised and updated at any time. Cards for withdrawn materials could be removed. The arrangement of the card catalog in drawers made it convenient for many people to consult the catalog at the same time. The size of the catalog card made it possible to provide a large amount of information on each book title. The major disadvantages of the card catalog were the time involved in filing large numbers of catalog cards, the possibility of misplacing cards, and the necessity of keeping the card catalog in one location.

In 1901, the Library of Congress began to publish cards that contained the cataloging information for new books added to its collection and made the cards available for library purchase. This availability of prepared cataloging influenced the rapid adoption of card catalogs by United States libraries and standardized the catalog-card format.

The advent of the computer with its capabilities for rapidly updating information and printing it has brought the book catalog back into libraries. Libraries that can afford a computer-produced book catalog can make many copies of it available at many locations for the convenience of their users. These catalogs can be revised frequently and easily and can sometimes be kept more up-to-date than manually maintained card catalogs.

The computer has also been used to produce computer-output-microform (COM) catalogs. These catalogs provide a record of a library's catalog information on microfilm or microfiche and are used by libraries for their public catalogs. COM catalogs can be updated and reprinted more cheaply than book catalogs. The development of reasonably priced, good-visibility microform equipment (particularly high-speed microfilm readers) has encouraged libraries to adopt them for catalogs.

Some libraries are installing on-line computer catalogs in which a user directly searches a computer's memory by using a terminal. On-line catalogs may be tied in to the library's computerized circulation system. Thus, when looking up a title, the patron may be able to tell if the item is on the shelf or if it is charged out and also when it is due. Such capabilities are so useful that on-line catalogs will probably become more common as they become more refined and less expensive.

The type of catalog a library chooses depends on the needs of its users and the finances of the library. No matter what type of catalog is chosen, it should serve as an index to all the materials in the library and should fulfill the following three purposes: (1) provide the location of materials in the library, (2) record all the books and materials in a library by their title and author, and (3) provide subject access to all the materials. In order to provide this triple access, the library card catalog usually includes an author card, title card, and subject card for every title in the collection. (The COM catalog lists the item in these three ways, too.) Each of these cards will always include the call number, or shelf location, of the book.

These cards may be arranged in many ways in a card catalog depending upon a library's objectives and needs. The two most common arrangements are the dictionary catalog and the divided catalog. The dictionary catalog is arranged with all catalog cards in one alphabetical order, like a dictionary. If the card catalog contains a great number of cards, some libraries have found it more useful to divide it into several catalogs. Usually, the subject cards are filed in one catalog and the author, title, and other types of catalog cards (there are a large number of them, as the student will learn in the next sections) are filed in the other catalog. Some large libraries even divide the author and title cards into separate catalogs.

The dictionary and divided catalogs are arranged alphabetically, but classed catalog cards are arranged by the classification number (first part of the call number) in numerical order. Since the classification numbers were assigned to place books logically within a subject area, this arrangement provides a systematic subject approach to the collection in contrast with alphabetic arrangement of subject headings. The arrangement of cards in a classed catalog then corresponds to the arrangement of books on the shelves. In order for the patron to use a classed catalog effectively, the major outline of the classification system should be prominently displayed near the catalog.

Catalogs intended for use by library patrons are often called the "public catalog" or the "official card catalog." Another type of catalog, designed primarily for use by the staff, is the shelflist catalog. This catalog is a classed catalog (i.e., arranged according to the call number and how the books are arranged on the shelves). It is usually kept either in the technical processes area or adjacent to the technical processes and reference areas. The shelflist catalog includes information about the number of copies owned by the library and how they were acquired, which usually does not appear on the public catalog cards. Besides being the library's official record of every copy of every item that it owns, the shelflist is also constantly used by catalogers in assigning call numbers to materials. This ensures that the same number will not be assigned to two different items and gives a distinctive call number to every item that the library has cataloged. (Even different editions and duplicate copies of the same title have slightly different call numbers.) The reference section often uses the shelflist as a classed subject catalog for locating information. In acquisitions and weeding, the shelflist is used to review the library's subject holdings. Because of the importance and use of this catalog, it must be kept up-to-date and accurate at all times. If any cards are pulled from the shelflist for use by the staff, dummy cards with the call numbers, titles, and authors written on them should be inserted. This maintains the integrity of the shelflist and ensures the accuracy of its call numbers.

The previous catalogs usually contain information for only one library. If a catalog contains information for the holdings or the locations of materials for two or more libraries, it is called a "union catalog." The most famous union catalog is the *National Union Catalog* (*NUC*), published in book and microfiche form for the Library of Congress. This catalog is a photographic record of main entries (in alphabetical order) of the catalog cards filed in the National Union Card Catalog at the Library of Congress. The cards represent books that have been acquired by the Library of Congress and other large U.S. libraries. Entries contain location symbols that indicate which libraries have the book.

Many individual libraries and library networks maintain union catalogs that show the holdings and locations of a library system or the holdings and locations of libraries within a region. These catalogs enable the staff and patrons to find out which library owns a needed title so that it may be borrowed on ILL. An individual library system may maintain a union card catalog at a central library showing the holdings of all agencies in the system. Staff members from the branches then contact the central library to see if another owns a particular item. Union catalogs may also be available in book, COM, or on-line form so that every library and agency knows immediately where an item can be located.

Library Cataloging Rules

The criteria and rules for the content and form of catalog cards have been codified by the ALA in the *Anglo-American Cataloging Rules* (1st ed.), 1968 and the *Anglo-American Cataloguing Rules* (2nd ed.), 1978 (*AACR2*). These rules are used by professional librarians to catalog materials. The library assistant should know enough about *AACR2* to understand the format and information found on catalog cards. Since the catalog card heading for the same item cataloged under *AACR* and *AACR2* might differ significantly, staff members should also understand some of the major differences between these two codes. Then they will be better able to locate materials in the library catalogs.

Cataloging rules establish one specific heading under which all the information about a particular item is recorded. This heading is called the "main entry." The main entry usually indicates the author or person responsible for the intellectual or artistic content of a work. If not a person, the main entry can be a corporation, an organization, or the title of the work. Once a form of entry has been established for a person or corporation, that same heading will be used throughout the catalog whether the name of the person or corporation is used as the main entry of a work or as its subject or for some other heading.

The catalog format used to designate the personal names of authors has been changed in *AACR2* to conform with the author information given on the chief source of information for the work, usually the title page. Earlier cataloging rules had required that the full and complete name of a person be given whether or not it was included in the item. Thus, persons who wrote under pseudonyms such as O. Henry and George Orwell were cataloged under their real names as "Porter, William Sydney," and "Blair, Eric Arthur."

AACR had changed this practice to allow pseudonyms to be used as main entries but still required, however, that the person's complete name be given. Thus, D. H. Lawrence and H. Allen Smith became "Lawrence, David Herbert," and "Smith, Harry Allen." If a person's forename (or forenames) were unknown, eight spaces were often left after an initial so that the information could be filled in at a later time. Also, a person's birth and death dates were added to complete the headings.

Instead, *AACR2* requires the form of name by which a person is identified, whether or not it includes initials. If conflicts occur between two names, the full form of the name can be added in parentheses, for example,

Lawrence, D. H.   (David Herbert)
Lawrence, D. H.   (David Horace)

Dates are only added to personal names if one heading is otherwise identical to another heading. Although these differences in headings may seem minor at first glance, they can cause a number of filing problems in a catalog.

The headings for corporations have also undergone a number of major changes under *AACR2*. Under *AACR*, corporations were used as main entries when they were responsible for the editorial content of the work. *AACR2* has replaced this concept of authorship with a concept of official corporate thought as expressed in administrative publications, legal publications, and reports of committees, commissions, conferences, etc. Sound recordings, films, and video recordings that are the results of the work of a performing group are also entered under a corporate heading (e.g., the name of the performing group). Other items issued by corporate bodies (including firms, organizations, associations, and governments) are entered under personal author or title main entries. This change in corporate authorship may mean that works formerly entered under corporate main entries will now be entered under other types of headings.

Even the format of the corporate headings has been changed by *AACR2*. Corporate bodies are now entered directly under the names by which they are predominantly identified. Corporate names are no longer transposed to fit the cataloger's rules. For example, universities are now entered under their official names as with "University of Pennsylvania" or "University of California, Los Angeles" rather than under "Pennsylvania University" or "California University, University at Los Angeles." Corporate bodies, particularly business firms whose names contain forenames or initials, are now entered under those forenames (e.g., "H. W. Wilson Co." and "Howard H. Sams and Co.") rather than transposed and entered under their surnames. These basic changes in corporate headings will produce many new headings incompatible with those already in a library's catalog.

The title of a work is used as a main entry when the personal authorship is unknown or diffuse or the work is published under editorial direction. Works that are published by corporate bodies but are not records of official thought are also now entered as title main entries. A work will also be entered under its title when responsibility for the work is shared among three or more persons or corporate bodies. Some works with various titles—for example, certain sacred works—may be assigned uniform titles by the librarian so that different or variant editions of the same title will be brought together.

Audiovisual materials are often cataloged by title main entry because there is seldom a personal author given. However, audiovisual materials that include personal responsibility for artistic content (such as artists, composers, or songwriters) may be entered under personal names. The title main entry of an audiovisual item will be followed by a "general material designation" indicating its format. These designations are listed in Rule 1.1C1 of *AACR2*; they are written in lowercase letters and enclosed in brackets after the title and before the subtitle. Sometimes, libraries may additionally identify AV items by using colored bands on the tops of the catalog cards.

Library Catalog Cards

Libraries use main entry headings and main entry cards to record all the information for a particular item in the library catalog (fig. 53a-h). However, in determining this main entry, the cataloger usually makes a choice among several different headings or access points. After such choices have been made, added entries are made for those headings or terms not chosen (fig. 53i). Thus, added entries are often made for (1) titles, if the main entry was a personal or corporate name; (2) personal names not used as main entries; (3) corporate bodies not used as main entries; (4) editors; (5) translators; and (6) series titles. These headings are added to extra copies of main entry cards (also called an official entry card or unit card) and the added entry cards make up a set of catalog cards (see fig. 53).

Every item in the library is represented by a set of catalog cards. Usually the set contains an author card, a title card, and from one to three subject cards (fig. 53a-d). If the headings on the subject and title cards are identical, libraries with dictionary catalogs may not make title cards, but libraries using divided catalogs must always use title cards. Since the cards are filed in the public catalogs by the top line of the card, the various cards from each set will be alphabetically separated in the catalog. This will enable the library patron to use any of the headings to find information about an item the library owns.

It is fairly easy to distinguish a main entry card from an added entry card because of the standardized spacings used to place information on the catalog card (see fig. 54). Libraries use standard three-by-five-inch cards and set the tabulations for three indentations (often the eighth, twelfth, and fourteenth spaces from the left hand margin of the card). The main entry (usually the author) is always typed at the first identation on a predesignated line at the top of the card (often the third or fourth line). If this main entry continues to a second line, it continues at the second or third identation so that it will stand out and be recognized easily. The added entry heading, such as the subject heading, is typed on a unit catalog card a line or two above the main entry at the second indentation. If it is longer than one line, it continues on the next line at the third identation. This format makes the added entry heading stand out from the main entry heading and makes both entries easy to recognize.

The format for the part of the catalog card following the main entry heading consists of paragraphs of information. These paragraphs are begun at the second indentation and are continued at the first indentation. The first paragraph begins on the first line under the main entry and is called the "body of the entry." It contains information transcribed from the chief source of information (for a book, this is the title page if there is one). The information is listed in standard order and separated by standardized punctuation, as follows: the title, subtitle, any statement of the names of authors, editor, illustrator, translator, or other person or orga-

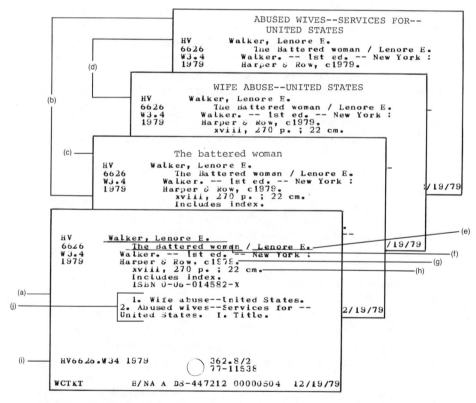

Fig. 53. Set of catalog cards.

(a) Main entry card (author entry); (b) Added entry cards; (c) Title card; (d) Subject cards; (e) Author main entry; (f) Title; (g) Imprint; (h) Collation; (i) Call number; (j) Tracings.

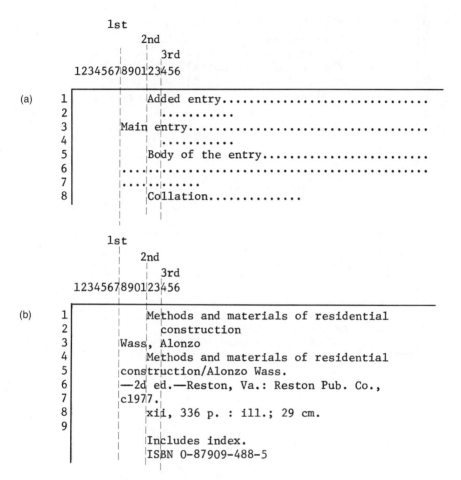

Fig. 54.   Main and added entry headings.

(a) With indentions; (b) With headings.

nization associated with the work. Any edition statement is listed next, followed by a dash and place of publication, publisher, and date of publication (fig. 55).

   If the title is used as the main entry, the main entry heading and the body of the entry form one paragraph. The paragraph begins on the main entry line at the first indentation and continues at the second to form a

```
12345678901|23456
```

```
(a)  1   _____
     2  | Call        |   |
     3  | No.    Main| entry............................
     4  |             |   | ..............
     5  |            Title........... : subtitle....... /
     6  | statements of responsibility. --
     7  | edition. -- Place : Publisher,  date.
     8  |            Collation........ -- (Series)....
     9  | ....|......
        |            Note...............................
        |            Note...............................
        | ....|......
        |
        |            Tracings.........................
        | ....|......
        |_____
```

```
12345678901|23456
```

```
(b)  1   _____
     2  | TJ          |   |
     3  | 163.4 Hayes, Denis, 1944-
     4  | U6          | Energy: the case for conservation/
     5  | H39   by Denis Hayes and James Wright. --
     6  | 1st ed. -- Washington : Worldwatch
     7  | Institute, 1976.
     8  |          77 p. : graphs ; 22 cm. --
     9  | (Worldwatch paper ; 4)
        |            Includes bibliographical references.
        |
        |          1.  Energy conservation--U.S.
        | I. Title.  II. Series.
        |
        |_____
```

Fig. 55.   Unit catalog card.

(a) Standard format; (b) Sample card (author-main entry card).

"hanging indentation," or inverted paragraph (fig. 56). The placement of the rest of the information on the card resembles an author-main-entry card.

The second paragraph contains the "collation" and the series statement. The collation is the physical description of the book and is as follows: the number of pages, the number and type of illustrations, and the size of the book in centimeters. The name of the series to which a work belongs is printed in parentheses after the collation. A series is a group of separate works usually related to each other by subject or in some other way and issued in a uniform format by one publisher.

Other paragraphs may follow that give pertinent or related information about the work, such as whether it has a bibliography, a list of contents, notes, etc. The last such note for a book is the ISBN (international standard bibliographic number) or publisher's identifying number for that edition. The price of a book may also be given although many libraries prefer to omit this in their public catalogs. The last note for an audiovisual material is usually a summary of the work and enables patrons and staff to find out what the material is about without having to preview it (fig. 56a).

The final paragraph of a catalog card consists of the "tracings." The tracings list all the catalog cards made for the work. Some tracings are coded, e.g., a tracing contains the word *title* rather than the title itself. That appears higher on the card. Sometimes tracings are put on the back of the catalog cards rather than on the front. The headings in the tracings that are preceded by Arabic numerals represent subject headings. The Arabic numerals signal the typist to type the heading in capital letters or with red ribbon (whichever form the library uses for subject added entries) at the second identation at the top of the card above the main entry. The numbers also tell the filer that the card typed in capital letters is a subject heading; though all subject cards are typed in capitals, not all headings in capitals are subject headings. (As an example, IBM 360 could be either a subject heading or the title of a book.)

Headings in the tracings preceded by roman numerals represent added entry headings other than subject headings. These headings may be for an editor, second author, illustrator, translator, title, or series, or they may show some relationship between this work and another that a patron might look up. Sometimes, the tracings may also show that analytic entries were made for parts of a work such as the individual volumes of a set of works included in a collection. Thus, if a patron looked up the title of a play or short story, he or she might find an analytic card for that play or short story contained in a collection that the library owns.

After the headings have been typed at the top of the other catalog cards for the work according to the tracings code, a small check should be made next to each tracing on the main entry card for which another card was made (fig. 56a). This records the complete set of cards that can be found in the catalog for a particular item. When an item is withdrawn

(a)

```
TS
227.7     Careers in welding (filmstrip-phonotape
C2.71x       cassette) -- rev. ed. -- Wichita, Kansas:
1977         Library Filmstrip Center, 1977.
             1 filmstrip 35mm color; 1 cassette 1 side
          (inaudible signal)  17 min   (Welding)

             Summary: Explains various types of welding
          and some of the good and bad features to be
          considered in choosing welding as a career.
                 ✓                              ✓
             1. Welding - Vocational guidance   2. Career
          education   I. Series ✓


                              12-77-7
```

(b)

```
                  Dictionary of economics and
                          business
       HB      Nemmers, Erwin Esser, 1916-
       61         Dictionary of economics and
       N4.5     business/ by Erwin Esser Nemmers. --
       1978     Enl. ed. 4th ed. -- Totowa, N.J. :
               Littlefield, Adams, 1878.
                  523 p. : graphs ; 20 cm. -- ( A
               Littlefield, Adams quality paperback
               ; no. 33 )

                  1. Economics--Dictionaries.
               2. Business--Dictionaries.
               I. Title.


       HB61.N45 1978                   330/.03
                                 (     78-16946
       WCTKT        B/NA A DJ-433452 00000023   01/18/80
```

Fig. 56.   Title cards.

(a) Title-main entry card with title at first indentation as hanging indention; (b) Title-added entry card with title at second indentation.

from the library, the main entry card is used as a record for withdrawing all the cards for the book from the catalog. The tracings have become useful reference tools as well as a processing record. A patron who wishes to know about other items on related subjects can search the catalog under other subject headings listed in the tracings.

The call number, which gives shelf location for an item, is placed in the upper left-hand corner of every catalog entry. This enables the patron to find the material on the shelves. The number may be assigned by a cataloger or may be obtained from other cataloging sources. If special shelf location symbols are used with the call number, a key to these symbols should be provided nearby for library patrons' use.

Besides main and added entry catalog cards, the library has "shelf-list" cards. A shelflist card is a main entry card with the addition of a record of the copies of a title that the library has. It often includes the item identification number, accession number (a number that may be given to an item when it is first added to the collection), copy or volume number, cost of the book, source or agent for the book, and date of acquisition (fig. 57). When a book is lost or withdrawn, this information is recorded on the shelflist card opposite the correct copy or volume information. The shelflist cards are filed in exact call number order in a catalog separate from the public card catalogs.

In the past, libraries typed most of their catalog cards and shelflist cards. As an economy measure, they put the complete catalog information only on the main entry card. The added entry cards and shelflist card were often typed in abbreviated form. However, when libraries began to get reproduced catalog cards at a reasonable cost, they used copies of the main entry card as a unit card to which an added entry heading or shelflist information was added. This trend has made catalog cards more complete and has increased their usefulness as a reference tool.

```
 R C           Lerner, Gerda, 1920-
 280               A death of one's own / by Gerda
 B 7           Lerner. -- New York : Simon and
 L4.8          Schuster, c1978.
                   269 p. ; 24 cm.
                   ISBN 0-671-24008-0

                   1. Brain--Tumors--Biography.
                   2. Lerner, Gerda, 1920-  I. Title.

    c.1  6-79  Baker & Taylor   7.69
    c.2  6-79  Baker & Taylor   7.69
    c.3  10-81  Baker & Taylor  8.35

 RC280.B7L48              ◯  616.9/94/810926  [ E ]
                              78-45

 WCTKT         B/NA A D4-264816 00000492  12/12/79
```

Fig. 57. Shelflist card.

Filing in Library Catalogs

Many people who try to use the library catalog consider it an enigma. They cannot find the item they are looking for or cannot find anything on a subject. Because the catalog is hard to use, patrons sometimes give up and leave the library, incorrectly believing that it does not have the material or information they seek. Even staff members get frustrated at times, trying to locate entries in the catalog for an item they know the library has. These problems often arise because the user does not understand how entries are filed in the catalog.

Catalog cards are filed alphabetically in the catalog by their top line, but as card catalogs grow larger and larger, there is a much greater chance that the alphabetizing will become confusing. There may be many cards that begin with the same word or heading. Cards may exist for George Washington as an author, George Washington as a subject, the title *Washington, D.C.*, and the Washington State Library as an author; all would be filed under the word *Washington* in the card catalog. If the catalog user does not know what rules or order the library follows in filing cards with such similar headings, he or she may never locate the desired information.

The advent of *AACR2* and its adoption by the Library of Congress in 1981 has not made the library catalog user's task any easier. Changes in the form of personal and corporate headings result in the existence of two different headings for the same person or corporate body, one prepared under the old rules and the other under the new. The Library of Congress and many libraries are solving this problem by closing their card catalogs as of a certain date. (The Library of Congress closing date was December 31, 1980.) This means that no more entries will be made in the closed card catalogs and that new library catalogs will be compiled. Many libraries plan to use on-line computer or COM catalogs for these new catalogs. Other libraries may just open new catalogs. A few small libraries may elect to superimpose, or type new headings above the old headings as they are added to the card catalog. Others may make cross-references from the old heading to the new heading. Whichever method libraries use to coordinate their old and new headings, they should be sure to inform and instruct their library catalog users on how to use the system.

In order to establish some order for filing entries in the catalog, libraries follow specified rules and guidelines. These rules have been codified by the American Library Association in the *ALA Filing Rules*. The most recent edition of this book was published in 1980 and will be used as the basis for this chapter. Some libraries still use the 1968 edition of the *ALA Rules for Filing Catalog Cards*.

This 1980 edition has incorporated many filing changes necessitated by the arrival of computer-based book, COM, and on-line catalogs. The earlier concept of filing entries "as they were pronounced" has been replaced by the concept that entries are filed "as they are written." Thus, under the new rules, entries for "Mister Roberts" and "Mr. Tracy" would not be filed near each other under "Mister" but would be filed separately in the catalog under "Mister" and "Mr."

In addition, the 1980 *Filing Rules* considers each entry or heading for a title to be an access point to a bibliographic record. Each access point is made up of character strings which are compared character by character to another access point in accordance with prescribed rules. In other editions of the filing rules, this process was referred to as filing "word by word." However, the new rules refer to character strings because that is the way a computer distinguishes between two different headings or access points. Thus, symbols such as *$$* or *&* or numbers such as *IX* or *19* are just sets of characters in the new filing rules rather than having meanings such as the word *dollars*, or *and* or the number *nine* or *nineteen*. Based on this concept, new rules have been devised for filing such characters and must be learned by both old and new library personnel.

The following discussion on filing catalog cards will introduce the major concepts of the 1980 *ALA Filing Rules*. This discussion should enable the reader to understand these filing rules. It will present the more commonly encountered filing patterns. This section should be read in conjunction with the filing rules themselves. It should enable the reader to understand the filing order of entries in the library's catalogs so that he or she can file and find information more easily and accurately.

How to file catalog cards

Accurate filing of catalog cards in a library is very important, because misfiling loses the point of access to an item provided by the card's heading. Catalog filers can develop their filing accuracy by studying the filing rules and by reviewing their knowledge of the alphabet before they begin filing. Because many people have difficulty filing a particular group of letters such as *P*, *Q*, and *R* or *W*, *X*, and *Y*, a brief review of the alphabet may help a filer become aware of any letters that he or she tends to interchange and approach them with more caution.

When a set of catalog cards is to be filed in a library's catalog, they are first separated according to the catalog in which they will be filed. Shelflist cards are arranged and filed in call number order. Cards for the public catalogs are filed by the top line, or access point, of each card. They, too, may be separated by type of catalog such as adult or juvenile, author and title, or subject. Then the cards for each catalog are arranged in alphabetical order. Libraries that use OCLC or other computerized cataloging systems may receive their catalog cards from these systems already arranged in alphabetical order and ready to be filed in their proper catalogs. However, most libraries need to separate the sets of cards manually and arrange them in alphabetical order.

If there is a large number of cards to file, it is easier to sort the cards into alphabetic groups by letter and then alphabetize each group. (There are commercial card sorters available to make this job easier.) If there are fewer cards for each catalog, the cards for each catalog can be sorted into groups as they are alphabetized. In this preliminary sorting, the filer should look for any cards that should not be included in the public catalogs and errors on the cards that should be corrected.

The card filer should follow the basic principles and rules described below when questions arise or when the entries are similar. Above all, he or she should refer to either the rule book or the librarian when uncertain about a rule or a card heading or access point. If any heading seems inaccurate or inconsistent with cards already in the catalog, it is the filer's responsibility to bring this to the supervisor's attention.

When the filer places cards in the catalog, he or she will notice that all catalog drawers have some sort of rod or holding device to prevent the catalog cards from falling out if the drawer is dropped or turned upside down. Libraries sometimes refer to this initial card filing as filing "above the rod" because the filer places the cards in their correct places but does not pull out the rod. Card filing is usually checked for accuracy by a second person called a "reviser." This procedure is sometimes called filing "below the rod" because the reviser pulls out the rod, drops the newly filed cards to the bottom of the drawer, and replaces the rod to lock the cards in place. Some libraries prefer to file all new catalog cards below the rod and place filing flag cards in front of each new card. The flag cards are then removed by the reviser. Beginning employees often file above the rod to familiarize themselves with the catalog; their filing is then reviewed by the librarian or by an LMTA with more experience.

Basic filing rules

Earlier editions of filing rules required that all headings be arranged alphabetically word by word and letter by letter as they were spoken, without regard to punctuation. The 1980 rules require that each word or character string be *filed as is*, i.e., as it is written, although punctuation is still ignored. This new approach changes the filing order for many entries in library catalogs. Headings pronounced the same but spelled differently are no longer filed together.

Headings, or access points, that have spelled-out numbers in them would be filed in their place in the alphabetical index. If the numbers are represented as numerals, however, they are filed in numerical order. If an access point begins with numerals, the headings are filed at the beginning of the catalog (before any headings beginning with letters), and they are arranged in numerical order from the lowest to the highest.

Following a similar pattern, characters for nonroman alphabets are filed at the end of the catalog after all of the entries in the roman alphabet. Such changes in the filing rules help simplify finding a heading if the written form is known. If only the spoken form is known, however, a person may have to look in several places before the correct entry is found. Generous cross-references to variant spellings or other headings may help refer the patron from a heading that he or she might use to another heading or access point that may also contain useful information.

In filing catalog cards, the basic filing principle is that every word or character string is filed exactly as it is written, including contractions, elisions, and variant spellings. Punctuation marks are usually ignored unless they separate character strings; then they are considered to be similar to spaces between words. Any variant personal or corporate headings caused by *AACR2* changes should be changed by the library so that all headings for the same entry will match.

The cards or entries in each catalog are filed alphabetically by the access point or heading on the top line of the card. This heading consists of the group of words or character strings that are set off at the beginning of the bibliographic record. If two or more entries have the same heading or access point, such as the same main entry, title, or subject heading, they are further alphabetized by the next element. Thus, personal and corporate main entries are subarranged by title, while title main entries are subarranged by date. Cards for title, subject, and series-added entries are subarranged alphabetically by their main entries, if they have the same heading. However, name-added entry headings for editors, translators, and so forth are filed by the top line of the card, then filed by the title of the entry, without regard to the main entry by author or uniform title. An example follows.

    Romeo and Juliet
Bernstein, Leonard
    West side story

    Romeo and Juliet
Shakespeare, William
    Romeo and Juliet

    Romeo and Juliet (Motion picture)

    Romeo and Juliet (Phonodisc)

Romeo, John
    Cooking with vegetables

Romeo, John
McGrath, Robert
Food fads and diets

Romeo, John
Living off the land

The basic principle is that if two cards have the same access point or heading, they are filed character by character until they differ. The following rules are then applied.

Arrangement by filing rules

The *ALA Filing Rules* call for *word-by-word* filing rather than *letter-by-letter* filing, which is used in many dictionaries. The space that separates the words is therefore important in library filing. It gives rise to the rule "nothing comes before something," meaning that a character followed by a space, or no character, is filed before the same character followed by or joined by another character. (In letter-by-letter filing, blank spaces are ignored.) In addition, punctuation marks that separate words have the same function as a space. Thus, words or compound names that have hyphens in them are filed as separate words. The following headings show a comparison between these two filing orders:

Word-by-Word	Letter-by-Letter
Book	Book
Book collecting	Bookbinding
Book-plate	Book collecting
Bookbinding	Book-plate
New	New
New, Richard	Newark
New York	New, Richard
Newark	New York

Headings that begin with the same words or character strings are compared alphabetically character by character until they differ from another heading (ALA rule 2.1). If headings or access points are identical, they are filed in the following order: (1) cross-reference cards for main and added entries; (2) main and added entries, which are interfiled; (3) cross-references for subjects; and (4) subject headings. Cross-references for subject headings and subject headings themselves are easily recognized because they are usually typed in capital letters (ALA rule 2.2).

Washington, D.C. see also	[cross reference]
Washington, D.C. (Filmstrip)	[period filed as a space]

WASHINGTON, D.C.	[subject entry]
Washington, George	[author main entry]
WASHINGTON, GEORGE	[subject entry]
Washington-Jones, David	[hyphen filed as a space]
Washington (State) Library	[parentheses ignored]

The English articles *a, an*, and *the*, when they begin a heading, are disregarded in filing. Instead, the card is filed by the second word. Articles in every language, such as *der, die*, and *das* in German or *le, la*, and *l'* in French, are disregarded when they begin a heading. Articles within an entry, however, are always regarded in filing (ALA rule 4.1).

    The Living cell
       Living on a budget
       Living on Puget Sound
       Living on the river

Sometimes, however, initial articles in headings form an integral part of a place name or a personal name, such as Las Vegas and La Fontaine; such articles *are* regarded in filing. Also, names with prefixes such as El Greco, De La Mare, Van Doren, or McDonald are filed character string by character string exactly as they are written.

La Belle dame sans merci	La Fontaine, Jean
De la Mare	M'Ilvaine
De la Tour	Macdonald
Delamare	McDonald
Delatour	Van Doren
El Greco	Vance
Electricity	Vanderbilt
La France et Paris	

To help patrons find some of the headings that are pronounced the same but spelled differently, the library should provide cross-reference cards in the catalog, e.g.,

    For names beginning with Mac, see also
       names beginning with Mc.

Some headings include abbreviated forms such as initials (A.L.A. Yearbook, I.B.M. 360), abbreviations (Dr., Mr., Mrs.), and signs ($, &, %). The principle to follow when filing such forms is to file them as they are written (ALA rule 5). Initialisms (acronyms formed from initial letters) written as distinct, single-letter words are filed as separate words, e.g., I. B. M. is filed as three capital-letter words with spaces between.

Thus, they are filed in alphabetical order before longer words beginning with the same character. The word *I* is the common single-letter word, but the letter *A* may sometimes also be a single-letter word. Some initials and abbreviations are written and pronounced as words. These are called "acronyms." These acronyms are filed as they are written, e.g., FORTRAN, AMACOM, UNESCO library bulletin.

Signs and symbols such as *$$* or *%* are disregarded in filing (ALA rule 1.2). An exception to this rule may be made for the ampersand or the symbol *&*, which represents the word *and*. If a library adopts ALA optional rule 1.3, this symbol may be filed as if it were spelled out in the language of the heading.

A cappella choir songbook   [A is a single-letter word]
A.L.A. glossary of library
    terms
A & P Company   [& disregarded in filing]
& furthermore   [& filed by optional rule 1.3]
And now Miguel
$$$ and sense   [$$$ disregarded in filing]

Doctor Zhivago
Dr. Faustus
Fort McNair
FORTRAN   [acronym filed as a word]
I am woman (phono-disc)
I. B. M. 360   [initials filed as single-letter words]
The Ibis is a sacred bird
Mister Roberts
Mistress of Flanders
Mr. Tracy
Mrs. 'Arris goes to Paris
Ten % down
Ten little indians
U.N. see United Nations   [initials filed as single-letter words]
UNESCO library bulletin   [acronym filed as a word]
United Nations

Headings or access points that contain numerical designations can be filed in several ways. If the numeral is written out in words such as *ten*, the numeral is filed alphabetically. If the numeral is expressed in digits or numbers such as *1984*, the number is filed in order of numerical value (from lowest to highest) before alphabetic character strings. Digits expressed in roman numerals are interfiled with their equivalents in Arabic numerals. Any headings that include dates are filed in chronological order (ALA rule 8).

<u>3</u>M Company
The <u>13</u> steps
<u>20</u>th Century Fox
<u>101</u> dalmations
<u>1001</u> Arabian nights
Henry <u>II</u>, King of England
Henry <u>IV</u>, King of France
Henry <u>VIII</u>, King of England
<u>One h</u>undred and one Christmas ideas
<u>One t</u>housand best love poems
<u>T</u>wentieth Century Limited

Because a patron might not know if a numeral is written as a word or expressed in numbers, the library should provide cross-reference cards for the more commonly used numerals, e.g.,

> Entries for One hundred and one . . . or One thousand and one . . . may also be found under 101 . . . and 1001 . . . at the beginning of the card catalog before any entries that begin with the letter A.

When numbers show a chronological or numerical arrangement in identical headings or entries, they should be filed in alphabetical order first and then in numerical order with the lowest number or earliest date first (ALA rule 8.7) as follows:

A.L.A. filing rules. 1st edition.
A.L.A. filing rules. 2nd edition.
U.S. Army. 1st army.
U.S. Army. 3rd cavalry.
U.S. Army. 5th army.
U.S. Army. 7th cavalry.
U.S. ARMY—HISTORY—1865–1898
U.S. ARMY—HISTORY—1933–1945

Rules for order of entries

Entries for the same surname should be filed alphabetically by the forenames. If there are different surname entries for the same person due to *AACR2* changes, the entries should be changed to match each other. For example, if a heading already exists for "Lincoln, Abraham, Pres. U.S., 1809–1865" and a new heading for "Lincoln, Abraham, 1809–1865" is added, the words *Pres. U.S.* can be neatly lined out. Birth and death dates in the entries should be used to distinguish two personal names that are otherwise identical (e.g., Stevenson, Adlai E., 1835–1914 and Stevenson, Adlai E., 1900–1965). The person's name with the earliest birthdate should be filed first.

The main and added entries for a person as an author, editor, and so forth would be interfiled in one alphabet before any subject entries for that person (ALA rule 2.2). The subject entries in a dictionary catalog are, therefore, filed in a second alphabet and subarranged alphabetically by their main entries. Entries for the same surname are subarranged alphabetically by titles. If a short title is identical to the beginning of a longer title, the short title comes first; subtitles should be ignored. If there are two editions of the same title, the cards are filed chronologically by the edition number or publication date; the earliest one is first.

> Brown, John. Accounting.—1st ed. 1969.
> Brown, John. Accounting.—2nd ed. 1971.
> Kahn, Gilbert. Progressive filing.
> Kahn, Gilbert. Progressive filing and records management.

Analytics, or author-title entries for portions of a work such as a collection of plays or chapters in a book, may be entered in the catalog. For filing purposes with such entries, the author-title portion replaces the main entry and title elements of the complete collection or book. Thus, the author-title analytics would be interfiled with any main entries and any other analytic entries for the work that form that portion of the collection; these entries are subarranged according to their dates of publication (ALA rule 2.3).

> O'Neill, Eugene
>   The ice man cometh. 1960.
>
>   O'Neill, Eugene
>   The ice man cometh (in)
> Gassner, John
>   Twentieth century plays. 1967.
>
>   O'Neill, Eugene
>   The ice man cometh (in)
> Malcolm, Karl
>   Modern plays of the 20th century. 1972.

Title cards are of two basic types—main entries and added entries. If title main and title added entries are identical, the title main entries should be filed first and subarranged by their publication dates. Identical title added entries are subarranged by their main entries; different editions of the same title are further subarranged by their publication dates. Sometimes, uniform headings have been assigned to titles of anonymous classics such as the Bible. Such headings should be filed in straight alphabetical order, and any dates in the headings should be filed chronologically with the earliest date first.

The Bible and the common reader.
    Bible. English. 1961. [dates filed chronologically]
    Bible. English. 1970.
    Bible, John   [author main entry]
Bible. New testament.
Bible. Selections.

Series entries are subarranged alphabetically by their main entries unless they are numbered. If numbered, they are then filed numerically or chronologically.

    Life Science Library
Modell, Walter
    Drugs

    Life Science Library
Owen, Wilfred
    Wheels

    Representative American Speeches, 1968–69

    Representative American Speeches, 1969–70

Subject entries are very important; many patrons use them as a first approach to the catalog. Libraries use reference books on subject headings to establish uniform and standardized subject headings. The two major subject authorities, the *Sears List of Subject Headings* and the *Library of Congress List of Subject Headings* are valuable as reference tools. The catalog user can refer to them to determine the form of subject heading used by the library for the information needed.

Most libraries file their subject entries alphabetically. Identical subject headings are subarranged alphabetically by their main entries and then by their titles. Subject headings with subdivisions are filed according to the following basic order (see fig. 58). Subject headings without any subdivisions are filed first. Next, the subject headings with time divisions are filed chronologically; the earliest is filed first. These period divisions may be designated by dates or by distinctive phrases if these are more commonly used than the dates might be (e.g., U.S.—HISTORY—REVOLUTION; U.S.—HISTORY—CIVIL WAR). If two period entries cover the same time period, the longer period comes first. Period designations that are open-ended (e.g., 1918–) are considered to continue to the present time and precede other periods beginning with the same date (e.g., 1918–1933). Libraries use authoritative books for establishing these period divisions. The reader should refer to ALA rule 8.7.2 for a list of the period subdivisions used for "U.S.—HISTORY." After the chron-

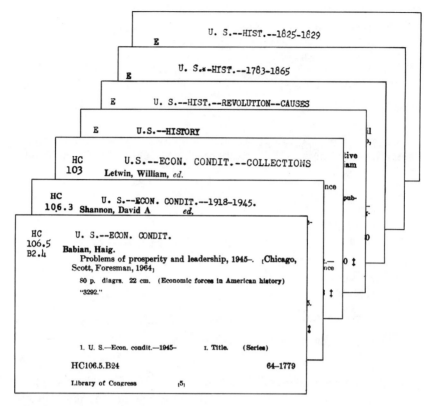

Fig. 58.   Subject catalog cards.

Subject without subdivision filed first, then time period divisions, then other subdivisions.

ologically arranged group of period subdivisions, the other subdivisions are filed alphabetically word by word.

Because the filing rules are based on how headings are written rather than on how they are spoken, cross-reference cards should be provided in order to make the catalog as useful as possible. Cross-reference cards should be filed alphabetically in their places in the catalog. They will precede their respective entries under the same heading or word (ALA rule 2.2).

> EDUCATION
>   see also
> SCHOOLS
>
> EDUCATION
> Mayer, Martin

The format of library catalogs has changed over the years and will probably change more in the future. However, libraries try to standardize headings and entries that are filed and arranged in these catalogs. *The Anglo-American Cataloguing Rules*, 2nd edition, introduced many changes in personal and corporate headings that libraries should accommodate by either closing or modifying their catalogs compiled prior to publication of *AACR2*. In addition, the 1980 *ALA Filing Rules* introduced many changes in the filing order of both the new and the old library headings. Since all libraries file their similar headings according to these established library filing rules, it is the responsibility of the LMTA to understand these rules. Then the LMTA should see that they are systematically applied in an individual library's catalog.

Maintaining Library Catalogs

Catalog cards should be filed on a regular basis. This can be scheduled weekly or daily depending on the accumulation of a certain number of cards. If cards are accumulated, they should be kept in some kind of alphabetical order so that they can be consulted. If cards are filed on a scheduled basis, filing should be frequent enough that patrons can locate information for new books. It is most frustrating to be unable to locate information on a new book because the catalog cards are not yet filed.

Cards may be filed by clerks, pages, or volunteers who understand the basics of library filing. No person should ever file cards for more than one or two hours at a time—fatigue sets in and filing accuracy deteriorates rapidly. This filing of cards should be revised by another person to verify the correct filing order and because it is so easy to make alphabetical mistakes. The cards may be filed above the rod for the reviser to place below the rod or filed below the rod with filing flags used to designate newly filed cards. This latter method eliminates the danger of patrons moving the catalog cards before they are revised.

The library catalogs must be maintained as well as filed with new cards. As cards are added, the drawers get full so that cards need to be shifted to other drawers, or new guide cards may be needed. These problems should be noticed at the time cards are filed and attended to.

When catalog cards need to be shifted for more than one or two drawers, a systematic procedure should be followed. The cards to be shifted should be measured and the total available drawer space measured. The drawers should only be filled two-thirds to three-quarters full to allow for future additions. Cards should be separated at natural divisions rather than into exactly equal numbers of cards in each drawer (e.g., "South" rather than "Southall" or "Schools" rather than "Schoolhouse"). Filing flags can be used to mark the separations ahead of time so that a few drawers at a time can be shifted, and the entire catalog is not out of use at one time.

New labels should be made immediately for drawers that have been shifted. These should be legible and accurate! Each label should not only show the contents of the drawer but also represent the part of the alphabet included. For example, if the letter Q is included within a drawer, its label should include Q. Labels may be colored to facilitate returning the drawers to their proper place. It is highly recommended that the catalog drawers be numbered.

If the catalog is divided, the different catalogs should have color-coded drawers and be clearly marked to show that they are author-title or subject drawers.

Guide cards should be placed in catalog drawers to enable the user to easily locate a particular part of the alphabet. Guide cards are usually placed every one to two inches. The headings may alternate from left to right in the catalog drawer. Some libraries now use guide cards with headings as wide as the card itself. These are used especially in divided catalogs by libraries that type subject headings on guide cards rather than on the cards themselves. The library staff should (by some means) inform the user whether the guide cards are only local guides or are the only presentation of the subject headings. Many patrons believe the library has no information on a subject if there is no guide card with the desired heading.

The term chosen for a guide card should be a simple, short word that relates to many cards, not just to the card immediately behind it (e.g., "Birds" rather than "Bird Nests"). The library should choose places for guide cards that are meaningful for that particular library's users. A library for library-science students would put a guide card at "School Libraries" rather than "School Laboratories." When surnames are used on guide cards, only the last name should be used. Large card catalogs might make an exception by adding initials with very common names such as "Smith."

The library should provide as many explanatory guides as would be useful for the user. Each drawer could contain a card explaining how to use the card catalog, and signs or posters placed near the catalog can also explain its use. (It would astound many staff members to know how few users really understand how to use the catalog or the information on the catalog cards.) If any filing "options" have been used, explanation cards should be placed in the catalog in their correct alphabetical locations. Cards explaining that numerals are filed before the beginning of the alphabet are very helpful.

The object of maintenance is to make the catalog as orderly and clean as possible to interest the library user. This includes replacing worn or dirty guide cards and messy labels and shifting full drawers. The catalog must be kept up-to-date with uniform subject headings, necessary guide and explanatory cards, and accurate card filing. The catalog should contain cards only for materials that are actually in the collection, so cards for withdrawn and lost books should be weeded from the catalog as soon as possible. This catalog maintenance should be done on a regular basis, preferably as the responsibility of one particular person such as the filing reviser.

Library catalogs—COM, on-line, book, or card—are important reference and control tools for a collection. They must be designed so that they can be most easily and effectively used by the library patron and staff member alike. To achieve this purpose, libraries have codified the criteria and rules for organizing information about a work in a standard format and have systematically arranged this information in catalogs for library users. However, though these rules are known by librarians, they are rarely known by other staff members and even more rarely by the patrons. Library patrons usually fumble through a library catalog without understanding the principles of its arrangement or what information is included in it. The library must be responsible for remedying this, partly by educating everyone in the use of this key to the library collection.

The library staff at the circulation and reference desks should accept this responsibility and approach a patron using the catalog with an offer to help him or her locate information. If the patron has already used the catalog, the staff member can tactfully suggest they return to the catalog together to look for information under another heading. This will give the staff member an opportunity to verify the information and perhaps instruct the patron in the use of the catalog. A staff member should never tell the patron to "look up the information in the card catalog" without being sure the patron knows how to do this.

The rules for cataloging and filing cards are complex; any catalog user can become confused or fail to locate needed information. It is up to the library staff to maintain a catalog that, as much as possible, will eliminate this confusion and make the catalog user's search rewarding rather than frustrating.

Conclusion

Catalogs provide access to a library's vast collection of information. Although the format of these catalogs has changed over the years, the information has remained generally the same. Catalogs provide access to the collection by author, title, and subject; catalog cards and entries usually include the author, title, edition, publishing information, collation, and series and subject headings. This information is included in a catalog entry according to standardized cataloging and filing rules. Although these rules are currently changing, libraries should update and maintain their catalogs so that patrons will be able to find the information they need.

Student Work Unit

The student should use chapter 8 and the *ALA Filing Rules*, second abridged edition, to think about the problems presented below, look up the applicable rule, and then perform the objectives. The student will be able to accurately solve the following problems.

1. Identify the distinguishing characteristics of each of the following types of library catalogs: dictionary, divided, classed, public, shelflist, and union.
2. Label the numbered elements on fig. 59.
3. Using fig. 59, correctly list below the call numbers as they would be filed in a shelflist.
   (1)   (2)   (3)   (4)
4. Correctly number the filing order for the catalog cards in fig. 60.
5. Designate the correct filing order for the headings listed:
   - no. _____ Lord-Jones, Alexander
   - Princes in the tower
   - _____ Lord of the flies
   - Golding, William
   - _____ Lord, Walter
   - Incredible victory
   - _____ Lord, Walter
   - Day of infamy
   - _____ Lord, Richard
   - Great day in the morning
   - _____ Lord, Jim
   - Conrad, Joseph
6. On fig. 61, number the catalog cards in their correct filing order.
7. Number the catalog cards in their correct filing order on fig. 62.
8. Number the correct filing orders of the catalog cards on figs. 63 through 72.

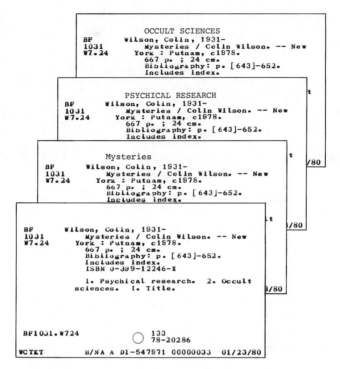

Fig. 59.   Set of catalog cards.

Label the following items on the catalog cards:

1. Main entry heading
2. Added entry cards
3. Title card
4. Subject cards
5. Title
6. Author
7. Imprint
8. Collation
9. Tracings

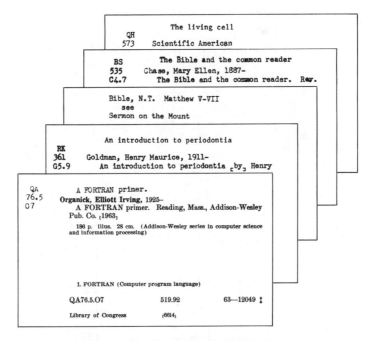

Fig. 60.   Correctly number the filing order for the catalog cards.

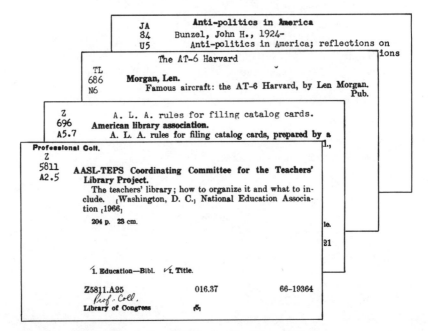

Fig. 61.   Number the catalog cards in correct filing order.

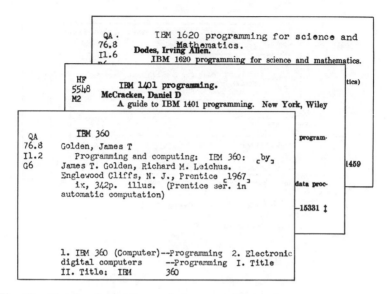

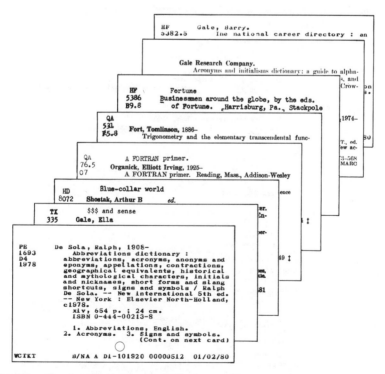

Fig. 62.   Number the catalog cards in correct filing order.

Fig. 63.   Number the catalog cards in correct filing order.

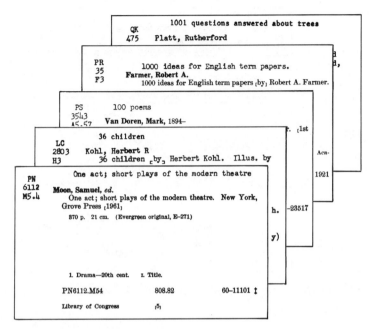

Fig. 64.   Number the catalog cards in correct filing order.

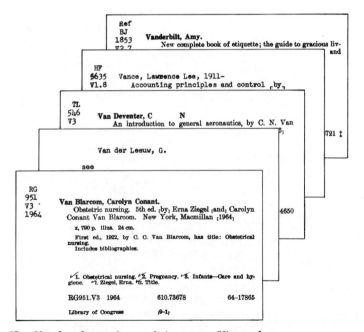

Fig. 65.   Number the catalog cards in correct filing order.

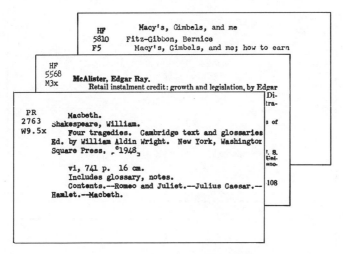

```
        HF          Macy's, Gimbels, and me
        5810    Fitz-Gibbon, Bernice
        F5          Macy's, Gimbels, and me; how to earn
```

```
     HF
     5568
     M3x     McAlister, Edgar Ray.
                 Retail instalment credit: growth and legislation, by Edgar
```

```
  PR          Macbeth.
  2763     Shakespeare, William.
  W9.5x       Four tragedies.  Cambridge text and glossaries
             Ed. by William Aldin Wright.  New York, Washington
             Square Press, 1948

                vi, 741 p.  16 cm.
                Includes glossary, notes.
                Contents.--Romeo and Juliet.--Julius Caesar.--
             Hamlet.--Macbeth.
```

Fig. 66.   Number the catalog cards in correct filing order.

```
     Ref
     HF
     5381    U.S. Department of Labor.
     U5.8x       Dictionary of occupational titles, 1965.
     1965    3rd. ed.  Washington, U.S. G.P.O.,  1965.
                 2 vol.  xxiv, 809p, vii, 656p.

                 Contents: Vol. I Definitions of titles.
             Vol. II Occupational classification.



     OCCUPATIONS
     Title
```

```
     HF
     5381    U.S. Department of Labor.
     U5.8x       Dictionary of occupational titles.  2nd
     1949    ed.  Washington, D.C.,  G.P.O.,  1949.
                 2 vol.

                 Contents. V.1 Definitions of titles.
             V.2 Occupational classification and industry
             index.



             1. Occupations            I. Title

                                              5/67/3
```

Fig. 67.   Number the catalog cards in correct filing order.

```
                EDUCATION
      LB
      1025   Bode, Boyd H
      B6x        Modern educational theories.  New York,
                Vintage Books ⌐1927⌐
                   351p.  (Caravelle ed.)




             1. Education    I. Title


                                            2/69/4
```

```
              EDUCATION
                 see also
           HIGH SCHOOLS
           VOCATIONAL EDUCATION
```

Fig. 68.   Number the catalog cards in correct filing order.

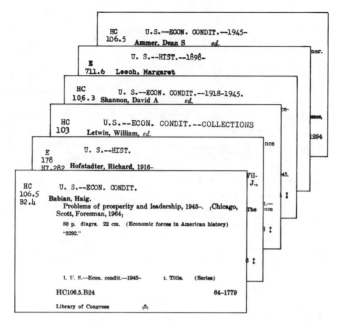

Fig. 69.   Number the catalog cards in correct filing order.

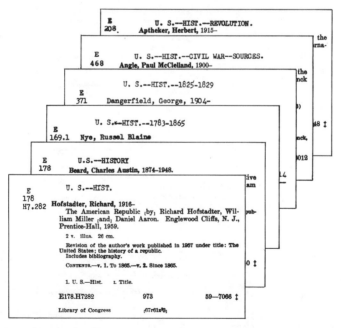

Fig. 70.   Number the catalog cards in correct filing order.

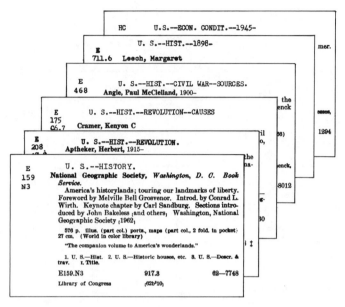

Fig. 71.   *Number the catalog cards in correct filing order.*

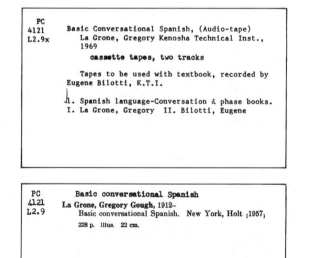

Fig. 72.   *Number the catalog cards in correct filing order.*

Teaching Unit

The teacher should assign exercises and assignments to give the students practice in filing catalog cards correctly. The teacher could assign exercises in practicing the alphabet, such as writing parts of the alphabet or writing the alphabet backwards. Students could correctly alphabetize the names of class or staff members. They also could write out numbers and dates as they would be filed. Practice in alphabetical filing should be given before filing rules are practiced.

Students should practice filing catalog cards in shelflist order. They should practice filing catalog cards according to the *ALA Filing Rules*, 2nd edition. The teacher should provide as many cards as possible to illustrate the most important filing rules. Students could revise each other's filing to gain practice in this task.

The student work unit should be used as a learning exercise. The teacher should correct it with the students and clarify any problems that may arise.

9 Processing Library Materials

Unit Outline:

Materials Selection
Materials Acquisition
Receiving Materials
Cataloging Materials
Processing Materials
Conclusion
Student Work Unit
Teaching Unit

Unit Objectives:

Identify the major elements that should be included in a policy for material selection.

List the advantages and disadvantages of ordering from a jobber and ordering direct from a publisher.

Explain the two major ways in which libraries verify library materials.

Identify the basic elements in the procedures for the receipt of library materials.

Discuss the place of gift materials in a library and the bases on which they should be accepted.

Describe the various methods for obtaining catalog cards.

Identify the steps in processing an item after it has been cataloged.

Many of the procedures discussed in the preceding chapters are performed in the public services department. In order for this department to function effectively, however, it must be supported and assisted by a technical services or technical processing department. The technical services department is primarily responsible for ordering, receiving, cataloging, and processing library materials. It takes the combined efforts of both departments for a library to provide the right material at the right time.

To help achieve this objective, a technical services department should design its procedures so they will serve its library's objectives as well as satisfy its patrons' needs. For example, procedures should be designed so materials will be made available to the patron as soon as possible after they have been received. This might mean that reserve materials would be rushed through the processing steps as quickly as possible rather than be processed in the order received. Such procedures indicate that a technical services department should be as committed to providing good library service as the public services department.

Materials Selection

For technical services to contribute effectively to library services, every staff member should understand the materials selection policies and procedures. The selection of library materials may be the joint responsibility of public and technical services; alternatively, the responsibility of selections may belong to public services, while the function of ordering materials is the responsibility of technical services. In either case, the library should have established a written policy on materials selection that is used as a basis for selecting its library materials. This policy should indicate who will select the materials, what type of materials will be selected, and the basis on which they will be selected. Many policies also include the philosophy and objectives that guide the development of their libraries' collections. They may describe the community or the institution being served and include statements concerning intellectual freedom and the people's right of access to all information. In addition to selection criteria, libraries may include criteria for weeding as well as any statements concerning the addition of gifts (or donated materials) to their collections. Such written policies on materials selection will provide direction for the people who are selecting a library's materials so they will develop a collection to serve that library's needs.

Written policies on materials selection are also important to know for the rest of the staff and the library's community. If all the people concerned with the library were aware of the policy for selecting its materials, they could better understand why particular materials are purchased. For instance, such knowledge might explain why a periodicals or audiovisual media budget was high. In fact, the criteria for materials selection might be shown to patrons complaining about an item that they found offensive. Thus, the selection policy should be an integral part of a library's operations and should govern its selection and acquisitions procedures.

A selection policy usually indicates who will select a library's materials and what type of materials will be selected. Selection differs for the major types of libraries. In academic libraries, faculty members may select most of the materials; in special libraries, the members of the institution (such as researchers or management) may select the materials. In both of these libraries, however, such requests may be reviewed by the professional librarians to see that they fall within the budget or the needs of the collection. In school libraries, faculty members and administrators may request materials; often, however, the school media specialists either make suggestions to the faculty or make the selections themselves if it is their responsibility. Professional librarians make the selection in most public libraries although they usually consider requests from patrons in making their selections.

All those responsible should select materials within their libraries' budgets and according to established guidelines. These guidelines have been established to ensure that a library's collection will be developed to meet a particular community's needs. All selectors should know and consider these needs when they review and select materials for a collection. Before selecting any materials for purchase, selectors should learn as much as possible about the many published materials that are available. They will then be able to make informed decisions to satisfy their libraries' needs.

Each selector may use reviewing magazines, publishers' brochures, and advertisements (or other sources) to help in the selection of library materials. Such review magazines as *Library Journal, School Library Journal, Choice, Booklist, Kirkus Reviews*, and *Publisher's Weekly* are often used, as are other professional journals in other subject fields. Library materials will usually be selected if they add depth or fill a gap, provide a new approach or new information on a subject, and fit within the library's budget. This selection process is very important because no library can afford to buy all the materials available that could satisfy its needs. Usually, selectors must choose carefully because they can only buy a small portion of what they would like to select.

Materials budgets in libraries and the ways they are divided vary from library to library. In academic libraries, the budgets may be divided between books and periodicals; audiovisual materials may be controlled and purchased by another department. In public and school libraries, all media might be purchased. The proportion spent for AV materials may be much greater in a school library than in a public library. Each library breaks down its materials budget into specific categories so that the selectors know how much money can be spent on each. These categories may be by academic department or subject such as chemistry or business; by department such as adult or juvenile; or by type of material such as fiction, nonfiction, periodicals, and AV. In addition to this budget breakdown, more specific guidelines may also be established.

A percentage or ratio of a budget may be set aside for building up a special subject area or for replacing worn-out or outdated materials. For example, a budget for juvenile materials might be divided into two-thirds replacements and one-third new materials. Some libraries do not buy paperback editions unless hardbound copies are unavailable. Other libraries prefer to stretch their budgets by purchasing paperback editions.

Libraries usually establish a policy concerning the number of copies of an item they will buy. In academic libraries, this is often based on the number of students in a subject requiring an item; public libraries may base this figure on the number of reserves on an item. Most libraries are reluctant to purchase textbooks that are used locally although it is convenient for its patrons if an academic or school library includes one copy of each current textbook in its collection. Once the guidelines for expending the budget have been established and the selectors have accordingly made their selections, the requests for materials are turned over to the acquisitions or order section of the technical services department.

Materials Acquisition

The technical services department is usually divided into several main activities, or sections—acquisitions or ordering, cataloging, and processing. (Serials and binding are often also included in this department.) The purpose of the acquisitions section is to order materials after they have been requested, maintain the budgetary records, and receive the materials. However, ordering library materials involves some very important preliminary steps before an order is placed with a supplier. Each request for a library material must be checked, or verified, to see if the order information is correct and whether or not the library already has a particular item.

Verification of material requests

A library may receive its requests to purchase materials from many different sources, and these requests may be incomplete or contain inaccurate information. Therefore, a library will usually verify a materials request in two different ways (fig. 73). It will first check the title, author, and publisher or producer information to see that it is correct. Then it will check the library's records to see whether it is a new addition to the collection or would be a duplicate copy. Although automated systems such as OCLC may make it possible for a library to perform both these procedures in one step, most libraries will divide them into separate procedures. Libraries perform these procedures because it is less costly to verify an order than it is to buy and catalog duplicate copies of unwanted materials. Staff members who perform these procedures should be aware of this fact and of the need for great accuracy in these verification procedures.

To verify the existence of an item and the accuracy of its bibliographic information, a library will usually check or verify this information in a standard bibliographic source. Books are usually verified in the

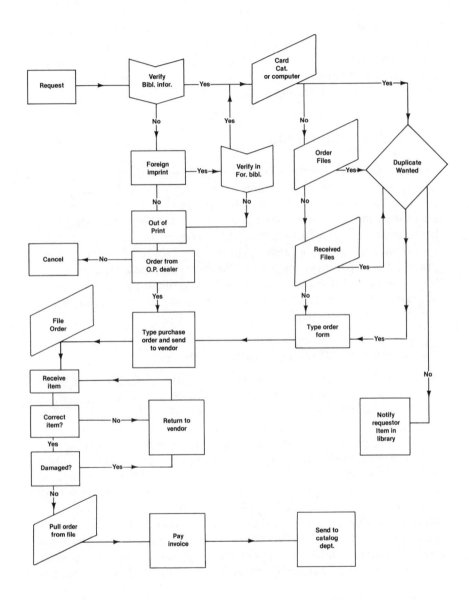

Fig. 73.   Acquisitions flowchart.

current edition of *Books in Print* (*BIP*) or its companion volumes *Paperbound Books in Print, El-Hi Textbooks in Print*, and *Children's Books in Print*. If they are not listed in these sources but seem to be new books, the information should be looked up in *Forthcoming Books* or the *Weekly Record*. These sources, or tools, include information provided by major U.S. publishers and give the title, author, publisher, date of publication, editions, prices, Library of Congress card number, and international standard book number (ISBN) for each title. If the title is not found in these tools, it may be from a small publisher not covered by the major current bibliographies. If the title of an older book from a major publisher cannot be found in *BIP*, it may be out of print and unavailable from the publisher. (In such a case, libraries might be able to borrow an item from another library for their patrons' use, or they might be able to locate a copy for purchase through a bookseller specializing in out-of-print books.)

Libraries may also use other sources to verify their materials requests. Sources such as *Schwann's Record and Tape Guide* may be used to verify records and audiotapes. Current publishers' or producers' catalogs and review magazines may provide accurate information as well as the current price and publication data. Some bibliographies, such as *Fiction Catalog* and the *NICEM Indexes* for audiovisual materials, provide accurate author and title information but do not include the current price or publication data. Libraries usually need this information; unless a current publisher or producer is known, the library usually cannot order an item.

Once an item has been verified in a bibliographic tool and complete information for it has been accurately recorded, a library will usually verify to see if it already owns the particular item. This verification procedure includes checking the library's official records such as its card catalogs, on order or orders-outstanding files, received or in-process files, and any standing order or serial files. These files should contain data on all the materials that the library owns or has on order. If a card for the item is located in the files, the request can be returned to the librarian or original requester to see if a duplicate copy should be ordered. Such careful checking can prevent unnecessary duplication.

Verification procedures

Requests to purchase library materials come to the order or acquisitions section from many different sources and in many different formats. Library patrons may ask the librarian to purchase particular items by giving their titles and their authors. Sometimes, patrons or selectors send in lists of materials they want purchased. At other times, a review magazine or publisher's catalog may be forwarded that someone has checked for recommended purchases. Because these requests come in so many shapes and forms and in such various stages of completeness or accuracy, libraries have tried to standardize them. Libraries usually transfer all the information given for the requested item, including the source of the request, onto a standard material request card. Some libraries prefer to transfer this information directly onto an order form, usually a three-by-five-inch card (fig. 74). The use of such cards or forms ensures that the library will gather all the necessary information. Also, the compact format enables the cards to be easily alphabetized and handled during the verifying process. (It is very difficult to check a nonalphabetized list of items against three or four sets of files.) Once the requests have been transferred to the cards, the original requests can be filed in a folder according to the month in which they were processed. These can be kept for a period set by the library, usually six months; it is almost another "library law" that the information on an order may be incorrect, so the library needs to check the original request. After the request cards have been written, the verification process begins.

The actual steps of this process differ from one library to another depending upon its size and complexity. Libraries that are heavily automated may be able to key the title and author information into a computer system for the system to verify the bibliographic data, check the library's catalogs and files, and place an order if the library does not own the item sought. Libraries that are less automated may be able to perform some of these tasks by computer. However, the majority of libraries must still rely upon staff members to perform these verification procedures manually.

Each library establishes its own sequence for performing the following steps based upon its own needs. Some libraries verify their orders in *BIP* before they check their library records. If the information for most of the requests comes from fairly reliable sources such as current review magazines, a library may prefer to check its library records first. Because libraries want to decrease any duplication of effort as quickly as possible, they usually perform those verification steps first that tend to catch the largest number of duplicate requests.

Libraries usually alphabetize the request cards as the next step in the verification procedures. Many times, these cards are alphabetized by title because libraries have found that titles can be more distinctive and take less time to verify than author-title entries might take. However, in order to verify by title, all the library's files must be arranged by title and the catalogs must have a title card for every item in the library.

Most libraries then separate the request cards by type of media and verify them in their appropriate bibliographic tools. For example, requests for books are checked in the appropriate *BIP*. The information in *BIP* should be used to replace any incorrect information on the card. (Sometimes a library may establish acquisitions preferences for buying

(a)

Janitch, Valerie. **Dolls for Sale.**
Faber & Faber. 1980. 79p. color photogs. by
Rob Matheson. illus. $15.95; pap. $6.95. CRAFTS
Small character dolls made primarily of
felt and decorative trim can easily be
made in quantity for bazaars and other
commercial ventures. Janitch gives detailed instructions for 20 dolls along
with hints for selling. Her gnomes, sol-
diers, and friars are as clever as those
in her *Storybook Dolls* and are certain
to find a ready market.—*CAF*

*Constance Ashmore Fairchild, Univ. of
Illinois Lib., Urbana*

Library Journal/January 1, 1981   50

(b)

Class No.	Author (surname first) *Janitch, Valerie*	Date requested *Jan. 12, 1981*
Accession No.	Title *Dolls for Sale*	
No. of copies ordered	SBN *0-571-11536-5*	
Date ordered	Publisher and Place *Faber + Faber*	Year *1980* / List Price *$6.95 pb*
Dealer	Edition or series Volumes *(order from Merrimack Bk. Service*	No. of Copies
Date received	Requested by *bec*	Notify
Cost	Reviewed in *LJ, 1/1/81 p. 50*	
L. C. card No.	Approved by *✓BIP*	Fund Charged *ANF*
GAYLORD 101-L		PRINTED IN U.S.A.

Fig. 74.   Order request.

(a) Example source for material to be ordered; (b) Example material request card
for this material after it has been verified in *BIP*.

library bindings rather than trade bindings or trade editions rather than paperbacks or textbook editions—*BIP* indicates whether such preferences can be exercised.) Any new information should be added and a notation made on the card that the item was verified in *BIP* (see fig. 74). If the book title is not found in *BIP*, this should be noted as *O BIP* so that the acquisitions or order librarian or technician will know that it may be a new book, out of print, or that the publisher is not a major American publisher. During this verification step, the searcher should be particularly aware of any discrepancies such as misspelled words or names, wrong editions and publishers, and incorrect price and ISBN.

After the requests have been verified in the bibliographic tools, they are usually checked against the library's catalogs and files. Again, the sequence for checking these files differs from one library to another. The library's public or union catalogs are usually checked first. Any person who performs this step should be well versed in the library's filing rules. If a library has placed notification of its on-order material in its public catalog, the verification procedure may be reduced by one step. Otherwise, the order file should be checked next, then the received or in-process files. This step may be more complicated than it seems. The verifier should check to see that there are no orders waiting to be filed and that the file for received items contains orders for all the materials in processing. If a title is found in the catalog or any of the library's files, the verifier should check carefully to see that the items match exactly, that is, that the title, authors, publishers, and editions are the same (see fig. 75). This information should then be indicated on the request card.

Once these standard files have been checked, the orders should be reviewed to ensure that no special files were overlooked. The request may then be turned over to a supervisor, who may notice some special characteristics about the work. For example, the work may be published on an annual basis or be part of a series or serial for which the library has a standing order, by which it receives each item as it is published. The request may also be for a textbook that can be received from the college bookstore. The supervisor may also note that a title was not found in *BIP* or *Schwann's* because the publisher or producer was foreign or too small to be included in the source. After such possibilities have been reviewed, the requests can be separated into two categories—one category for material the library owns and the other for materials not owned. The duplicate requests can be returned to the initial selector to decide if another copy is needed. If appropriate, all the requests can be returned to the department head or requester for final review and selection before the items are finally ordered. This last step enables the selector to review selections and purchase those items that best fit the library's needs and budget. Once the selections for purchase have been verified and reviewed, they are ready to be ordered.

(a)

LRC Call No. **F**	**Date:** Ordered **K has 1979 ed.**
1754.7	**Rec'd** _____ **Cat** _____
D5.6	**Title:** **Complete travel guide to Cuba**
Edition _____	
CIP _____ No Cds _____	
LC Cd No. _____	**Author/Editor:** **DiPerna, Paula**
ISBN No. **0-312-15862-9**	
GPO Doc No. _____	
Program **Trav Agt**	**Publisher & Place:** **St. Martin's**
Campus ____**k**____	
Copies __**1**__	
Dup _____ Repl __✔__	**Price:** **19.95** Copyright Date **1981**
BIP __✔__	Volume _____ Copy # _____ Media _____
Source **pub. cat.**	**Requested By:** **bec**
Date **Fall 1981**	
Page __**20**__	Date of Request: **Oct. 1981**

(b)

```
F          DiPerna, Paula.
1754.7         The complete travel guide to Cuba /
D5.6       by Paula DiPerna, with the assistance
           of the Center for Cuban Studies and
           the Cuban National Tourism Institute.
           -- New York : St. Martin's Press,
           c1979.
               275 p. : ill. ; 21 cm.
               Includes index.
               ISBN 0-312-15862-9  ISBN 0-312-
               15863-7 pbk.

               1. Cuba--Description and travel--
           1951- --Guide-books.  I. Center for
           Cuban Studies.  II. Instituto
           Nacional de Turismo (Cuba)  III.
                              (Cont. on next card)



WCTKT          B/NA A D9-519520 00000451  11/14/79
```

Fig. 75. Verifying a request.

(a) Completed material request card; (b) Catalog card for earlier edition of the item requested.

Ordering library materials

Libraries usually order their materials in one of three ways. They may order materials directly from the publisher or producer; they may order materials from a jobber or wholesaler; or they may use a combination of these methods. There are advantages and disadvantages to any of the methods.

Sometimes libraries place direct orders because the publisher or producer does not sell materials through jobbers. Libraries may also place direct orders because they thereby receive materials sooner. When ordering directly, the library can take advantage of any prepublication and promotional prices that the publisher offers. The library may also receive a good discount if a specified number of copies or titles are ordered at one time. However, the number and variety of publishers and producers makes it very cumbersome for a library to order all its materials directly unless it is a very large institution. Since there are hundreds of major U.S. publishers and many more minor publishers, a library that chooses to order directly must send purchase orders to many addresses, receive materials from many publishers, and conduct correspondence with many different people. In addition, the library pays postage and any handling charges for each item.

To avoid some of these disadvantages, many libraries place their orders through jobbers or wholesalers. These libraries can place orders with many different publishers or producers with one jobber on one purchase order. They can also receive many items at one time from a jobber through shipping companies that charge low rates. Finally, any claims or problems can be taken care of by corresponding with only one claims department. However, there are some disadvantages to ordering entirely through a jobber. Not all jobbers order material from every publisher, so an order placed with a jobber may be returned several weeks later with the message to order direct. Also, jobbers may not have the item in stock, and so an order with a jobber may take longer to receive than an order placed with the publisher.

There has been discussion among librarians as to which provide better discounts—jobbers or publishers—but the answer seems to depend upon a library's buying patterns. Jobbers and publishers both base their discounts on the volume of orders a library places with them. Such discounts range from 0 to 40 percent. The more money a library spends, the greater the discount it is likely to receive. Jobbers are able to provide discounts to libraries because publishers give them large discounts for placing such large orders. The jobbers then pass on some of these discounts to their customers.

To compete with publishers and with each other for a library's business, jobbers also provide many services—accepting orders by phone, providing special billing to suit each library's needs, and providing computerized acquisitions services involving a cathode ray tube (CRT) terminal in a customer's library. Because jobbers compete heavily with each other, a library should continually evaluate and review its jobber's costs as well as its services. For example, some libraries may subscribe to a rental service for new books from one jobber, while others may decide it is cheaper to buy such books outright from another jobber. Such competition among jobbers and publishers benefits the library and its budget.

The technical services librarian together with the order librarian or technician usually determines the library's policy for ordering from the various sources. The order technician separates the orders according to this policy. If the library wants more than one copy, such orders should be placed at the same time so they will be received and processed together. Orders for books may go to one jobber and orders for AV media to another, or all orders may go to the same jobber. Orders to publishers that only sell directly are set aside to be sent to each publisher. The order technician may also note that a publisher's name is missing or incomplete on a material request form. Because this information must be correct and complete to order an item, the publisher's name and address will usually be verified in the publisher listing found at the end of *Books in Print: Titles*, Volume 2.

Once the material request cards have been separated according to the source for purchase, they are ready to be typed on order forms or entered into a computer system. It is very important that all the information on the request card be transferred to the order form—this is usually a multicopy form. This information may be very useful if there is a problem with the order at some point. For example, if an incorrect publisher is recorded, the original source for the request may provide the correct publisher information. Order forms also usually include the date of the order and a purchase order number or budget account that should be charged. The orders to be placed with each source are typed as separate orders. If the material request cards have been kept in alphabetical order, each group of orders will remain in alphabetical order.

After the order forms have been typed, it is very useful to verify the order form against the material request card to see that the order was typed correctly. Although this extra step takes time, it may prevent the frustration of an incorrect or incomplete order. After this verification, the multicopy order forms can be separated into several groups of order slips. These copies are usually color-coded. Several copies are sent to the publisher or jobber, one copy is filed in the card catalog, one copy is sent to the requester to indicate that the item was ordered, and several copies are filed in the on-order file. Libraries have found it very useful to file these copies for new orders in the order file or card catalog before mailing orders; this procedure provides a final check that may turn up enough orders already filed to make it worthwhile.

At the time an order is typed, it is given a budget account number or assigned a purchase order number. The cost of the items on the orders may then be added to see how much money must be encumbered, or reserved, for expenditures. If libraries expect an average discount from a particular source, this discount can be subtracted from the total list price before the amount is encumbered. Such discounts range from 30 percent or more for trade books to 5 to 10 percent for juvenile books with library bindings to 0 to 10 percent for technical books. A library must evaluate its previous orders to determine the average discount percentage to be used. The amount to be spent on the materials ordered should be recorded in the library's account books so that the selectors know how much of their budget has been encumbered. As items are received, their prices should be deducted from this encumbered amount and added to another account that records the amount expended.

After the orders have been typed, their amounts encumbered, copies filed in the order file, and copies mailed to the proper sources, the major order steps are complete. The next steps include sending copies of orders to the original requesters with a budget update of the balance in their materials budgets. In addition, the order technician must monitor the orders that have been sent. Unless a library has a computer system that automatically prints out claims notices for items that have been on order for a certain period of time, the technician should periodically search the files for items not received. The library may instruct some jobbers to cancel any orders not filled within certain time periods and to send cancellation notices to the library. However, a library may want to claim any unfilled orders before this time period expires, claiming orders at three months rather than waiting until they are cancelled at six months. Also, a library will usually claim direct orders because they are not automatically cancelled.

An easy method for claiming such overdue materials is to send one of the multiple copies of the order, or a photocopy of it, to the source. An exact copy will help the source's claims department locate the original copy of the order more easily. The jobber or publisher usually responds to such claims with a form giving one of a number of standard explanations for its inability to fill the order; the source may reply that the item is out of print (OP), out of stock (OS), not yet published (NYP), or not our publication (NOP). Depending upon the library's policy, such orders can either be cancelled or held until the publication becomes available. If the response is NOP, the original source of the order should be reviewed to see if the wrong publisher information was given on the order form. Any items that are cancelled should be deducted from the encumbered budgets, and the final selectors should be notified about them.

The order technician should set up an order routine so that requests are received, verified, and ordered as quickly as possible on a regular basis. The smooth operation of the entire technical services department often depends upon receiving a steady stream of library materials. Although some school libraries place their orders at one time so they will be received and processed in the summer months, few other libraries follow this practice. In fact, even this practice may be detrimental to a school's faculty and students; they may need material in January or February rather than in the following September. It will be useful for the order technician to consider the patrons' needs when establishing such routines.

Acquiring special library materials

Most libraries receive materials donated by patrons, organizations, government officials, or special-interest groups. The number of these gifts may be large or small. Donations may be either solicited or unsolicited. In recent years, more and more libraries have begun to solicit donations to expand their collections or to provide expensive materials that the library could not afford to buy. The library staff should understand that most gifts are accepted only within the guidelines of the library's material-selection policy. This means that a library does not put an item on its shelf if it is not very likely to be selected for purchase. For example, gifts of religious books or books that represent only one group's point of view might not be added to the collection. Such a policy should be explained to every donor offering an item to the library.

Oftentimes, people offer to donate a very old or a rare item to the library. Such gifts may be discouraged by a library if it has no collection of rare books or does not collect materials on the gift's subject. If an item is truly rare, it often needs a climatically controlled room in order to be preserved. More often than not, the item is not that old or rare or is in poor condition, perhaps even mildewed. A library offered such items might do better to refuse them if it knows they would not be added to the collection. On the other hand, libraries may accept rare materials in such areas of interest as local history.

Gifts may be a big business in a large library with a long "wish list" and a staff to solicit such gifts. They may be a small business in other libraries, where a short letter of appreciation may satisfy a patron. In either case, the library should avoid getting involved in appraising donated materials. Donors often want to use the appraised value of materials as a deduction for income taxes, but because the library is an interested party in the donation, a court would view an appraisal made by the library suspiciously. If the donation is evidently greater in value than several hundred dollars, the donor may wish to hire a professional appraiser to evaluate the donation; the appraiser's fees are deductible, too. Patrons sometimes request letters from the library indicating receipt of a donation. The library may send such a letter, but it can thank the donor for "ten psychology books" rather than mention any monetary value. It is only considerate for the library to send an originally typed letter of appreciation to any person who donates materials.

Once gift materials have been accepted by the library, the order staff usually checks all the library's records to see if the item is already owned. If it isn't, the item may then be turned over to the appropriate librarian or selector to determine if it should be added to the library's collection.

Sometimes, libraries want to purchase out-of-print materials. If so, a request is usually sent to out-of-print dealers or antiquarian booksellers to learn about the availability and cost of the item. A library staff may also search through catalogs of such dealers to see if they can locate needed items. If such items are found, the library will have to find out their condition (which may range from very good to very poor) and decide if it is willing to pay the asking price. Prices of out-of-print materials (especially books and periodicals) depend upon how much the market will bear rather than upon the original cost of the item.

The last type of special material represents materials not yet published. Orders placed for these materials are called "standing orders." Such open-ended orders are often placed for materials such as reference books published annually or biannually. Their receipt can cause confusion in an order department because they do not have the library's order slip attached and the library may have no order in the on-order file. (Some libraries, however, make a cross-reference to the standing-order file or even combine the two files.) The receiving clerk should learn to recognize the type of book most likely to be a standing order, and a periodic review of the titles in the standing-order file may also be very useful.

Receiving Materials

The process of receiving and checking in library materials is very important and requires a great deal of accuracy. That a library has received an item does not necessarily mean that it ordered the item. Publishers and jobbers both tend to make mistakes in filling and sending orders to their customers. Also, publishers may have changed the title of a work or even its author so that a book that does not seem to be on order may really be long overdue. The receiving clerk must be very alert to catch such discrepancies and to verify each item as it is received.

The physical condition of materials should be examined as they are unpacked from their shipping containers. A quick inspection of a book can determine if the cover or spine is damaged, if the binding is intact, and if the contents have been placed correctly in the casing. A quick inspection of audiovisual materials can verify the title of each item with its container as well as verify that all items have been received. Any damaged items can be set aside to be taken care of after other materials have been checked in. Quick inspections when materials are unpacked will speed up the claiming process and forestall misunderstandings that can arise if any damages are discovered later.

The verification process also includes checking to be sure that each received item is the exact item that was ordered. Although the sequence of the following steps varies from library to library, each step is usually performed at some time during the receiving process. After an item has been unpacked and inspected, it should be checked off on the supplier's invoice for the order shipment. This step may not be as easy as it sounds—sometimes invoices are mailed separately from orders. If this happens and the order arrives before the invoice, it may be a good idea to wait until the invoice arrives before unpacking the shipment. Since the invoice is the supplier's official record or bill that an item has been shipped to a library, it is important to verify the items actually received against the bill that the library will have to pay.

It is useful to locate the original order for each item after it has been checked off on the invoice. This step can be expedited if the jobber or supplier has been instructed to place a copy of the library's multicopy order form in each item shipped. Such a copy will give the exact entry or title under which the library has filed an order. This can be very useful if the title of the ordered item differs from the received item. If such a copy is supposed to be in an item and is not there, a receiving clerk should be very wary. Although the library may have such a title on order, the absent order slip may indicate that the supplier still has the order open in its records. A second, unwanted copy with an order form could therefore be received in the future.

If an order form is in the received item, the clerk should then pull the library's copy of the order form from the on-order file and compare it carefully to the item received. Each element of the order form should be carefully checked. For a book, the title, author, publisher, edition, and date should be verified. For an audiovisual item, the title, date, producer, and format should be verified. (For example, is the film received a super 8 or standard 8 film? Is it a videotape?) If a library orders catalog cards or receives its materials partially or fully processed, the accuracy of this processing can also be verified at this time.

Receiving incorrect editions, receiving similar titles by the wrong authors, and not receiving all of the volumes or parts of a title that have been ordered are common problems. If other problems or discrepancies are found, they can be brought to the attention of the order technician. In addition, the library may receive materials that require special handling.

For example, libraries may order some materials as rush orders; these should be cataloged and processed as soon as they are received. In addition, on-approval items may be received; this means that the selector wants to review an item to see if it should be added to the collection. These items can all be set aside to be taken care of after all the remaining materials in an order have been checked in.

Once all of the items in an order have been checked in, the materials are arranged in the order requested by the catalog section. The correct materials should then be delivered to the catalog section. Problems or special materials should then be considered at this time. Approval items should be forwarded immediately to the selector. The receiving clerk will have to keep track of approval items; if the selector decides against purchase, they must be returned within a specific period of time. Damaged or incorrect materials may be returned to the supplier. If items to be returned came from a jobber, the library can complete the return form provided by the jobber; the reason for the return should be stated and the items should be shipped with copies of the form back to the jobber. (The library should keep a copy of the completed form.)

Sometimes, items cannot be returned for credit without prior permission and shipping instructions. (This category may include items ordered directly and items from a jobber who does not have the publisher on an approved list.) In such cases, the receiving clerk should write a letter to the order department of the supplier stating the problem with the item, giving the invoice number, and asking for shipping instructions. The library probably has a standard letter for such occasions upon which the clerk can model a more specific letter. An item should never be returned without such information—because the item may never get to the correct department of the publisher or jobber, and the library may still be charged for it.

A final step in receiving is stamping the date on which the item was received on the order form and filing a copy of the form in the orders-received file. If libraries do not file their orders in the card catalog, the orders-received file can be very important because it provides a record for a title from the time it is received until it is cataloged.

An individual library's receiving procedures will be designed to fit its own needs. All libraries should, however, check the physical condition of the material. In addition, they should verify that an item was actually received from a supplier, and they should verify that the correct item was received. In addition, when all of the items on an invoice have been received, they should mark the appropriate purchase orders "received" and authorize payment of the invoice. The amount is then usually transferred from an encumbered account to an expenditures account. This financial accounting is usually the last step in the receiving process for most library materials.

Cataloging Materials

The cataloging function in a technical services department has changed greatly in most libraries. In the past, catalogers in each library generally received each item, examined it carefully, and prepared an original catalog record for it. This original cataloging described the item and assigned it a call number and subject headings. If published catalog information was available for the item, the cataloger would compare this information to the book in hand, check if the call number was acceptable for the individual library, and verify that no other book in the library had the same call number.

Over the past twenty to thirty years, however, libraries have reduced their large staffs of professional catalogers, replacing them with technical and clerical staffs that support one or two professional librarians. This change has been brought about by several important developments. One of these developments was the shortage of librarians in the 1950s and early 1960s. At that time, there were not enough catalogers to serve all of the libraries' needs. Into this gap stepped industrious library jobbers and suppliers who began to sell catalog cards along with books. These cards were based upon Library of Congress catalog cards or upon cataloging prepared by the suppliers' professional catalogers. Such cards could be customized to an individual library's criteria. The jobbers also began to sell library materials already processed so that they could be placed on a library's shelves as soon as they were received. These catalog card and processing services appealed to librarians and administrators who had large amounts of money (particularly federal money) to spend in short periods of time. The costs of such services compared favorably with cataloging personnel costs. In fact, many libraries found it cheaper to purchase prepared library cards and materials and have them processed by support staff under the direction of a technical services librarian than to pay the salaries of several professional catalogers.

A second major development was the acceptance of Library of Congress (LC) cataloging as the standard, combined with improvements in its availability. This acceptance is probably due to the quality of LC's cataloging as well as to the size of the collection that it catalogs. Because LC receives copies of everything copyrighted in the U.S. and many foreign materials, it catalogs a major portion of the world's publications and recordings. The availability of LC cataloging improved because of the activities of jobbers and library supply houses, sale of catalog cards and proof slips by LC itself, and the inclusion of LC cataloging information in bibliographic tools such as *Weekly Record, American Book Publishing Record*, and *Booklist*. As more and more libraries used LC cataloging, they began accepting it without making many changes at the local library. This development has also enabled support staff rather than catalogers to add materials to a library's collection. Library of Congress cataloging and the information of its companion machine readable cataloging (MARC) tapes are available from a great variety of sources.

One source of LC cataloging may be the newly purchased book itself. The cataloging-in-publication (CIP) data often found on the verso of a title page has been prepared by LC from proof copy supplied by the publisher. These data provide the main entry, title, call numbers, tracings, and any notes that should be included on a catalog card (figure 76a). The rest of the information needed for cataloging can be gathered from the book itself. Although libraries have noted errors in this cataloging, it still can be an excellent source for cataloging a book.

Other useful sources of LC cataloging are *Weekly Record* and the *American Book Publishing Record* (*BPR*), which provide LC's complete cataloging information for books published by major American publishers. This catalog information needs only to be translated into correct card format (fig. 77a-b). In addition, *Booklist*, a review magazine published by the American Library Association, also includes LC cataloging for each book reviewed. The easy accessibility of these printed cataloging sources makes it understandable that libraries have begun using them as authoritative sources for their cataloging.

The availability of computerized cataloging systems is another important development that hastened the shrinkage of cataloging departments. The major supplier of computerized cataloging is OCLC, Inc., but other vendors such as RLIN (Research Libraries Information Network) and the Washington Library Network (WLN) also provide such services. Since 1971, OCLC has enabled libraries to use a CRT terminal in their libraries to access a computer that is now in Dublin, Ohio, and obtain cataloging for their materials. This computer contains bibliographic and cataloging information for millions of items, some cataloged on MARC tapes, some by OCLC member libraries. In using OCLC, a staff member enters the item information in the terminal; the CRT then responds with the cataloging if OCLC has a record for the item (figure 78). The cataloging information can be edited to fit a library's format. The staff member then instructs the computer to print catalog cards for that item. The cards are printed in Dublin and mailed to the library in a week to ten days. When the cards arrive, they are already arranged alphabetically and separated according to the catalogs in which they will be filed, such as adult, juvenile, and shelflist. Some libraries enter OCLC or MARC cataloging information directly into their own on-line, computerized catalogs; they may also have book or COM catalogs produced rather than have cards printed.

All these developments have enabled libraries to reduce their professional staffs, modify their costs, and streamline their procedures. Commercially produced catalog cards and cataloging from other sources have

(a)

Library of Congress Cataloging in Publication Data

Chernik, Barbara E., 1938-
    Introduction to library services for library
technicians.

    (Library science text series)
    Includes index.
    1. Library technicians--United States.
2. Library administration--United States.
I. Title. II. Series.
Z682.C534   023'.3   81-15663
ISBN 0-87287-275-0   AACR2
ISBN 0-87287-282-3 (pbk.)

(b)

```
023.3     Chernik, Barbara E.
Che           Introduction to library services
          for library technicians. / by Barbara
          E. Chernik. -- Littleton, Colo. : Li-
          braries Unlimited, 1982.
              187 p. ; ill. -- (Library science
          text series)

              Includes index.
              ISBN 0-87287-275-0
              1. Library technicians--United
          States.  2. Library administration--
          United States.  I. Title.  II. Series.
```

Fig. 76.   Cataloging in Publication.

(a) Cataloging in Publication (CIP) data; (b) Catalog card taken from the above
CIP and the book itself.

(a)
```
       CASCIERO, Albert J., 1941-                    025.3
       Introduction to AV for technical assistants / by
       Albert J. Casciero and Raymond G. Roney ; illus-
       trations by Bruce Cheeks.  Littleton, Colo. :
       Libraries Unlimited, 1981. p.   cm.  (Library
       science text series)  Includes index. [Z674.4C37]
       19 81-13690 ISBN 0-87287-232-7 ; 23.00
       1. Instructional materials centers. 2. Audio-visual
       library service.  3. Instructional materials per-
       sonnel.  I. Roney, Raymond G. II. Title. III.
       Series.
```

(b)

```
 Z
 674.4   Casciero, Albert J., 1941
 C37         Introduction to AV for technical assistants /
         by Albert J. Casciero and Raymond G. Roney ; ill.
         by Bruce Cheeks. -- Littleton, Colo. : Libraries
         Unlimited, 1981.
             225p. : ill. ; 24 cm. -- (Library science
         text series)

             Includes index.
             ISBN 0-87287-232-7

             1. Instructional materials centers. 2. Audio-
         visual library service.  3. Instructional materials
         personnel.  I. Roney, Raymond G.  II. Title. III.
         Series
```

Fig. 77. **American Book Publishing Record** *entry.*

(a) Example *American Book Publishing Record (BPR)* entry; (b) Example catalog main entry card from this *BPR* entry.

reduced the amount of time and money spent in cataloging each individual item. Although computerized systems have not reduced a library's cataloging costs, they have enabled libraries to shift more staff to work directly with the patrons. Cataloging procedures have been streamlined because the number of library materials that must be originally cataloged by a professional has become very small. For example, public libraries that use the OCLC system report that 98 percent or more of their materials are located in the database; this includes video cassettes, games, and toys as well as records and books. Cataloging with prepared matter is quicker than original cataloging. If commercial catalog cards are purchased, there is no need to type cards. Companies that customize cards for a library can even add the call number and tracings to each card.

```
OCLC: 7835246       Ord stat: n  Entrd: 810922    Used:820120
Type: a Bib lvl: m Govt pub:    Lang: eng  Source:    Illus:
Repr:    Enc lvl: 8 Conf pub: 0 Ctry: con  Dat to: s M/F/B:10
Index: 1  Mod rec:  Festschrift: 0  cost:
Desc: a Int lvl:    Dates: 1982,
1010                81-15663
2040                DLC #c DLC
3020                0872872750 : #c $23.50
4020                0872872823 (pbk) : #c $16.50
5039                2 #b  3 #c3 #d3 #e3
6043                n-US---
7050                Z682  #b  .C534
8080                023/  .3  #2  19
9092                #b
10 049              IHZA
11 100 10           Chernik, Barbara E.
12 245 10           Introduction to library services for library
technicians /#c by Barbara E. Chernik
13 260 0            Littleton, Colo.: #b Libraries Unlimited,
                    #c 1982.
14 263              8201
15 300              p. cm.
16 440              Library science text series
17 500              Includes index
18 650 0            Library technicians   #Z  United States
19 650 0            Library administration #Z United States
```

Fig. 78.   Example OCLC entry.

Such capabilities have enabled libraries to increase their efficiency at a time when their personnel budgets are being curtailed.

Cataloging procedures

When the cataloging section receives new materials from the receiving section, the staff may look over the items to determine which ones should be cataloged and processed first. The staff may check to see if there are several copies of a title to be processed at the same time. Libraries usually process reserve materials and rush orders first, then new editions and reference books. It is useful for a library to set some priorities for cataloging, for there is a human tendency to process a favorite subject or easier items first. A schedule may be necessary to ensure that the majority of the items received first are cataloged first. Also, if there is a backlog, it is very useful to arrange items in some order so that a requested item can easily be located. Because large backlogs sometimes occur, some libraries provide minimum processing of an item when it is received (or perhaps when it is searched in OCLC) and allow it to circulate until it is ready to be fully cataloged and processed.

Some form of cataloging is available for most of the items received. No matter where this cataloging comes from, the same information must be verified against the item itself. The staff member should check that the main entry, title statement, author statement, edition statement, and publisher or producer statement are all correct. If there are minor differences (e.g., edition or date) between the item on hand and the cataloging, the cataloging can be changed to match the item. However, care should be taken to ensure that the cataloging really does match a particular item, for a book with the same title by a different author is not a match. Most libraries today will accept the call number given on this cataloging. (Small libraries often shorten the Dewey decimal classification number.) Some libraries add more subject headings if they think their patrons might search under the additional headings. School libraries might prefer to use less complicated subject headings based on the *Sears List of Subject Headings* rather than the LC subject headings that are usually given in prepared cataloging. Some libraries may not use particular tracings given in the cataloging or may modify such tracings. Some libraries do not use cards for joint authors. Some drop the subdivision "Juvenile Literature" from subject headings. The principles for assigning subject headings and call numbers will not be discussed here, for there are a number of excellent books available such as Elrod's *Classification* and Wynar's *Introduction to Cataloging and Classification*.

If prepared cataloging accompanies the item when it is received, the cataloging staff can easily compare it to the item on hand. If the cataloging is a set of processed cards, the staff can indicate any changes that need to be made and send the item to the processing section. If there are no cards with a book but the book has CIP information, a main entry card should be made that can be used as a master for producing the complete set of catalog cards. CIP data usually includes necessary information except for the number of pages and whether or not the book is illustrated; this can be learned from the book itself and included on the catalog card. The information is then placed in standard format for catalog cards. (See chapter 8 and figure 75b.)

Sometimes the cataloging is not included with an item when it arrives in the cataloging section and must be located elsewhere. If a library has OCLC or a similar system, one of a variety of computerized indexes can be searched to locate the cataloging information. The most used access points are an author-title code, LC card number, and ISBN. Libraries without OCLC may turn to *Weekly Record, BPR*, or *Booklist*. Entries in these periodicals may be found in the issues for the year in which a book was published (or the year before or after the publication date). Some catalog information for AV materials such as the main entries and producers may be obtained from *Schwann's Guide* for tapes and records or the *NICEM Indexes* for other AV materials. The information from these sources should be transferred into standard catalog card format on a main entry card. (See chapter 8 and figure 76b.)

If there is no prepared cataloging at all available for an item, an assistant may follow one of several procedures depending upon the policies of the library. In some libraries, the item may be turned over to a librarian or cataloger for "original cataloging." This means the librarian would determine the main entry, identify the bibliographic information that correctly identifies the item, and assign the subject headings and call numbers. In small libraries, the assistant may determine this original cataloging by following established guidelines and by comparing the item in hand to similar items in the collection or to prepared cataloging for similar items. This original cataloging may then be reviewed by a librarian.

Once the cataloging has been located and verified, the item should be checked in the shelflist to be sure that the library does not already own it. The items can then be sent with their cataloging to the processing section.

Processing Materials

The processing section is usually responsible for completing the sets of catalog cards, adding the entries to the shelflist, filing the cards in the catalog, and preparing the material for the library's shelves. Each item will come from cataloging with either a full set of catalog cards or a typed master card which is used to prepare the set. Even if the cards themselves are included with the item, the typist may add or change any entries or headings as the cataloger has indicated. This may include typing the call number on each card, typing the added entries above the main entry, and adding shelflist information on the shelflist card. (See chapter 8 for the correct format.)

Producing catalog cards

If a master card has been prepared, it is used for reproducing as many cards as are needed to complete a set of catalog cards. This set usually includes one card for the main entry, one card for each heading in the tracings, and a shelflist card. Other cards may be needed for special catalogs such as union catalogs. These cards may be reproduced in a variety of ways. Some libraries type the main entry cards for several items onto card stock which is then photocopied to produce catalog card sets. Other libraries type a main entry card on a memory typewriter or a word processor. When a main entry is typed on these machines, they produce a tape or program which can be used to type additional cards automatically. The machine can be programmed to stop on each card so that the heading can be typed in. Libraries with smaller budgets may still use small duplicating machines that take stencils the size of cards. The main entry cataloging is typed on a stencil and then all the cards needed can be run off. Although this process is more time-consuming than the other methods, it is still usually cheaper for a library than typing each card individually.

After the catalog cards have been reproduced, the headings for added entries will be typed on each card if this is not already done. Shelflist information will be typed on the shelflist card; this usually includes the price of the item and the date it was added to the collection. Any item identification number, copy number, or accession number is added both to the item itself and to the shelflist card at this time. (They should not be added at an earlier step because the item may turn out to be an unwanted duplicate.) If a library has a union catalog or shelflist, the item identification or copy information may need to be added to a shelflist card that is already in the catalog. Similarly, new editions of standing orders or cataloged serials may need to have the item information added to existing shelflist and catalog cards. When these steps have been completed, a copy of the catalog card or the whole set may be put with the item so that it is ready for final processing.

Preparing materials for the shelves

Each library decides how much or how little processing will be done with its library materials. Usually, such processing is determined by the format of the material. Processing may add anything ranging from an ownership stamp and a strip of tape down the spine of a periodical to a book card and pocket with author and title information and a plastic jacket. (The last practice is often called "full processing.") In order to make such processing as efficient as possible in terms of both time and money, libraries are constantly evaluating their processing methods. Some libraries have found that changes in their circulation systems enabled them to revise and streamline some procedures. For example, because transaction systems do not use charge cards, libraries can use a small label giving the book identification information or even use a copy of the catalog card as the pocket for the transaction slip. Libraries that use computer identification lables may need only a pocket to hold the due date card. Many libraries use timesaving materials such as preglued book pockets that bear the library's ownership information (fig. 79). Most important of all, libraries try to evaluate the projected use of their materials and provide the best processing to withstand that use.

Therefore, a library may set different standards for different items in each format. For example, periodicals that are heavily used may be reinforced with several strips of plastic and have a card and pocket made

Fig. 79. Example processed book.

for each issue. Periodicals that do not circulate very much may not be processed except for an ownership stamp. Similarly, fiction paperbacks may be reinforced with plastic coatings, while more scholarly paperbacks may not be. Some libraries that buy children's books in library bindings may not put plastic jackets on their picture books because the covers themselves are so colorful. Other libraries, such as college libraries, may not place jackets on any of their books because they do not need the eye-catching covers to attract readers to a book that public libraries might need.

Libraries that do use plastic jackets to cover their books' dust jackets can choose among a variety of types to attach to their books. Plastic jackets come in single sheets the size of books so that one sheet fits one book, or they may come in rolls of various sizes and are cut to fit each book. These jackets are usually folded around the book's dust jacket and attached to the book itself with a heavy filament tape that will not tear easily. Sometimes, libraries may even seal a clear plastic sheet onto the cover or book. The type of protective covering a library chooses depends upon the skill of its staff and the variety of materials sizes it receives.

In addition to processing books and printed matter, libraries also process other types of material. The library will usually purchase sturdy library containers to house these materials. Whether the containers should be cardboard or plastic depends upon their expected use, the number of AV items that a library intends to purchase, and the size of the supply budget. Some materials such as audio cassettes and records may be housed in their original containers. However, record albums are usually inserted into heavy-duty plastic covers. Materials that are usually transferred to library containers include films, filmstrips, slides, and videotapes. Sometimes, materials such as art prints, sculpture, and games are placed in special containers when they are checked out.

No matter what type of material it is or how it is finally prepared for the shelf, libraries usually take the following precautions. The catalog cards are kept with the material so that the correct identification information can be placed on the items. (The order form should never be used for this step because there are too many changes from the order to the catalog cards.) This information should be placed on every piece of an item except for puzzle or game pieces—every book in a set, every record or tape in an album, and every slide in a slide set. The information usually put on each item includes the library's name and the call number or item identification number. If there is room on the item, the title (and perhaps the author) and copy number or accession number may also be included. If the circulation system needs a book card and pocket, the call number and author and title of the material are often typed on these and they are placed on the items. The call number is also typed on a label that is placed on the spine of a book or the container of an audiovisual item. This label may be protected by a thin layer of glue brushed over it, or it might be sealed with a heating iron. Many libraries then put plastic jackets on their books.

At this point, most libraries have completed their material processing. However, some libraries add one more step somewhere along the way; they may *accession* the item, or assign a distinctive number to it. This is often based on the year of acquisitions as in 82-305, 82-306, and so on. These numbers are particularly helpful in distinguishing between similar materials or two copies of the same item. Libraries that do not use accession numbers based on the year of acquisition sometimes stamp the date on a newly processed item. This helps in the weeding and inventory processes and also helps to identify books ready to be removed from the shelf of new books. When all the processing steps are completed, the processed material should be double-checked against the information on the catalog cards. If everything is correct, the catalog cards should be pulled from the materials, separated by type of catalog, and set aside to be filed in their proper catalogs. The materials themselves should be separated by department and delivered to their proper places. The work of the technical services department is then completed.

Conclusion

Although many patrons are never aware of the technical services department, its role is vital if a library is to provide the right material at the right time. The smooth and efficient movement of an order should be the chief concern of everyone involved in the technical services department. The ordering section must be particularly alert in the verification, ordering, and receiving processes. The cataloging section should send materials through its section as speedily as possible; it should also provide catalog information that will be useful for patrons and help them to easily locate any particular item. The processing section is responsible for the final product. This section will provide the cards for all of the library's catalogs and judiciously process the library's materials. These activities should expedite delivery of requested materials to the library's patrons.

Student Work Unit

Based on chapter 9, the student will be able to:

1. Obtain a copy of a local library's policy on materials selection and compare it with the major elements identified in this chapter.
2. Using fig. 80, record all the appropriate information on the sample request card for the requested item.

(a)

> ✓ Murphy, Bruce W. & Ana G. Lopo.
> **Lampmaking.**
> Sterling. 1980. 192p. illus. bibliog. $14.95; pap.
> ($7.95).
>   CRAFTS
> This is the book for the person who has
> always wondered just how old coffee
> grinders and stoneware jugs are turned
> into lamps. Step-by-step instructions
> for about 20 such conversions plus four
> early American chandelier projects are
> given. All can be done with a few tools
> and basic lamp parts. An interesting
> picture section of early lamps unfortu-
> nately does not relate well either to the
> text or to the lamp projects.—*CAF*
>
> 50   LIBRARY JOURNAL/JANUARY 1, 1981

(b)

Class No.	Author (surname first)		Date requested	
Accession No.	Title			
No. of copies ordered	SBN			
Date ordered	Publisher and Place		Year	List Price
Dealer	Edition or series	Volumes	No. of Copies	
Date received	Requested by	Notify		
Cost	Reviewed in			
L. C. card No.	Approved by		Fund Charged	
GAYLORD 101-L				PRINTED IN U.S.A.

Fig. 80.   Order request for study unit.

(a) Example source for material to be ordered; (b) Example material request card.

3. Using the completed request card in fig. 79, verify the information as it is found in *Books in Print*.
4. Following the teacher's guidelines, verify ten orders in the library or laboratory files.
5. Following the teacher's guidelines, check in three items that have been received in the library or laboratory.

6. Write a letter asking to return an item because it was not the item ordered.
7. Using fig. 81 and chapter 8, type a complete set of catalog cards for the item given in fig. 81.

```
DAY, David,  1947-                   591.042
The doomsday book of animals / David Day.
New York : Viking Press, 1981. p. cm. (A Studio
book) Includes index. [QL88.D39] 19 81-43018
ISBN 0-670-27987-0 : 40.00
1. Extinct animals. 2. Rare plants. 3. Wildlife
conservation--History. I. Title.
```

Fig. 81. **Example American Book Publishing Record (BPR)** *entry.*

Teaching Unit

The teacher may set up a laboratory unit using example card catalogs, on-order files, and received files. Students may be given material request forms for ten items that they should verify in the appropriate bibliographic tools and in the files. These ten items might include several that require the student to make decisions. The teacher may also set up a sample order and its attendant files and invoices for students to check in. Some problem items may be included so that students could use them to write letters requesting permission to return an item.

10 Library Files and Supplies

Unit Outline:

Pamphlet Files
Library Office Files
Supplies
Equipment
Conclusion
Teaching Unit

Unit Objectives:

Describe the purposes and uses of pamphlet files and the types of material included in them.

Identify the principles for developing and maintaining library office files.

Describe methods for organizing files for their most efficient use.

Describe policies and procedures for inventorying, ordering, and maintaining supplies and equipment.

Discuss the principles and methods used in budgeting supplies and equipment.

In addition to supervising and maintaining the library's book, audiovisual, and serial materials, the library staff also maintains the pamphlet files, office files, supplies, and equipment. Maintenance of these materials and equipment requires unique procedures. Pamphlet files for the public's use and library files for the staff's use require constant weeding to keep them relevant. Library supplies require constant monitoring so they are always on hand when needed. Equipment records must be accurately kept so that equipment is maintained on a regular basis and replacements are provided for in the budget. This chapter covers guidelines and procedures that every staff member should know and follow to make the library's files and supplies contribute to the efficient functioning of the library.

Pamphlet Files

Many materials are important in a library collection that are not cataloged and placed on the library's shelves. These materials are usually of transient interest. Many are frequently replaced by new editions or new information. They may also be published in unusual formats and might be lost if they were shelved with the books or audiovisual materials. Such materials as pamphlets (written material of less than 50 pages), pictures, maps, charts, and other flat materials are usually shelved instead in pamphlet or vertical files or stored flat in large drawers.

Library pamphlet files can add an important dimension to a library's collection. Along with serials, pamphlet files can provide information that is too recent to be contained in books, especially since information may take two years to be published in book form. Pamphlets can also supplement the book collection by providing materials on special aspects of a subject for which the library could not afford to buy an entire book. They can provide duplicate or additional information on subjects that have a heavy demand at certain times. This is particularly useful for supporting class assignments or providing holiday materials. Pamphlet files may also include information of local interest that is clipped from magazines and newspapers. In addition, pamphlet files provide quickly accessible information for important but seldom-used material such as a company's or city's budget.

Pamphlet files also provide many types of graphic materials to support the rest of the library collection. Pictures, graphs, charts, diagrams, tables, and maps are just a few of the materials found in most pamphlet files. Pictures are particularly useful because they can be used in many ways and in many different subject areas. Pictures of Thanksgiving pilgrims can be used for American history classes, for holiday pictures, or for costume design by drama students. Maps are used not only in school libraries for class study but also for planning vacations as well as for the actual traveling. The pamphlet files also contain many materials in colors and formats that are hard to publish in book form. Color charts that rotate, colored posters, large-scale diagrams of frogs or automotive engines, large-scale maps of the moon, blueprints, and dioramas (pictures that pop out or have moving parts) can easily be stored in vertical pamphlet files. All these materials can not only be used to supplement a library's collection, but they can also be used in the production of new audiovisual materials.

Libraries get their pamphlet file materials from many different sources. Pamphlets are produced by many companies for informational, promotional, and educational purposes. Some must be purchased; some are "free for the asking" from such sources as publishers, government agencies, business corporations, and nonprofit organizations. Although pamphlets may contain some advertising and should be evaluated to be sure that they are not biased or propagandistic, most pamphlets from these sources are factual and objective. Many business firms publish company information such as annual reports and financial statements (useful in library business collections) as well as useful pamphlets about the subjects to which their activities relate. For example, pharmaceutical companies may publish pamphlets on diseases or scientific discoveries. Travel agencies may donate travel posters, brochures, and pamphlets about every part of the world. In addition to providing pamphlets, these sources and others may sell or give away such graphic materials as posters, wall charts, or pictures suitable for framing.

Libraries often find suitable pamphlet materials available in their own collections. Withdrawn and discarded books may provide colorful illustrations, reproductions of famous paintings, and other materials that can be easily removed and added to the pamphlet files. Libraries may look through their old newspapers and magazines for useful pamphlet file information before discarding them. If anything worthwhile is found such as local maps, charts, or pictures, they can be clipped out and laminated or mounted for protection from wear and tear. Sometimes, libraries notice useful articles in current periodicals on subjects that are in heavy demand. If the libraries would like duplicates of copyrighted articles, they can often order them from the periodical publisher or copy them with the publisher's permission. Photocopying without permission, however, is illegal if its effect is to substitute for the purchase of another copy.

In selecting materials for pamphlet files, libraries should follow several important guidelines. First, the materials should support the objectives of the library and its parent institution. There is a great deal of pamphlet material available that is both interesting and enjoyable. If it is unlikely to be needed in a particular library, however, it should not be added to the library's collection. Too often, the pamphlet file ends up being a catchall for material that the staff cannot bear to throw away.

Material selected for the pamphlet file should add to the dimensions of the library's collection. That is, pamphlets should not duplicate information already available in the library unless such duplication is needed. Material added should not be of such fleeting interest that it will be outdated in several months. The shortest acceptable shelf life is equal to the time between weedings of the pamphlet collection. The material itself should be durable and legible; the printing and the graphics should be sharp and clear. The language of any written material should be interesting, understandable, and informative. The writing should also be objective and factual rather than subjective or slanted. If controversial topics are discussed, the discussions should not include propagandistic or derogatory comments. Graphic representations should be accurate in detail, artistically executed, and aesthetically pleasing. All these factors are important in selecting pamphlet materials if this collection is to contribute to fulfilling the library's objectives.

Once selection guidelines for pamphlets are understood by an LMTA, he or she can use them and any additional guidelines set by the librarian to make the preliminary selection of materials for the pamphlet files. The LMTA can search indexes such as the *Vertical File Index* and *Public Affairs Information Service* as well as pamphlet listings in new periodicals, *Selected U.S. Government Documents* listings, and recent bibliographies to locate possible pamphlet acquisitions. Because such materials become obsolete quickly, the list should be reviewed by the librarian and the orders sent out as soon as possible.

Orders for pamphlet materials are often more informal than book orders. Since many pamphlets may be ordered free, a form letter may be sent requesting the material. A form letter should give complete information for the item being requested as well as the title, date, and page of the source of information about the item. This latter information assists the publisher in filling a request and gives the company feedback about its publicity efforts. Other items may not be free but have only nominal charges. These may often be ordered by a letter of request with the amount enclosed. (Libraries may often use petty cash to pay the small charges for these materials.) More expensive items, over three or four dollars, may be ordered by requisition or purchase order just as books are ordered.

When these materials are received, they should be processed quickly and minimally so they can be added to the pamphlet files as soon as possible. Since their importance in the collection is due to their timeliness, they should not be cataloged or delayed in processing. Processing of pamphlet materials can easily be done by the LMTA and reviewed by the librarian.

Each item should be assigned a subject heading from the subject authority listing. Many libraries use the same authority list as that used for the card catalog. Some libraries use the *Readers' Guide to Periodical Literature* to provide currently used headings for new subject areas. Unless the pamphlet files are very extensive, a more general subject heading should be preferred to a very specific heading. Thus, a pamphlet or chart of the heart's circulation could go under "Heart" rather than "Heart—circulation" or "Blood." The chosen heading can then be printed on the material or printed or typed on a label that is placed on the material. Labels should be affixed so as to be visible even when the item is in the folder. The date the material is processed should also be stamped next to the subject heading.

If the date of publication is not printed on the item, it should be added. For example, newspaper clippings and magazine articles should include their publication dates. The item should then be stamped with a library ownership stamp and filed in the pamphlet files by subject heading. If the heading is new to the files, the assistant should make a new subject folder. If there is an index to the pamphlet file, an entry should be prepared for any new heading. A cross-reference card may be placed in the card catalog that will say "HEART. For further information on this subject, see the PAMPHLET FILE."

Material should not stay in the pamphlet files forever. The files should be weeded annually and old materials withdrawn or updated. Sometimes, information may be retained because it has not changed (e.g., material on George Washington), or because it may give a historical perspective (e.g., annual reports for a local manufacturer). However, much of the information will soon become outdated or superseded by information contained in books or in new pamphlet acquisitions. This material should be weeded on a preliminary basis by the LMTA and set aside for the librarian to review. By following these procedures, the LMTA will help ensure the development of an up-to-date, usable collection.

Library Office Files

Libraries have internal records, reports, and correspondence; jobbers', publishers', and suppliers' catalogs; brochures; and other information that must be organized to be useful. These records are usually arranged in library office files for use by the staff. When such files are established, the library staff should determine what purposes the files will be used for and what types of material they should contain. Answers to such questions as Who will use the files? and Why? will help determine the types of materials that will be kept. For example, acquisitions personnel might need to keep publishers' flyers used in ordering materials. The pamphlet file assistant might need to keep the copies of all letters requesting pamphlet materials.

In determining what types of material and how much material should be kept, the staff should ask other important questions. For example, should the files contain all library correspondence from "year one" or should they contain only correspondence of certain types for the last year or two? Should every piece of promotional literature be kept, or only certain types needed by specific personnel? It is useful to determine the length of time items should be kept in the files and to set up a schedule for weeding the files. Once such answers have been determined, it is easier for the staff to develop and maintain useful files. Decisions such as whether to keep or discard an old supply catalog when the new one arrives would then be based upon the needs of the supply assistant rather than purely upon chance.

Libraries may divide their office files into two types. One may concern internal library operations—library records, correspondence, statistics, and projects in progress. These are sometimes kept separately from the other files and maintained by a secretary or office clerk. The other type of library file usually contains information relating to all aspects of the library's operations. Such material as information brochures; catalogs on supplies, materials, and equipment; bibliographies; and information for publicity releases may be included. These files are often kept in the library's workroom or in some location where the entire staff has access to them. They are usually maintained by library assistants or clerks. Even if all files are kept in one location, the business files may be separate so as to be more easily accessible. These files are usually consulted more often than the other library files.

Once the scope of the files has been determined, their organization should be kept simple and flexible. Libraries have found it most useful to arrange these files alphabetically by subject rather than by individual company or correspondent. Since the subject heading under which a person looks up information may not be the heading under which it has been filed, general headings already established by the library's book of subject headings should be used. These headings can be filed according to library rules rather than business rules. This enables all staff members to understand the filing order and provides a subject authority index for the headings used in the files. These general subject headings may be subdivided to allow for any needed expansion of the files and headings without disruption of the current arrangement. A list of headings can be taped to the filing cabinets to further enable staff members to find needed subject headings quickly and easily.

In arranging the materials in the files, the following methods can be followed. Small libraries with limited files could arrange subject folders in alphabetical order behind guide cards for letters. A "miscellaneous" folder for each guide letter could be filed at the end of each section to hold those items for which there is not enough material to make a complete file folder. Libraries with larger files may provide guide cards for subjects and then place folders alphabetically behind the subject guides by subdivisions, correspondents, business firms, libraries, or even letters of the alphabet. Miscellaneous information on a subject may be filed in a "subject miscellaneous" folder at the beginning or end of each subject section.

The material in each folder should be filed in a designated order. If the folder is for a subject, the items included in it should be filed alphabetically by name of business, correspondent, or some other distinguishing characteristic of the material such as the type of supply or equipment. If the folder is for a letter of the alphabet or is a miscellaneous folder, the items in it should be filed alphabetically by company name. These items and folders for correspondents should then be subarranged by date with the most recent date at the front. This will provide an orderly arrangement of materials in the files and make them easier for other people to use.

If a folder is removed from the files, an "out" guide can be put in its place while it is in use. This guide indicates who has the folder and the date it was taken so others may know it is in use and not lost or misplaced. If any item is removed from the folder, it should be replaced in its proper place, not at the front of the folder. Sometimes, staff members responsible for maintaining library files prefer the user to place the used item in a "to be filed" basket. Then the file clerk can personally refile the item to ensure the integrity of the files.

The mechanics of adding material to the files should be as simple as possible while still providing maximum use. To do this, every item should be dated with the month, day, and year it was received. The subject heading should be quickly printed or indicated on the material so it will always be replaced in its proper folder. The date and heading should be recorded in the upper right-hand corner of the material. This will make it visible when the material is placed in the folder so that its top is on the left-hand side of the folder. Placing the material in the folder in this way makes it easy to read when the folder is opened. When material is placed in a folder already in a file, pulling the folder up slightly can prevent the material from being inadvertently placed between two folders.

A special type of material often included in library files is the materials catalog. Catalogs can be filed on shelves or in files arranged alphabetically by company or by type of catalog. They may be most useful when they are filed by general type of catalog such as supply and equipment, audiovisual, or new book; this is often the approach used to find them. They would then be arranged alphabetically by company.

If materials contain information on two subjects, several courses can be followed. A larger subject heading that includes both subjects can be assigned to the material (e.g., "technical processes for cataloging and acquisitions"). Material with two subjects can also be filed under the first or most prominent subject. If material is so important that it should be found under two subjects, a simple solution might be to photocopy it and place one copy in each subject file (e.g., "serials budget data" under both "budget" and "serials").

The library files should be maintained regularly and weeded periodically. Obsolete and superseded materials, outdated correspondence, and other items should be discarded. The library files should include only useful records. Unnecessary duplicates and records should be withdrawn or placed in inactive files. Library files should not be storage places for archives but usable files of current developments, correspondence, and available materials.

Supplies

The supplies needed in any library will differ depending upon the size of the library and the systems it uses. Even the amount of supplies used from year to year in a particular library may vary. To provide the right amount of supplies when they are needed, taking a careful inventory and planning a budget are necessary. It should be the responsibility of one staff member to maintain library supply inventories and orders and to work with the librarian at budget time on the library's supply needs.

The library should have some official record of supplies needed and used. This list could be the basis for an inventory of supplies on hand, ordered, used, and needed. It should be arranged so that a supply item can be found easily and quickly. The easiest arrangement is to assign general headings to supplies so that similar supplies will be grouped together (e.g., cards, catalog; cards, book). These headings can then be arranged alphabetically or grouped together by the section they will be used in—circulation, cataloging, acquisitions, and so forth. Such a list will be useful at budget time to review the supplies needed by the library.

Libraries will usually need types of supplies as follows:

Cataloging supplies (cards, guide cards, etc.)
Acquisitions supplies (order forms, etc.)
Circulation supplies
Mending supplies
Bookends
Vertical file or pamphlet cabinets and supplies
Display materials
Office supplies such as paper, pencils, pens, note pads, paperclips, etc.

They may also use such supplies as plastic covers, ribbons, rubber bands, explanatory signs and labels, record jackets, and AV containers.

Most of these supplies can be purchased from commercial supply houses such as Gaylord, Demco, or Brodart. These companies provide library supply catalogs, inform their customers of new developments in the field, and will usually work with a library on its special supply problems. Lists of these national suppliers can be found in the *Bowker Annuals* and in the annual "Purchasing Guide" that appears in the *Library Journal*.

In choosing a supplier, the following criteria should be considered. The library should determine what type of supplies will satisfy its needs and what specifications these supplies should meet. Such considerations as quality, durability, and quantity are among these specifications. Once these are determined, the library can compare the supplies available from various suppliers. Since most prices are comparable, the library should choose the best quality supplies that meet its specifications. The next major consideration for choosing a supplier should be the speed and quality of service a supplier provides. If supplies are needed, the library does not want to wait three months to receive them.

Besides ordering supplies from a library supply house, the library should investigate local suppliers to see if they can provide comparable quality at a lower price. Sometimes local dealers can provide quicker service or can provide special orders more reasonably than a national suppler. The library could also query library suppliers on the possibility of special rates for large or frequent supply orders. After comparing quality, service, and prices, the library should then be able to order its supplies with confidence.

Once the library has received needed supplies, it should determine the quantity of supplies it will want to keep on hand in the future. For example, some supplies can be purchased a year in advance while other supplies should not be ordered in too great a quantity because they have shorter shelf lives. The librarian should determine this need, and the assistant can then maintain a running inventory of these supplies. The staff members can also be instructed to inform the supply assistant when supplies get to a certain level or to note the needed supply on a request list. Either a formal inventory record or informal notation should be kept of the number of supplies used. An inventory record of the dates on which supplies were ordered or needed will be invaluable in planning the library's supply needs for the next year's budget (fig. 82).

It almost seems to be a "library law" that supplies and the supply budget run out simultaneously before the end of the budget year. Careful planning is needed to avoid this predicament. The supply assistant should use the present and past years' inventories to help plan the quantity and type of supplies that should be requested in the next year's budget. He or she can use the inventory dates that show when supplies were ordered or used to find out if supplies are being used faster or slower than was planned for the present budget. Most libraries operate on a fiscal year (often July–June) rather than on a calendar year, and the assistant should know when the fiscal year begins in order to make supply requests for a budget. The budget request should cover supplies to last from the beginning of a budget year until supplies arrive that will be paid for under the next year's budget. All these factors, as well as estimates of future needs, should be used to determine the supply budget.

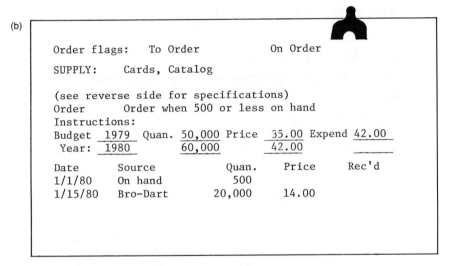

(a)

SUPPLY	INVENTORY

Cards, Book
Cards, Catalog
Cards, Guide

(b)

Order flags: To Order   On Order

SUPPLY: Cards, Catalog

(see reverse side for specifications)
Order   Order when 500 or less on hand
Instructions:
Budget 1979 Quan. 50,000 Price 35.00 Expend 42.00
  Year: 1980   60,000   42.00

Date   Source   Quan.   Price   Rec'd
1/1/80   On hand   500
1/15/80   Bro-Dart   20,000   14.00

Fig. 82. Example supply inventory records.

(a) Informal running inventory; (b) Formal inventory record card.

The librarian should be notified in advance of any extraordinary outlays that will be needed in supplies. Such items as special order forms or new equipment to house supplies or library materials are expensive items that may need to be budgeted separately from the supply budget.

Once the budget has been requested and approved, the assistant and librarian may want to establish priorities for ordering supplies. In any case, most supplies should be ordered at the beginning of the fiscal year and, if possible, all supplies should be ordered by mid-year. General library expenses have a habit of running higher than they were budgeted for, and the supply budget is often the first part of the budget to be cut.

No matter how carefully supplies have been budgeted for, they may run out if the entire library staff is not instructed in their proper use. The supply assistant can encourage the reasoned use of supplies and explain that supplies have specific uses and should not be used otherwise (e.g., if tissues are supplied to clean up paste in mending, they are not for the personal use of staff members). The assistant can also encourage staff members to indicate when supplies are getting low. This teamwork is essential if supplies are to be available when they are needed.

Equipment

It is surprising how much equipment other than furniture can be found in a library. This equipment should be inventoried and stamped with the library's ownership label for identification purposes.

Some typical types of library equipment include:

Card catalog and shelflist catalog
Typewriter (elite type preferred for typing catalog cards)
Copying machines
Filing cabinets
Audiovisual equipment
Audiovisual storage cabinets (for films, filmstrips, microforms, etc.)
Bulletin boards
Book trucks

An inventory record of the equipment can be kept on cards. It should include the date of purchase, price, and source of the equipment as well as any repair and maintenance record (fig. 83). This information, especially the repair and maintenance records, could then be used for comparison when similar new equipment is purchased.

One assistant should be responsible for library equipment. He or she would take inventory of the equipment and be responsible for maintaining it. The assistant should keep the equipment clean and in good condition and see that the supplies needed to use the equipment are always on hand. He or she should instruct others in the proper care and use of the equipment and related materials and place printed instructions on the equipment to decrease the possibility of improper use. When any equipment needs professional repair or maintenance service, the assistant should also be responsible for contacting the service companies and following up until the equipment is satisfactorily repaired.

Since the purchase of new library equipment can be expensive, the assistant should inform the librarian far ahead of budget time if any old equipment needs to be replaced. He or she can assist the librarian by preparing a justification report for this equipment that could be attached to the budget. The assistant could gather all the information concerning a particular piece of equipment by reviewing catalogs and library litera-

(a)

```
EQUIPMENT:  TYPEWRITER

Accession    Company &          Purchase
Number       Model              Date          Price

20           Adler electric     2/5/79        $469.
             #356201
21           Adler electric     2/5/79        $469.
             #356202
35           Adler electric     10/9/79       $475.
             #428697
```

(b)

```
EQUIPMENT:  TYPEWRITER                        Acc.   35
                                              No.

Company &   Adler electric
Model:      #428697

Date:       Source                            Price
10/9/79     Wettengel's Bus.                  $475.
            Machines

10/80       Wettengel's: cleaned
            and stuck keys fixed              30.
```

Fig. 83. Example equipment inventory records.

(a) Composite equipment inventory record; (b) Individual equipment inventory record.

ture. The *Library Technology Reports* published by ALA are particularly useful in providing in-depth studies of library equipment. Then the assistant could state the reasons for needing the new equipment, list the advantages and disadvantages of the particular models, and present comparative prices and specifications for each. The librarian can then use this information to select and order library equipment.

Conclusion

Library files, supplies, and equipment contribute to the functioning of the library. If files are poorly arranged, out of order, or obsolete, they can be worthless to the library. If needed supplies are used up halfway through the budget year and the supply budget is exhausted, many library activities can be stopped or severely handicapped. Equipment that is always broken or malfunctioning can render thousands of dollars worth of library materials completely useless. For these reasons, persons in charge of these areas should keep accurate records and develop procedures for maintaining library files, supplies, and equipment, so they support rather than hinder the library's objectives. In addition, every staff member should understand the purposes of these activities, communicate any problems or needs to the proper assistant, and use the materials correctly.

Teaching Unit

1. Students may select two free pamphlets from *Vertical File Index* or a similar source and write letters requesting these pamphlets according to the guidelines presented.
2. Students may search old magazines for articles that are appropriate to add to a particular library's collection. They can then process these materials, choose appropriate subject headings, and make a subject file folder.
3. Students may make inventory records of the supplies and equipment used in a library or laboratory. They can determine what supplies would be needed to replenish those used in a laboratory for the library procedures course and prepare the supply order. (Such supplies would include circulation and mending supplies.)
4. Students could organize library or laboratory files according to the guidelines and methods discussed in chapter 10.

Appendixes

Appendix A
    Categories of Library Personnel (from *Library Education and Personnel Utilization* statement of ALA)

Appendix B
    Library Media Technical Assistant Job Description approved by Council on Library/Media Technical Assistants (COLT)

Appendix C
    Circulation Duties of Personnel (reprinted with permission from *Tex-Tec Syllabi*, edited by Louis Shores)

Appendix D
    September–November, 1980, Calendar

Appendix A

TITLE FOR POSITIONS REQUIRING:		BASIC REQUIREMENTS	NATURE OF RESPONSIBILITY
LIBRARY-RELATED QUALIFICATIONS	NONLIBRARY-RELATED QUALIFICATIONS		
Senior Librarian	Senior Specialist	In addition to relevant experience, education beyond the M.A. [i.e., a master's degree in any of its variant designations: M.A., M.L.S., M.S.L.S., M.Ed., etc.] as: post-master's degree; Ph.D.; relevant continuing education in many forms	Top-level responsibilities, including but not limited to administration; superior knowledge of some aspect of librarianship, or of other subject fields of value to the library
Librarian	Specialist	Master's degree	Professional responsibilities including those of management, which require independent judgment, interpretation of rules and procedures, analysis of library problems, and formulation of original and creative solutions for them (normally utilizing knowledge of the subject field represented by the academic degree)

CATEGORIES OF LIBRARY PERSONNEL—SUPPORTIVE

TITLE		BASIC REQUIREMENTS	NATURE OF RESPONSIBILITY
Library Associate	Associate Specialist	Bachelor's degree (with or without course work in library science); OR bachelor's degree, plus additional academic work short of the master's degree (in librarianship for the Library Associate; in other relevant subject fields for the Associate Specialist)	Supportive responsibilities at a high level, normally working within the established procedures and techniques, and with some supervision by a professional, but requiring judgment, and subject knowledge such as is represented by a full, four-year college education culminating in the bachelor's degree.
Library Technical Assistant	Technical Assistant	At least two years of college-level study; OR A.A. degree, with or without Library Technical Assistant training; OR post-secondary school training in relevant skills	Tasks performed as supportive staff to Associates and higher ranks, following established rules and procedures, and including, at the top level, supervision of such tasks
Clerk		Business school or commercial courses, supplemented by in-service training or on-the-job experience	Clerical assignments as required by the individual library

Reprinted by permission of the American Library Association from *Library Education and Personnel Utilization*, A Statement of Policy Adopted by the Council of the American Library Association, June 30, 1970; revised 1976 by the Office for Library Personnel Resources Advisory Committee.

Appendix B

Library Media Technical Assistant Job Description

1. The library media technical assistant (LMTA) is a graduate of a two-year college program with an associate degree in library technology. This formal training prepares the LMTA to work under the guidance of a professional librarian. As a supportive member of the library staff, the LMTA must have an understanding of the philosophy underlying library service and a practical knowledge of the library tools, methods, and procedures that contribute to the success of library service.

2. The LMTA may be responsible for the supervision of other members of the library supportive staff and other specified groups. It is important that an LMTA have the capacity and desire to work comfortably with the people who constitute the community served and with other members of the staff.

3. Examples of work assignments:
   A. Technical services:
      1. Ordering, preparing, and maintaining library materials.
      2. Organizing and maintaining library files and records.
      3. Performing elementary descriptive cataloging and classification.
      4. Supervising clerical, volunteer, and student personnel.

   B. Readers' services:
      1. Performing responsible activities in connection with the loan of library materials.
      2. Providing bibliographic assistance to library patrons and staff.
      3. Providing basic information and guidance in the use of library resources.

   C. Audiovisual services:
      1. Participating in the selection, maintenance, and operation of office and library equipment.
      2. Creating displays, exhibits, and other instructional materials.
      3. Scheduling and maintaining audiovisual materials and equipment.

The variety of activities performed by an LMTA will vary according to type, size, and personnel requirements of the various employing libraries.

4. Salary
The salary scale for a library media technical assistant may begin below the maximum for the clerical level but should not exceed two steps above the minimum professional level. Consideration must be given for prior training and experience. In addition, the same fringe benefits provided other personnel should be extended to the LMTA position in an established classification plan.

Guidelines recommended by the committee appointed by the chairman of the COLT Workshop at Bethlehem, Pennsylvania, 1970.

Appendix C

Circulation Duties of Personnel

1. Professional
    a. Establishes and supervises policies concerning systems, equipment, loan periods, penalties, and records.
    b. Determines which statistics and analyses are useful and directs compilation of same.
    c. Acts as liaison with other departments and, when pertinent, with the public in relation to complaints or compliments.
    d. Directs work of all subordinates, either directly or through line delegation.

2. Technical assistant
    a. Schedules personnel and supervises circulation desk operations to ensure adequate coverage.
    b. Assists in registering, charging, discharging, filing, checking, searching, reserving, etc.
    c. Trains new clerks and other technical assistants in library circulation procedures for the specific library.
    d. Maintains detailed control system, reserves, renewals, overdues, and adjustments of claims including telephoning.
    e. Handles routine borrower complaints and adjustments.
    f. Plans and supervises inventories of materials and equipment, including reports of lost and missing items.
    g. Maintains equipment and supplies used in circulation operations.
    h. Compiles and submits statistical reports as directed.
    i. Maintains interlibrary loan files, including recall and return as well as borrowing of materials.
    j. Schedules and maintains shelving operations and shelving routines.
    k. Explains borrowing rules and registers patrons. Explains library service areas.
    l. Introduces professional help when needed.

3. Clerk or aide
    a. Sets up desk for the day.
    b. Charges and discharges materials.
    c. Types overdues.
    d. Helps compile and tabulate statistics as directed.

e. Does simple filing under supervision.
f. Assists with borrower registration and telephone duty.
g. Inspects books for damage or repair needs.
h. Reserves books and searches shelves for specific titles.
i. Shelves returned books in proper order.
j. Reads shelves to maintain proper sequence.
k. Helps maintain facility by straightening chairs, picking up trash, shifting books, etc.
l. Mail pickup and distribution.

Reprinted from Louis Shores, *Tex-Tec Syllabi: Courses of Study for Library Technical Assistants* (Washington, D.C.: Communication Service Corp., 1968), pp. 130–31, 136.

Appendix D

September–November, 1980, Calendar

(For use with student work units)

September

Sun	Mon	Tue	Wed	Thu	Fri	Sat
	1	2	3	4	5	6
7	8	9	10	11	12	13
14	15	16	17	18	19	20
21	22	23	24	25	26	27
28	29	30				

October

Sun	Mon	Tue	Wed	Thu	Fri	Sat
			1	2	3	4
5	6	7	8	9	10	11
12	13	14	15	16	17	18
19	20	21	22	23	24	25
26	27	28	29	30	31	

November

Sun	Mon	Tue	Wed	Thu	Fri	Sat
						1
2	3	4	5	6	7	8
9	10	11	12	13	14	15
16	17	18	19	20	21	22
23	24	25	26	27	28	29
30						

References

1. The Library

American Library Association. *Code of Ethics for Librarians*. Chicago: ALA, 1938.
————. Library Education Division. *Criteria for Programs to Prepare Library/ Media Technical Assistants*. Rev. ed. Approved by ALA Council, June 1979. Chicago: ALA, 1979.
————. Office for Library Education. *Library Education and Personnel Utilization*. A statement of policy adopted by ALA Council, June 30, 1970. Chicago: ALA, 1976.
Butler, Pierce. *Introduction to Library Science*. Chicago: Univ. of Chicago Pr., 1961.
Gates, Jean. *Introduction to Librarianship*. 2nd ed. New York: McGraw-Hill, 1976.
"Library Education and Manpower: ALA Policy Proposal." American Libraries 1 (1970): 341–44.
Lyle, Guy R. *The Administration of the College Library*. 4th ed. New York: Wilson, 1974.
Maloney, R. Kay. *Personnel Development in Libraries*. Issues in Library and Information Science. New Brunswick, N.J.: Rutgers Univ. Pr., 1977.
Ricking, Myrl, and Robert Booth. *Personnel Utilization in Libraries: A Systems Approach*. Chicago: ALA, 1974.
Special Libraries Association. *The Library: An Introduction for Library Assistants*. Edited by William Petru. New York: Special Libraries Assn., 1967.
Strauss, Lucille. *Scientific and Technical Libraries: Their Organization and Administration*. 2nd ed. New York: Wiley, 1972.
Wallace, Sarah Leslie. *Patrons Are People*. 2nd ed. Chicago: ALA, 1956.

2. The Circulation Department

Bloomberg, Marty. *Introduction to Public Services for Library Technicians*. Littleton, Colo.: Libraries Unlimited, 1976.
Fry, George, and Associates, Inc. *Study of Circulation Control Systems: Public Libraries, College and University Libraries, Special Libraries*. Chicago: ALA, 1961.
Geer, Helen Thornton. *Charging Systems*. Chicago: ALA, 1955.
Kirkwood, Leila H. *Charging Systems*. New Brunswick, N.J.: Rutgers Univ. Pr., 1961.
Library Technology Reports: Evaluative Information on Library Systems, Equipment, and Supplies. Bimonthly. Chicago: ALA, 1965– .
Special Libraries Association. *The Library: An Introduction for Library Assistants*. Edited by William Petru. New York: Special Libraries Assn., 1967.

Stevens, Rolland E. *Supervision of Employees in Libraries.* Urbana: Univ. of Illinois Pr., 1979.
Tauber, Maurice. *Technical Services in Libraries.* New York: Columbia Univ. Pr., 1953.

3. Circulation Procedures

American Library Association. *Circulation Policies of Academic Libraries.* Chicago: ALA, 1970.
Bloomberg, Marty. *Introduction to Public Services for Library Technicians.* Littleton, Colo.: Libraries Unlimited, 1976.
Carpenter, Ray. *Statistical Methods for Librarians.* Chicago: ALA, 1978.
Fry, George, and Associates, Inc. *Study of Circulation Control Systems: Public Libraries, College and University Libraries, Special Libraries.* Chicago: ALA, 1961.
Geer, Helen Thornton. *Charging Systems.* Chicago: ALA, 1955.
Kirkwood, Leila H. *Charging Systems.* New Brunswick, N.J.: Rutgers Univ. Pr., 1961.
Knight, Nancy H. "Theft Detection Systems Revisited: An Updated Survey." *Library Technology Reports,* 15 (May–June 1979): 221–38.
Lancaster, Frederick. *The Measurement and Evaluation of Library Services.* Washington: Information Resources, 1977.
Lyle, Guy R. *The Administration of the College Library.* New York: Wilson, 1974.
Murphy, Marcy. *Handbook of Library Regulations.* New York: Marcel Dekker, 1977.
Special Libraries Association. *The Library: An Introduction for Library Assistants.* Edited by William Petru. New York: Special Libraries Assn., 1967.
Thompson, Sara Katharine. *Interlibrary Loan Procedure Manual.* Chicago: ALA, 1970.

4. Shelving and Inventory

American Library Association. *A.L.A. Glossary of Library Terms.* Chicago: ALA, 1943.
Cohen, Aaron. *Designing and Space Planning for Libraries: A Behavioral Guide.* New York: Bowker, 1979.
Ellsworth, Ralph. *Economics of Book Storage in College and University Libraries.* Metuchen, N.J.: Scarecrow, 1969.
Harrod, L. M. *Librarian's Glossary and Reference Book.* Boulder, Colo.: Westview, 1977.
Humenuk, Stanley. *Automatic Shelving and Book Retrieval: A Contribution toward a Progressive Philosophy of Library Service for a Research Library.* Occasional Papers, no. 78. Urbana: Univ. of Illinois Pr., 1966.
Jesse, William H. *Shelf Work in Libraries.* Chicago: ALA, 1952.

Slote, Stanley J. *Weeding Library Collections*. Littleton, Colo.: Libraries Unlimited, 1975.
Small Libraries Project, ALA. *Weeding the Small Library Collection*. Small Library Project #5, Supp. A. Chicago: ALA, 1966.

5. Audiovisual Media and Equipment

American Library Association. *Guidelines for Audiovisual Materials and Services for Large Public Libraries*. Chicago, ALA, 1975.
———. *Recommendations for Audiovisual Materials and Services for Small and Medium-sized Public Libraries*. Chicago: ALA, 1975.
Cataloging, Processing, Administering AV Materials: A Model for Wisconsin Schools. Madison: Wisconsin Assoc. of School Librarians, 1972.
Library Technology Reports: Evaluative Information on Library Systems, Equipment and Supplies. Bimonthly. Chicago: ALA, 1965– .
Orange County (Calif.) Department of Education. *School Library Media Center: A Handbook for Aides*. Santa Ana, Calif., 1974.
Rosenberg, Kenyon C. *Media Equipment: A Guide and Dictionary*. Littleton, Colo.: Libraries Unlimited, 1976.
Schroeder, Don. *Audiovisual Equipment and Materials: A Basic Repair and Maintenance Manual*. Metuchen, N.J.: Scarecrow, 1979.

6. Mending and Binding

"Binding Procedures and Programs in Libraries." *Encyclopedia of Library and Information Science*. New York: Marcel Dekker, 1969.
Cunha, George. *Conservation of Library Materials*. Metuchen, N.J.: Scarecrow, 1972.
Gaylord Brothers, Inc. *Bookcraft: A Complete Manual on Book Repair*. Syracuse, N.Y.: Gaylord, 1971.
Horton, Carolyn. *Cleaning and Preserving Bindings and Related Materials*. 2nd ed. Chicago: ALA, 1969.
"How Books Are Bound." *The Bowker Annual of Library and Book Trade Information*. New York: Bowker, 1967, 1968.
Library Scene. Quarterly. Boston: Library Binding Inst., 1972– .

7. Serials

Ayer and Son's Directory of Newspapers and Periodicals. Annual. Philadelphia: Ayer, 1880– .
Davinson, Donald. *The Periodicals Collection*. 2nd ed. Boulder, Colo.: Westview, 1978.
Katz, Bill. *Magazines for Libraries*. 3rd ed. New York: Bowker, 1979.

Mayes, Paul. *Periodicals Administration in Libraries: A Collection of Essays.* Hamden, Conn.: Shoestring, 1978.

Microforms in Libraries: A Reader. Edited by Albert James Diaz. Weston, Conn.: Microform Review, 1975.

New Serial Titles: Supplement to Union List of Serials. Washington, D.C.: Library of Congress.

New Serial Titles 1950–1970. Subject Guide. 2 vols. New York: Bowker, 1975.

Osborn, Andrew D. *Serial Publications: Their Place and Treatment in Libraries.* 2nd ed. Chicago: ALA, 1972.

Special Libraries Association. *The Library: An Introduction for Library Assistants.* Edited by William Petru. New York: Special Libraries Assoc., 1967.

Standard Periodicals Directory. Annual. New York: Oxbridge, 1964– .

Ulrich's International Periodicals Directory. Biennial. New York: Bowker. 1932– .

Union List of Serials in Libraries of the U.S. and Canada. 3rd ed. New York: Wilson, 1965.

8. Filing in Library Catalogs

American Library Association. *Anglo-American Cataloguing Rules.* 2nd ed. Chicago: ALA, 1978.

———. *ALA Filing Rules.* Chicago: ALA, 1981.

———. *ALA Rules for Filing Catalog Cards.* 2nd ed. Chicago: ALA, 1968.

Elrod, J. McRee. *Filing in the Public Catalog and Shelf List.* Chicago: Education Methods, 1967.

Hoffman, Herbert H. *What Happens in Library Filing?* Hamden, Conn.: Linnet, 1976.

Morse, Grant W. *Filing Rules: A Three-Way Divided Catalog.* Hamden, Conn.: Shoestring, 1971.

9. Processing Library Materials

Bonk, Wallace J. *Building Library Collections.* 5th ed. Metuchen, N.J.: Scarecrow, 1979.

Broadus, Robert N. *Selecting Materials for Libraries.* 2nd ed. New York: Wilson, 1981.

Collection Development Committee. Resources and Technical Services Division. *Guidelines for Collection Development.* Chicago: ALA, 1979.

Conway, Suzanne. *Selection and Acquisitions Manual.* St. Louis: Washington Univ. Medical Library, 1978.

Downing, Mildred H. *Introduction to Cataloging and Classification.* 5th ed. Jefferson, N.C.: McFarland, 1981.

Elrod, J. McRee. *Choice of Main and Added Entries: Updated for Use with AACR2.* 3rd ed. Metuchen, N.J.: Scarecrow, 1980.

————. *Classification: For Use with LC or Dewey*. 3rd ed. Metuchen, N.J.: Scarecrow, 1980.

Foster, Donald. *Managing the Catalog Department*. Metuchen, N.J.: Scarecrow, 1975.

Futas, Elizabeth. *Library Acquisitions Policies and Procedures*. Phoenix, Ariz.: Oryx, 1977.

Grieder, Theodore. *Acquisitions: Where, What, and How—a Guide to Orientation and Procedures for Students in Librarianship, Librarians, and Academic Faculty*. Westport, Conn.: Greenwood, 1978.

Hindle, Anthony. *Developing an Acquisitions System for a University Library*. New York: State Mutual Bk., 1981.

Lane, Alfred H. *Gifts and Exchange Manual*. Westport, Conn.: Greenwood, 1980.

Manhaimer. *Cataloging and Classification: A Workbook*. New York: Marcel Dekker, 1980.

Melcher, Daniel. *Melcher on Acquisition*. Chicago: ALA, 1977.

Piercy, Esther. *Commonsense Cataloging*. 2nd rev. ed. New York: Wilson, 1974.

Wynar, Bohdan. *Introduction to Cataloging and Classification*. 6th ed. Littleton, Colo.: Libraries Unlimited, 1980.

10. Library Files and Supplies

Collison, Robert L. *Indexes and Indexing*. 4th ed. London: DeGraff, 1972.

Gould, Geraldine. *How to Organize and Maintain the Library Picture-Pamphlet File*. Dobbs Ferry, N.Y.: Oceana, 1968.

Kahn, Gilbert. *Filing Systems and Records Management*. New York: McGraw-Hill, 1971.

Library Technology Reports: Evaluative Information on Library Systems, Equipment, and Supplies. Bimonthly. Chicago: ALA, 1965– .

Miller, Shirley. *Vertical File and Its Satellites: A Handbook of Acquisition, Processing and Organization*. 2nd ed. Littleton, Colo.: Libraries Unlimited, 1979.

Wynar, Bohdan. *Introduction to Cataloging and Classification*. 6th ed. Littleton, Colo.: Libraries Unlimited, 1980.

Index

Mary H. Davis

interagency loans. *See* interlibrary loans
interest in others, 7, 33
Interlibrary Loan Code, 74
interlibrary loans, 28, 70–77, 160
internal records, reports, correspondence. *See* office files
International Standard Book Number. *See* ISBN
International Standard Serial Number. *See* ISSN
intershelving, 119
inventories, 105–8, 250, 252
inventory records, 250, 251, 253
ISBN, 185
ISSN, 163

jackets, books. *See* book jackets
jobbers, 161, 222–23
judgment, 8
juvenile. *See* children as users

keypunched computer cards, 20
Kirkus Reviews, 214

laser beams. *See* light pens
LBI. *See* Library Binding Institute
LC. *See* Library of Congress classification
ledger circulation system, 14
lesser-used materials. *See* little-used materials
letter-by-letter filing, 192
librarians, 3, 6, 27, 141
libraries
  academic. *See* academic libraries
  definitions. *See* definitions of libraries
  functions. *See* objectives of libraries
  goals. *See* objectives of libraries
  objectives. *See* objectives of libraries
  policies. *See* policies of libraries
  public. *See* public libraries
  research. *See* research libraries
  school. *See* school libraries
  sizes. *See* sizes of libraries
  special. *See* special libraries
  types, 2

library aides. *See* aides, library
library associates. *See* associates, library
Library Bill of Rights, 9, 10
Library Binding Institute, 143, 151
library bindings. *See* binding
library boards. *See* boards of trustees
library catalogs. *See* catalogs, library
library cards. *See* cards, patron
library clerks. *See* clerks, library
Library Education and Personnel Utilization, xi
Library Journal, 134, 157, 159, 214, 249
library media technical assistants, 6–7
Library of Congress, 176, 178, 188
Library of Congress cataloging, 229
Library of Congress classification, 98–99
Library of Congress List of Subject Headings, 197
library pages. *See* pages, library
library stacks. *See* stacks
library systems. *See* cooperative systems
Library Technology Reports, 130, 253
light pens, 21, 22, 23, 42
liking for people, 7
limiting policies. *See* policies of libraries
list prices. *See* prices
lists of books. *See* standard lists of books
lists of manuscripts. *See* catalogs, library
little-used materials, 94, 109, 152
Little Used Materials Specifications. *See* LUMSPECS
LMTA. *See* library media technical assistants
loan periods, 40–41, 69
lost in inventory. *See* missing materials
lost materials. *See* missing materials
lounge areas, 96, 121
LUMSPECS, 143, 152

machine-readable cataloging. *See* MARC

public libraries (*cont.*)
  research collections, 157
  reserve collections, 70
  selection, 214
  statistics, 50
Public Library Catalog, 110
public relations, 8–9, 12, 28–30, 48–49, 56, 58, 62
Publisher's Weekly, 214
Purchasing Guide in *Library Journal*, 249
purposes. *See* objectives of libraries
puzzles. *See* games

quarto, 96
questions
  directional, 29
  reference, 29, 30, 69

ranges of shelves, 92, 93
rare materials, 94, 95, 140
Readers' Guide to Periodical Literature, 158, 245
realia, 102, 116, 117
rebinding. *See* binding
recalls, 13
receiving materials, 226–28
record-keeping, periodicals, 158, 160, 161–63, 164–68
record players. *See* audiovisual equipment
Recordak, 15
records. *See* phonograph records
records of borrowers. *See* borrower records
reel to reel tapes, 115
Reference Books for Small and Medium-sized Public Libraries, 110
reference materials, 73, 95, 96
reference questions. *See* questions, reference
reference searches, 30
regional medical libraries, 160
Regiscope, 15, 19
registration files. *See* borrower records
registrations of borrowers. *See* borrower registrations
renewals, 40–41, 44–46, 47
rentals of films. *See* films

reordering. *See* replacements
repairs
  AV materials, 130–33
  books. *See* mending
replacements, 60, 109, 110, 140
research collections, 157
research libraries, 74
Research Libraries Information Network, 230
reserve collections, 53, 64, 69–70, 71, 95
reserve requests, 13, 64–70, 125–30
  telephone, 68–69
reserved money. *See* encumbered money
reshelving, 56, 100
responsibilities in circulation. *See* personnel, circulation duties
restricted access areas, 70, 119
restrictive loan practices. *See* policies of libraries
return boxes. *See* book return boxes
revisers, 190, 201
ribbon shelving, 96, 97
RLIN. *See* Research Libraries Information Network
Rolodex, 59
routing, 171–72

saddle stitching. *See* sewn bindings
saddle wire stitching. *See* sewn bindings
sampling, 51–52
scale models. *See* realia
school libraries, 2, 98
  audiovisual materials, 116–17
  borrower registrations, 34, 39
  circulation, 13, 24, 50
  loan periods, 41
  ordering, 225
  overdues, 60
  policies, 4, 36
  research collections, 157
  reserve collections, 69–70
  selection, 214
  statistics, 50
School Library Journal, 214
Schwann's Record and Tape Guide, 217, 234